GASTON BACHELARD

The Poetics of Space

Translated by
MARIA JOLAS

Foreword by
MARK Z. DANIELEWSKI

Introduction by
RICHARD KEARNEY

PENGUIN BOOKS

PENGUIN BOOKS

Published by the Penguin Group
Penguin Group (USA) LLC
375 Hudson Street
New York, New York 10014

USA | Canada | UK | Ireland | Australia | New Zealand | India | South Africa | China
penguin.com
A Penguin Random House Company

First published in the United States of America by The Orion Press, Inc. 1964
This edition with a foreword by Mark Z. Danielewski and an introduction
by Richard Kearney published in Penguin Books 2014

Originally published in French under the title *La poetique de l'espace*
by Presses Universitaires de France, Paris.

ISBN 978-0-14-310752-1

Printed in the United States of America
27 29 28

Set in Sabon LT Std

PENGUIN CLASSICS

THE POETICS OF SPACE

GASTON BACHELARD was born in Bar-sur-Aube, in the Champagne region of France, in 1884. The son of shoemakers, he first worked as postmaster general, but soon left to earn his bachelor's and doctoral degrees. During his illustrious academic career, he became inaugural Chair in History and Philosophy of the Sciences at the Sorbonne, a position he held from 1940 to 1954. For his work in phenomenology, epistemology, and psychoanalysis, he earned the French Legion of Honor prize in 1951 and the Grand Prix National des Lettres in 1960. Bachelard's early work pioneered the concept of an "epistemological break," a notion that explains how obstacles to thinking interrupt the flow of knowledge, forcing the creation of new ideas. Yet, later in his career, he unexpectedly turned to studies of the imagination and consciousness in works like *The Psychoanalysis of Fire*, *Lautréamont*, and *The Poetics of Reverie*. While he is best known today for his development of "topoanalysis" in *The Poetics of Space*, his larger body of work influenced intellectual titans like Foucault, Merleau-Ponty, Deleuze, and Althusser. Perpetually questioning establishment ideas, Bachelard built his work upon conflict and complements: art and science; rationalism and idealism; experiment and experience; empiricism and rationalism. Among his myriad achievements, perhaps his lasting heritage is a renewal of emphasis on symbol and poetic meaning in fields like architecture that became overwhelmingly concerned with form and structure. Bachelard died in Paris in 1962, his legacy upheld by his daughter Suzanne, also a Sorbonne professor.

MARK Z. DANIELEWSKI is the author of *House of Leaves*. His other novels include *Only Revolutions*, a finalist for the 2006 National Book Award, and *The Fifty Year Sword*. He lives in Los Angeles.

RICHARD KEARNEY is Charles B. Seelig Chair of Philosophy at Boston College. He is the author of two novels, a volume of poetry, and more than twenty books on European philosophy and literature, including *The Wake of Imagination* and *Poetics of Imagining*. He is international director of the Guestbook Project.

MARIA JOLAS was born in Louisville, Kentucky, in 1893. She spent much of her lifetime in Europe, where she devoted herself to antiwar activism and translated many works. A member of James Joyce's Parisian literary circle, she cofounded the literary journal *transition* with her husband, Eugène Jolas. She died in Paris in 1987.

Contents

Foreword

MARK Z. DANIELEWSKI

For you without imagination, who can matter-of-factly claim that you're not the creative type—mind you, not proudly claim; for an imagination of ruin must burn beneath defiances against personal invention—then best put this book down and seek out instead some almanac of entertainment free from all such catalytic risks to a mind just mad enough to make out of one world another world.

Gaston Bachelard's book—published originally in 1957 by Presses Universitaires de France as *La poétique de l'espace*—has as little to do with the House, Cellar and Garret, the Hut, Drawers, Chests and Wardrobes, not to mention Nests, Shells and even Roundness (these from chapter titles), as it has everything to do with how our comprehension of space, however confined or expansive, still affords an opportunity to encounter the boundaries of the self just as they are about to give way.

"The lock doesn't exist that could resist absolute violence, and all locks are an invitation to thieves. A lock is a psychological threshold." Yet despite saying so, Bachelard does not turn to violence nor does he keep the company of thieves. There aren't even many locks. In fact it's hard, over the course of even one reading, not to detect the warmth of that rare personality who unmakes a thief simply by making every article of interest available. Sit down. Stay awhile. Something to nibble on? Generosity of spirit abounds. Doors swing open. Thresholds offer little impediment. All are welcome. And in return, Bachelard asks of us only to dream. Or rather he gives us the chance to dream. For a chamber is no more a cage than reverie is an escape. Improbable discoveries wait at every border. As when Bachelard extends René Char's invitation regarding

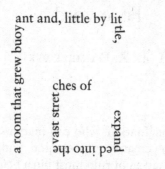

Discovery—not "hostile space"—concerns Bachelard. In the same way that Steve Erickson's *Days Between Stations* and Thomas Pynchon's *Against the Day* revive the sands of time as a medium intent on voyage, Bachelard gently addresses those settings we live in, and finally die in, with the lightness of why we live in the first place. Suddenly a chapter on miniatures offers a reflection on a hermit who while "watching his hour-glass without praying . . . heard the catastrophe of time." The matter of prayer seems incidental to the anecdote, and yet throughout these pages there arises something meditative. Call it a calculus of emotional continuity or a music that only the grieving can know because they chose to carry on: what warms the hearth long after catastrophe has razed both hearth and home.

The Poetics of Space is one of those books in the tradition of Edmond Jabès's *The Book of Questions*, Harold Bloom's *The Anxiety of Influence*, Anne Carson's *Eros the Bittersweet*, and Lewis Hyde's *The Gift*. Whether portraiture of Sarah and Yukel; the designs poets inscribe upon each other; Sappho; the Kula exchange of necklaces and armshells, each of these aforementioned books becomes so much more: an indispensable guide for anyone set on becoming an artist.

Over the years I have discovered that it is not uncommon to

mention Bachelard and hear in return a sigh of happy recognition. I have sat at tables crowded with journalists, graphic artists, urban planners, therapists, sculptors, and architects, all of whom carry some fond memory of their first encounter with *The Poetics of Space.*

The approval of architects seems the most obvious and at the same time the most odd. Despite the mention here of everything from floorboards to molding, names such as Isidore & Anthemius, Ictinus & Callicrates, da Vinci, Mansart, Gabriel, Soufflot, Garnier, Bartholdi, let alone Eiffel, Van Alen, Wright, Gaudí, Le Corbusier, or Pei, never appear. Instead the authorities vitalizing this work are Desbordes-Valmore, Caubère, Wahl, Caroutch, Poe, Barucoa, Morange, Clancier, Éluard, Milosz, Sand, Lafon, Duthil, Bosco, Monteiro, Proust, Spyridaki, Cazelles, Hartmann, Thoreau, Laroche, Guillaume, Bourdeillette, Richaud, Seghers, Supervielle, Wartz, Péguy, Rouffange, Vigée, Mallarmé, Bousquet, Goll, Ganzo, Shedrow, Valéry, Alexandre, Puel, Rouquier, Blanchard, Albert-Birot, de Boissy, Breton, Hugo, Bureau, Cadou, Patocchi, Rimbaud, Masson, Daumal, Vallès, Jouve, Guéguen, Baudelaire, Tardieu, Michaux, Pellerin, Barrault, Tzara, Rilke. Poets one and all. And why not? Just as stanza means "verse," it also means "room."

Though architecture prompted the recommendation, my own introduction to Bachelard came by way of poetry. A young woman I'd met one night in a roomy loft on Varick Street responded to my sonnets with news that in Italian her name meant "death"—A Non-Name Admittedly. Not that my interest was put off by this a.m. warning. Eventually I came to give her more than poems, including an early draft of my first novel. The seduction still failed and her stern advice to read Bachelard hardly seemed to make up for bruised desire. But what did I know? Thanks to love's failure—and here, really, is a belated thanks to her decades due—a necessary revision was set in motion thanks to a young woman whose name meant nothing more.

Of course, sometimes nothing more can mean so much more. And these pages offer just that. After all, here is a thinker who urges the reader to discover an excess of associa-tion: "And how should one receive an exaggerated image, if not by exaggerating it a little more, by personalizing the exag-geration? . . . in prolonging *exaggeration*, we may have the good fortune to avoid the habits of *reduction*." At every turn Bachelard encourages personal engagement: "A house that has been experienced is not an inert box. Inhabited space tran-scends geometrical space." Or here: "Sometimes the house grows and spreads so that, in order to live in it, greater elastic-ity of daydreaming, a daydream that is less clearly outlined, are needed." What would that have been like? To have had such a teacher who applauded you for letting your thoughts run wild? Encouraged you to live beyond gutters and margins, frames and apps, the limits of map and page? Well, this is that education.

A living creature fills an empty refuge, images inhabit, and all corners are haunted, if not

inhabited.

For the comet denies the palace, dust denies
marble, and worn objects deny splendor
and luxury. The dreamer in his comet
wrote off the world in a detailed
daydream that destroyed,
one by one, all the
objects in the
world.

Thus,
an immense cosmic house
is a potential of every dream of houses.

Winds radiate from its center and gulls fly from its windows.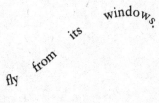

A house . . . allows the poet to inhabit
the universe
his house.
. . . the universe comes to inhabit

Note how Bachelard's Buddhistlike invocation creates out of the trap-of-the-corner a place to escape into the open of all that is not. Whether being there (*être-là*) or not there—or quoting Michaux, "*en dedans-en dehors*" (inside-outside)—by way of the house Bachelard grants access to the vastness of place while at the same time admitting within a vast inverse. Doors—ajar, in-between, mostly open—wait for us. Windows, however, seem less important, likely because of the way walls thin and nearly vanish. And I say "nearly" only because one senses that Bachelard believes that the invention of structure results in the transparency through which we need to view the world.

Above and beyond dwellings or even the inspirations of water and fire (see his *Water and Dreams*; *The Psychoanalysis of Fire*), image and language are central to Bachelard. He reveres image for its impact and the ecstasy it provokes just as he believes it is "the property of a naïve consciousness; in its expression, it is youthful language." (We can only imagine with what reservation he would observe our present-day addictions to jpegs and gifs.) Language, on the other hand, recalls time just as it suspends the ordination of time:

> We find ourselves experiencing in words, on the inside of words, secret movements of our own. Like friendship, words sometimes swell, at the dreamer's will, in the loop of a syllable. While in other words, everything is calm, tight . . . Words—I often imagine this—are little houses, each with its cellar and garret . . . To go upstairs in the word house is to withdraw, step by step; while to go down to the cellar is to dream, it is losing oneself in the distant corridors of an obscure etymology, looking for treasures that cannot be found in words.

For language is both image and text. The one tool we have capable of transcending both. Or as Bachelard so succinctly puts it, evoking childish delight over a discovery at the beach set against the immensity of ocean:

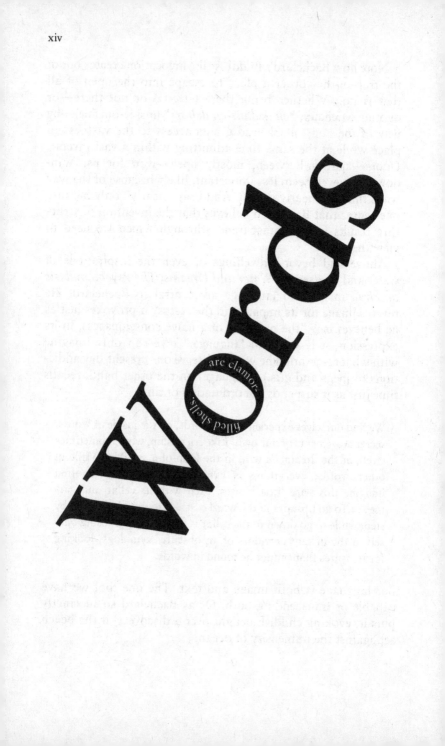

Perhaps the more clamor the better. That which we don't know provokes what we just might conjure. Or as Bachelard writes it: "A lost symbolism begins to collect dreams again."

What an inspiring pleasure then—with all this attention to paths and interiors leading to greater intimacies—to at the same time be reintroduced again and again to the outside. To suddenly discover D'Annunzio's hares awake at dawn, running across "silvery frost" only to pause, ears alert, and by gaze alone "confer peace upon the entire universe." And along with our own dreams of peace, ever beside such "animal peace," to discover soon enough trees, many trees, beautiful trees.

Make no mistake: for all this dreaminess and natural calm, Bachelard is not without bite. From the outset he shows little patience for psychologists or psychiatrists. Though a philosopher himself, he calls the philosophy of his day a "cancerization of the linguistic tissue." And yet in the final chapters he lets slip (a confession really) how if he "were a psychiatrist," he would recommend a poem by Baudelaire to treat "anguish." His squabble then is not with the purpose but rather the approach of a still-young profession. And of course, why not treat the power of great poems as something akin to "virtual 'drugs'"? Many today would not disagree.

Regardless though of correct protocols, it is this enduring desire to heal that is the heart of The Poetics of Space and it makes of these pages something far beyond pages. As comfortable as Bachelard might be at a table of chemists and physicists, he could just as easily join a conversation between the ghosts of Carl Jung and James Hillman. His distaste is for what impedes in the name of dogma. He values the imagination because he recognizes that understanding without imagination is doctrine without growth. And without growth, what chance is there to engage the complexity that bounds us?

Culture gives us our collective dreams—on stage, on screen, online—but daydreams grant us each the collective possibility of oneself. Bachelard wants his readers to find the courage to pursue that private and very personal becoming no matter how strange and unfamiliar the outcome may prove—if only because he recognizes that what must allways deny us in the end must forever remain strange and unfamiliar, too. And so, as I see it, Bachelard extends to anyone with even a flicker of desire to fashion something beyond the pettiness of themselves this wish:

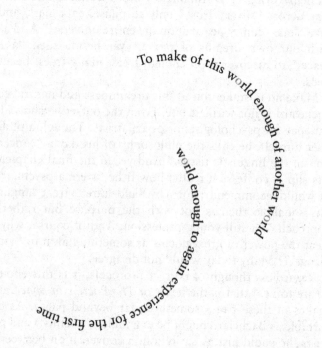

To make of this world enough of another world enough to again experience for the first time our world.

Introduction

Bachelard often praised imagination for its power of meta-morphosis. One could hardly think of someone more open to constant transformation than the author of *The Poetics of Space*. Born into a family of shoemakers, Bachelard began his career as a postman in the Champagne-Ardennes region of France before working his way to a professorship at the Sorbonne. Far from remaining satisfied as a philosopher of science, when he got there he went on to embrace the life of the imaginary in all its forms: poetic, visual, psychological and elemental. There were many mansions in Bachelard's mind and he occupied them all magnificently.

The house in which he took up ultimate residency was *The Poetics of Space*. This is a book that talks at length about homes. Or more precisely, their imaginary dimensions as underground cellars and dusty garrets, unlocked drawers and secret wardrobes, winding stairways and shadowy thresholds. For many years now, readers of all stripes have been attracted to Bachelard's poetic haunts: artists and architects, philosophers and analysts, writers and scholars, each finding what resonates with his or her own professional and personal interests. For some it is the phenomenology of roundness, for others the experience of insideness and outsideness, for others again the dream power of childhood or the collective unconscious: the way, for example, his favorite image—the tree—amplifies from root and bole to leaf and branch, offering nests to all sorts of imaginary dwellers. Bachelard paints a vast canvas, his sense of perspective ranging from the most intimate interior to the most vital expanse, moving easily—as only poetic imagination can—between the micro- and macro-cosmos. Nothing is alien to the Bachelardian home, be it elemental, human or sacred. His imagination is endlessly hospitable. In reverie the "not" no longer functions. All are welcome.

This Penguin edition of *The Poetics of Space* is timely and commendable. Its republication fifty years after the first English edition in 1964 comes at a moment when contemporary society needs imagination more than ever. So much of our experience today is processed by digital communication networks and social media, leaving little room for inner spaces of reverie and meditation—the sorts of places that Bachelard cherishes and celebrates in his poetic revisiting of basements and attics, nests and shelters, closets and stairwells, cupboards and chests. *The Poetics of Space* is about hide-and-seek places where the mind can go on holiday for a while and think about nothing—which means everything. Havens where the soul can pause, in silence, and free itself to dream. And let things be. Now more than ever we have need for intimacy, secrets, sites of interiority and contemplation where we can practice what Baudelaire—one of Bachelard's favorite poets—called the art of "fertile laziness" (*la paresse féconde*). Without such nooks and crannies to muse and mope, to linger and loiter, there is nowhere to begin anew. No place for rapt attention.

Amidst our culture of broadcast and bigness, Bachelard recommends that we rediscover the immense in the most intimate of things. In a world where Facebook and Twitter expose our most private thoughts to public view, and where so many places of work and habitation are featureless, climate-controlled and quarantined against surprise, Bachelard shows us ways of dwelling again in the flesh of space, of dreaming our homes as nests and shells, of reimaging hidden gardens and caverns where we can delve back into a world of natality, newness, beginning.

This book invites us to become readers and writers of our lives. And Bachelard is both. He is an author who *loves* reading, and no reader can enter the imaginary realms he opens up without falling in love with the world again. To follow Bachelard on his poetic meanderings is to be led through homescapes

and landscapes of reverie and repose. It is to wander medita-
tively through new fields and forests of imagination where we
revisit our experience as if it were the first day of creation.
Rilke, another Bachelard favorite, has the artwork summon
the reader with the words "Change your life."[1] Such change
occurs, for Bachelard, when we re-enter the dwelling of the
soul and intensify the transformation of being: "Our soul is an
abode. And by remembering 'houses' and 'rooms,' we learn to
'abide' within ourselves."[2]

The Poetics of Space is the most concise and consummate
expression of Bachelard's philosophy of imagination. His
famous turn toward poetics began in the late thirties when
Bachelard decided to supplement his work on scientific epistemology (almost thirteen volumes) with an exploration of the
life of art and creation. He had become increasingly dissatis-
fied by what he called the "growing rationalism of contemporary science" and was eager to investigate the "ecstasy of the
newness of the image."[3] This meant breaking with the strict
habits of scientific research—which placed new discoveries
always in the context of acquired bodies of evidence—so as to
expose oneself to the novelty of the poetic instant. Because
"the poetic act has no past,"[4] we must be fully attentive to the
image at the very moment it appears, both as itself and as a
vibration of the psyche. A new methodology was called for.

The notion of attention was key. Bachelard was concerned as
much with the "material" image that stirs us in our depths as
with the "formal" image that we produce in response. Bachelard offers a poetics of both matter and form, whereas Aristotle
had originally defined poetics in terms of formal properties
of plot (*muthos*) and imitation (*mimesis*). Poetics comes from
poiesis, meaning "to make," and for Bachelard this is a two-way
process: we are made by material images that we remake in our
turn. We are inhabited by deep imaginings—visual and verbal,
auditory and tactile—that we reinhabit in our own unique way.
Poetics is about hearing and feeling as well as crafting and shap-
ing. It is the double play of re-creation. And this oscillating tension flies in the face of traditional dichotomies between subject

and object, mind and matter, active and passive, which inform the history of Western thought. Or to put it another way: Bachelard's sense of poetic creation transcends the traditionally opposed roles of the image as either "imitation" or "invention." For Plato and many medieval philosophers, imagination was construed primarily as a mimetic act of mirroring, representing, copying. This approach was often associated with deceit and illusion, with confounding original realities with secondary substitutes. By contrast, for Kant and the romantics—including German idealists and existentialists like Sartre—imagination was hailed as a productive force in its own right, the source of all true meaning and value. Bachelard resisted both extremes. For him imagination was at once receptive and creative—an acoustic of listening *and* an art of participation. The two functions, passive and active, were inseparable. The world itself dreams, he said, and we help give it voice.[5] "The image [is] the specific phenomena of the speaking creature."[6] The highest act of imagination is the will to attune oneself to the saying of being itself.

Hence Bachelard's refusal of Jean-Paul Sartre's argument in *The Imaginary* (1940) that perception and imagination are two radically opposed modes of intentionality. Where Sartre spoke of imagination "unrealizing" the world and replacing it with a solipsistic consciousness, Bachelard celebrated imagination's power to realize the unrealized potential of the world. Where the Sartrean imagination involved a radical negation of things—issuing in an essential "poverty of being"—Bachelard saw imagination as the coming into being of language. Not non-being but surplus-being: being as incessant birthing of newness through images.

For Bachelard the cosmos, no less than the human psyche, is brimming with the force of the imaginary. And to return to his favorite example of the house, he maintains that the poetic re-imagining of stairs, passageways, porches or dressers brings together powers of memory, perception and fantasy that criss-cross in all kinds of surprising ways, sounding previously untapped "reverberations" (*retentissements*). Imagination is a laboratory of the possible inviting us—through reverie and poetry—to give a future to the past. And it is not just a matter of a private past (though Bachelard's memories of his home-town of Bar-sur-Aube ghost his work) but of a shared reser-voir of resonances bequeathed to us by the great poets from Homer and Ovid to Rilke and Valéry.

Bachelard is in his element in poetics, and his poetics is of the elements: water, fire, air and earth. The list of his works on the "elemental imaginary" is hugely telling in this regard, ranging from *Water and Dreams, Air and Dreams, Earth and the Rev-eries of the Will, Earth and the Reveries of Repose* right up to his final works, *The Flame of a Candle* and *Fragments of a Poetics of Fire*. The term "element" does double duty for Bach-elard as both a material and metaphysical substance. Elemental space is something we dwell in with body and soul. It is to be found—shaped and formed—in the "material paradise" of the protective dwelling as well as in the abyssal immensity that seems to breathe and blow through the house, at times dissolv-ing its doors and enclosures. *The Poetics of Space* is no less than the fruition of a chapter entitled "The House of Our Birth and the Oneiric House" that Bachelard had written in his last book on the elements, *Earth and the Reveries of Repose* (1948). Both elemental notions haunt *The Poetics of Space*—the homey exis-tential one, and the more expansive cosmological one. Bache-lard writes about the house blown by the winds, or the airy house of words, as well the house rooted in soil and rock.

Bachelard's philosophy was eclectic. Though primarily inspired by phenomenology, he was discreetly drawn toward Eastern philosophies and even mysticism, evident in his continuous pursuit of a "philosophy of repose" over against the *Angst* that ghosted much European culture during his lifetime. He stated this preference as early as his *Dialectic of Duration* in 1936 and as late as *The Flame of a Candle* in 1962. Yet, as a modest phenomenologist—with the ingrained discipline of a labora-tory scientist—Bachelard steered away from explicitly spiritu-alist or religious language as much as he did from political discourse (or any language that risked becoming tendentious). Instead, he made a sustained effort *to think always from the beginning*—focusing on the micro-phenomenon of the poetic image "at the moment of its emergence" in the reader's waking consciousness. In this sense his writing and thinking are deeply democratic, available to everyone regardless of ideology or creed. It requires no academic degree to appreciate the genesis of the image in the individual consciousness. His imagination is capacious, nothing deemed ineligible if it stirs being into language and language into being. No reader is excluded: professional or amateur, expert or lay. Anyone who can read poetry can read Bachelard—a philosopher of the infinite in the infinitesimal, of the mystical in matter. Daydreams and fantasies are grist for poetic reverie as much as masterpieces by Dante or Baudelaire. "When we dream, we are phenomenologists without realizing it," Bachelard tells us.[7] We are born poets whether we like it or not, though what we do with it is our singular responsibility.

The Poetics of Space not only summarizes the author's previous approaches to literary language—serving as canopy for its intertwining branches—it also signals his clearest philosophical insights. It is here that Bachelard inaugurates the distinctions between a "phenomenology of soul" (intuition) as opposed to a "phenomenology of mind" (analysis) and between "superlative" imagination and "comparative" reason (poetic words, he notes, are not comparisons but transformations). And it is also in this work that he sharpens the crucial difference between harmonic values (indeterminate reverberation) and empirical facts (determinate observation). Its sequel, *The Poetics of Reverie*, will elaborate on these key phenomenological insights while incorporating themes from Jungian depth-psychology, including those of *animus* and *anima* and the importance of imaginary idealization in their reconciliation.

Bachelard's poetics of space equally entails a poetics of time. The temporality of the image is, he insists, that of the instant. Here we are concerned with epiphanies that riddle the continuity of time. Bachelard claims that every true poetic image breaks with linear clock time, introducing a dimension of verticality in depth and height.[8] Where prosaic time is evolving and continuous (like Bergson's), poetic time is disruptive and surprising. Echoing Coleridge's definition of poetry as the "balance or reconciliation of opposite or discordant qualities," Bachelard maintains that the poetic instant is a "harmonic relation between opposites."[9] Confronted by the successive antitheses of ordinary time, the poet refuses to comply, resisting the habit of chronological sequencing by transmuting opposition into instantaneous "ambivalence" (where contraries coexist). The poetic imagination thus substitutes simultaneity for succession. It calls for a radical transmutation of values in a gesture Bachelard calls "rapture" or "ecstasy." A genuine poetics of space explodes the continuum of the world's time, as happens in the reading or dreaming of a great fantasy. Just think, for example, of how the creative revisiting of a childhood room can provoke a sense of "involuntary memory" that renders the recalled image timeless and essential—the past suddenly transformed into a miraculous present, as in the Proustian remembrance of the mother's bedtime kiss. But for Bachelard the imagination even surpasses the limits of the personal past, embracing what he calls the "antecedence of being." His ruminations on the epiphanic power of dwellings—from nests and shells to cellars and attics—epitomize this ontological embrace.

But perhaps the most original contribution that *The Poetics of Space* makes to contemporary poetics is its exploration of the rapport between imagination and *language*. It is here that Bachelard clarifies his bold claim that images "speak" the emergence of being, setting verbs in motion and turning sensations into metaphors by inviting us to live figuratively. For this reason, he insists, images are more demanding and rewarding than ideas. They give logos to perception. So that, as he says, we can devote our reading being to an image that confers being on us. In fact, the image that is the pure product of "absolute imagination" is a specific phenomenon of the *speaking creature*.[10] Here, under the ancient Greek term *Logos*—with its metaphysical and biblical resonances—Bachelard brings together the fundamental notions of Being, Word and Creation. But the Logos that commands our attention speaks in the lower case of cadences and rhymes. Bachelard always sounds the extraordinary in the ordinary.

So where does this Logos speak from? Bracketing standard causal and metaphysical accounts, Bachelard adopts what he calls a phenomenological attitude of "daily crisis" that allows consciousness to be exposed to the moment's gift.[11] Resolved to let images speak for themselves, he resists all determinist models of explaining consciousness in terms of prior infantile, historical or behavioral events. One cannot, he says, explain "the flower by the fertilizer."[12] Or again:

> Poetry extends well beyond psychoanalysis on every side. From a dream it always makes a daydream [*rêverie*]. And the poetic daydream cannot content itself with the rudiments of a story; it cannot be tied to a knotty complex. The poet lives a daydream that is awake, but above all, his daydream remains in the world, facing worldly things. It gathers the universe together around and in an object.[13]

Thus a poet can, for example, condense cosmic wealth into the image of a slender casket, the universe into a miniature purse. Images captured from the past act as triggers into a timeless elemental unconscious, extending across individuals and generations, and opening up a limitless future. He writes: "The casket contains the things that are *unforgettable,* unforgettable for us, but also unforgettable for those to whom we are going to give our treasures. Here the past, the present and a future are condensed. Thus the casket is memory of what is immemorial."[14]

Bachelard's work had a considerable impact on his intellectual contemporaries. He influenced structuralists like Foucault and Althusser with his revolutionary notion of the "epistemological break" (the idea of radical rupture between different paradigms of knowledge), existentialists like Merleau-Ponty with his discovery of the imaginary as a cosmic-psychic "element," and hermeneutic thinkers like Ricoeur with the claim that the image is a four-way relationship between author, reader, text and world. Contrary to the formalist ideology of the absolute text (closed in on itself), Bachelard celebrated the interactive function of imagination as a symbolizing process involving someone saying something to someone about something. Poetics, for Bachelard, is not a matter of anonymous floating signifiers; it signals a relational dynamics between beings, involving vital dimensions of intimacy, secrecy, desire and repose. Imagination is at its best when it is incarnate, elemental, opening out into time and space, even when the space is elsewhere—before being, beneath being, beyond being, more than being. For Bachelard, images are not merely seen but lived. They are not just vision, but the cosmos itself as it expands and amplifies from the minute to the magnified, creating a "concordance of world immensity with intimate depth of being."[15] Images touch us at the deepest place of existence and remake the world again and again. Baudelaire—oft cited by Bachelard—expresses this with his notion of "correspondences" that transform vast expanses into the intensity of our inmost being. Correspondences institute "transactions between two kinds of grandeur"—inner and outer.[16] They draft peace treaties between self and world. "In the realm of images, there can be no contradiction."[17]

The ultimate task of a phenomenology of imagination is, Bachelard concludes, to capture images at their *inception,* as they begin anew. In this the phenomenologist and the poet are one, for they both know that imaginative contact with the outer world renews our inner being. To imagine going down into the water or wandering in the desert is to change space; and to change space is to change being.[18] To dream otherwise—even if it is for the moment of a reverie or poem—is to *exist* otherwise. And Bachelard invites each reader to join company with his walking companions—Rilke, Lautréamont, Mallarmé, Poe—on such grand imaginary journeys. Once you have entered the poetics of space there is no going back. The home you revisit is never the same again.

RICHARD KEARNEY

NOTES

1. Rilke, "Archaic Torso of Apollo."
2. Gaston Bachelard, *The Poetics of Space* (henceforth *PS*), trans. Maria Jolas (New York: Penguin, 2014), p. 21.
3. *PS*, p. 1. It is important nonetheless to note that Bachelard's turn toward poetics did not mean turning his back on science. His main career remained that of a philosopher of science and, while he saw poetic imagination and scientific reason as traveling on apparently separate tracks, he also saw interesting links between them, especially in their prioritizing of the possible over the real and in their transformation of ordinary language (see Roch Smith, "Gaston Bachelard and the Power of Poetic Being," in *French Literature Series,* vol. IV, [1977], pp. 235–37). It was Bachelard's hope to return to more writing on science after *The Poetics of Reverie* (henceforth *PR*). Also alluding to the subtle relationship between science and poetics in Bachelard, Etienne Gilson notes in his foreword to the 1963 edition of *The Poetics of Space* (Boston: Beacon, 1994): "[Bachelard's] whole career was founded upon his philosophical critique of scientific knowledge and his conception of a free type of rationalism, quite different from the abstract mode of thinking which the word usually designates, and wholly bent upon the art of using reason as an instrument to achieve an always closer approach to concrete reality" (p. viii).
4. *PS*, pp. 1–2.
5. As he later put it in *The Poetics of Reverie*: "The more subtle duality of the Voice and the Sound rises to the cosmic level of a duality of the breath and the wind. Where is the dominant being of the spoken reverie? When a dreamer speaks, who is speaking, he or the world? . . . 'All the being of the world, if it dreams, dreams that it is speaking' [Henri Bosco]. But does the being of the world dream? Ah! long ago, before 'culture,' who would have doubted it? Everyone knew that metal ripened slowly in the mine. And how can anything ripen without dreaming?" *PR*, trans. Daniel Russell (Boston: Beacon, 1971), p. 187. See also Richard Kearney, *Poetics of Imagining* (New York: Fordham University Press, 1998), pp. 109–10.
6. *PS*, p. 96. On sounding the vibrant Logos of being, see also *Poetics of Imagining*, p. 107 et seq., and Eileen Rizo-Patron's excellent study "Awakening the Inner Ear: Gadamer and Bachelard in Search of a Living Logos," *Translation and Literary Studies,*

ed. Marella Feltrin-Morris et al. (New York: St. Jerome Publishing, 2012), pp. 52–68, esp. pp. 57–61. See also Miles Kennedy, *A Concrete Bachelardian Metaphysics* (Oxford: Peter Lang, 2012).

7. *PS*, p. 122. See also *Poetics of Imagining*: in Bachelard "the authentic image . . . does not represent something, it addresses someone" (p. 109).

8. Bachelard, "Poetic Instant and Metaphysical Instant," in *Intuition of the Instant,* trans. Eileen Rizo-Patron (Evanston, IL: Northwestern University Press, 2013), pp. 58–63.

9. Bachelard, *Intuition of the Instant*, p. 59. On Bachelard's critique of Bergson's notion of time, see Jean-François Perraudin, "A Non-Bergsonian Bachelard," in *Continental Philosophy Review* 41 (2008): 463–79. See also Richard Kearney, "Bachelard and the Epiphanic Instant," in *Philosophy Today (SPEP Supplement),* vol. 33 (2008): 38–44.

10. *PS*, p. 96.

11. *PS*, p. 3.

12. *PS*, p. 14.

13. *PS*, p. 105.

14. *PS*, p. 105. On Bachelard's own past see the very poignant piece "Bachelard et sa fille," by Alain Garric, in Libellules, *Le Monde,* January 4, 2004. Here it is worth recalling Bachelard's comment on poetic time in *The Poetics of Reverie:* "In reverie we re-enter into contact with possibilities which destiny has not been able to make use of. A great paradox is connected with the reveries toward childhood: in us this dead past has a future . . . which opens before any rediscovered image" (*PR*, p. 112). Poetic reverie performs a double action of retrieving unactivated seeds of the past while simultaneously provoking crises and ruptures that break the conjunctive tissue of time and carve open new spaces of becoming (*PS*, p. 31).

15. *PS*, p. 207.

16. *PS*, p. 210.

17. *PS*, p. 219.

18. *PS*, pp. 221–23.

Suggestions for Further Reading

WORKS BY GASTON BACHELARD

Bachelard, Gaston. *Intuition of the Instant.* Trans. Eileen Rizo-Patron. Evanston, IL: Northwestern University Press, 2013.

———. *Dialectics of Duration.* Trans. Mary McAllester Jones. Manchester, UK: Clinamen Press, 2000.

———. *Lautréamont.* Trans. Robert S. Dupree. Dallas: Dallas Institute Publications, 1986.

———. *Air and Dreams: An Essay on the Imagination of Movement.* Trans. Edith Farrell and Frederick Farrell. Dallas: Dallas Institute Publications, 1988.

———. *Earth and Reveries of Repose: An Essay on Images of Interiority.* Trans. Mary McAllester. Dallas: Dallas Institute Publications, 2011.

———. *The Right to Dream.* Trans. J. A. Underwood. Dallas: Dallas Institute Publications, 1988.

CRITICAL SOURCES

Gilson, Etienne. "Foreword" to *The Poetics of Space.* Trans. Maria Jolas. Boston: Beacon Press, 1994, pp. xi–xiv.

Kaplan, Edward. "Gaston Bachelard's Philosophy of Imagination," *Philosophy and Phenomenological Research,* 1972, pp. 1–24.

Kearney, Richard. "Bachelard and the Epiphanic Instant." *Philosophy Today* 52 (2008): 38–45.

———. "The Poetical Imagination" (Gaston Bachelard). In *Poetics of Imagining.* New York: Fordham University Press, 1998, pp. 96–119.

Kennedy, Miles. *Home: A Concrete Bachelardian Metaphysics.* Oxford: Peter Lang, 2011.

McAllester Jones, Mary. *Gaston Bachelard: Subversive Humanist.* Madison and London: University of Wisconsin Press, 1991.

Rizo-Patron, Eileen. "Awakening the Inner Ear: Gadamer and Bachelard in Search of a Living Logos." *Translation and Literary Studies.* Ed. Marella Feltrin-Morris et al. Manchester, UK: 2012, pp. 54–68.

———. "*Regressus ad Uterum*: Bachelard's Elemental Hermeneutics." *Philosophy Today* 52 (2008): 21–30.

Smith, Roch C. *Gaston Bachelard.* Boston: Twayne Publishers, 1982. See especially the chapter "A Phenomenology of the Creative Imagination," pp. 116–34.

———. "Gaston Bachelard and the Poetic Power of Being." *French Literary Criticism* IV (1977): 235–38.

RELATED READINGS

Casey, Edward S. *Getting Back into Place: Toward a Renewed Understanding of Place-World.* Bloomington: Indiana University Press, 1993.

Merleau-Ponty, Maurice. "Space." *The Phenomenology of Perception.* Trans. Colin Smith. London: Routledge & Kegan Paul, 1962, pp. 243–98.

The Poetics of Space

INTRODUCTION

I

A philosopher who has evolved his entire thinking from the fundamental themes of the philosophy of science, and followed the main line of the active, growing rationalism of contemporary science as closely as he could, must forget his learning and break with all his habits of philosophical research, if he wants to study the problems posed by the poetic imagination. For here the cultural past doesn't count. The long day-in, day-out effort of putting together and constructing his thoughts is ineffectual. One must be receptive, receptive to the image at the moment it appears: if there be a philosophy of poetry, it must appear and re-appear through a significant verse, in total adherence to an isolated image; to be exact, in the very ecstasy of the newness of the image. The poetic image is a sudden salience on the surface of the psyche, the lesser psychological causes of which have not been sufficiently investigated. Nor can anything general and co-ordinated serve as a basis for a philosophy of poetry. The idea of principle or "basis" in this case would be disastrous, for it would interfere with the essential psychic actuality, the essential novelty of the poem. And whereas philosophical reflection applied to scientific thinking elaborated over a long period of time requires any new idea to become integrated in a body of tested ideas, even though this body of ideas be subjected to profound change by the new idea (as is the case in all the revolutions of contemporary science), the philosophy of poetry must acknowledge that the poetic act has no past, at least no recent past, in which its preparation and appearance could be followed.

Later, when I shall have occasion to mention the relation of a new poetic image to an archetype lying dormant in the depths of the unconscious, I shall have to make it understood that this relation is not, properly speaking, a *causal* one. The poetic image is not subject to an inner thrust. It is not an echo of the past. On the contrary: through the brilliance of an image, the distant past resounds with echoes, and it is hard to know at what depth these echoes will reverberate and die away. Because of its novelty and its action, the poetic image has an entity and a dynamism of its own; it is referable to a direct *ontology*. This ontology is what I plan to study.

Very often, then, it is in the opposite of causality, that is, in *reverberation,* which has been so subtly analyzed by Minkowski,[1] that I think we find the real measure of the being of a poetic image. In this reverberation, the poetic image will have a sonority of being. The poet speaks on the threshold of being. Therefore, in order to determine the being of an image, we shall have to experience its reverberation in the manner of Minkowski's phenomenology.

To say that the poetic image is independent of causality is to make a rather serious statement. But the causes cited by psychologists and psychoanalysts can never really explain the wholly unexpected nature of the new image, any more than they can explain the attraction it holds for a mind that is foreign to the process of its creation. The poet does not confer the past of his image upon me, and yet his image immediately takes root in me. The communicability of an unusual image is a fact of great ontological significance. We shall return to this question of communion through brief, isolated, rapid actions. Images excite us—afterwards—but they are not the phenomena of an excitement. In all psychological research, we can, of course, bear in mind psychoanalytical methods for determining the personality of a poet, and thus find a measure of the pressures—but above all of the oppressions—that a poet has been subjected to in the course of his life. But the poetic act itself, the sudden image, the flare-up of being in the imagination, are inaccessible to such investigations. In order to clarify the problem of the poetic image philosophically, we shall have to have recourse to a phenomenology of the imagination. By this should be understood a study of the phenomenon of the poetic image when it emerges into the consciousness as a direct product of the heart, soul and being of man, apprehended in his actuality.

II

I shall perhaps be asked why, departing from my former point of view, I now seek a phenomenological determination of images. In my earlier works on the subject of the imagination, I did, in fact, consider it preferable to maintain as objective a position as possible with regard to the images of the four material elements, the four principles of the intuitive cosmogonies, and, faithful to my habits as a philosopher of science, I tried to consider images without attempting personal interpretation. Little by little, this method, which has in its favor scientific prudence, seemed to me to be an insufficient basis on which to found a metaphysics of the imagination. The "prudent" attitude itself is a refusal to obey the immediate dynamics of the image. I have come to realize how difficult it is to break away from this "prudence." To say that one has left certain intellectual habits behind is easy enough, but how is it to be achieved? For a rationalist, this constitutes a minor daily crisis, a sort of split in one's thinking which, even though its object be partial— a mere image—has nonetheless great psychic repercussions. However, this minor cultural crisis, this crisis on the simple level of a new image, contains the entire paradox of a phenomenology of the imagination, which is: how can an image, at times very unusual, appear to be a concentration of the entire psyche? How—with no preparation—can this singular, short-lived event constituted by the appearance of an unusual poetic image, react on other minds and in other hearts, despite all the barriers of common sense, all the disciplined schools of thought, content in their immobility?

It seemed to me, then, that this transsubjectivity of the

image could not be understood, in its essence, through the habits of subjective reference alone. Only phenomenology—that is to say, consideration of the *onset of the image* in an individual consciousness—can help us to restore the subjectivity of images and to measure their fullness, their strength and their transsubjectivity. These subjectivities and transsubjectivities cannot be determined once and for all, for the poetic image is essentially *variational,* and not, as in the case of the concept, *constitutive.* No doubt, it is an arduous task—as well as a monotonous one—to isolate the transforming action of the poetic imagination in the detail of the variations of the images. For a reader of poems, therefore, an appeal to a doctrine that bears the frequently misunderstood name of phenomenology risks falling on deaf ears. And yet, independent of all doctrine, this appeal is clear: the reader of poems is asked to consider an image not as an object and even less as the substitute for an object, but to seize its specific reality. For this, the act of the creative consciousness must be systematically associated with the most fleeting product of that consciousness, the poetic image. At the level of the poetic image, the duality of subject and object is iridescent, shimmering, unceasingly active in its inversions. In this domain of the creation of the poetic image by the poet, phenomenology, if one dare to say so, is a microscopic phenomenology. As a result, this phenomenology will probably be strictly elementary. In this union, through the image, of a pure but short-lived subjectivity and a reality which will not necessarily reach its final constitution, the phenomenologist finds a field for countless experiments; he profits by observations that can be exact because they are simple, because they "have no consequences," as is the case with scientific thought, which is always related thought. The image, in its simplicity, has no need of scholarship. It is the property of a naïve consciousness; in its expression, it is youthful language. The poet, in the novelty of his images, is always the origin of language. To specify exactly what a phenomenology of the image can be, to specify that the image comes *before* thought, we should have to say that poetry, rather than being a phenomenology of the mind, is a phenomenology of the soul.

We should then have to collect documentation on the subject of the *dreaming consciousness*.

The language of contemporary French philosophy—and even more so, psychology—hardly uses the dual meaning of the words "soul" and "mind." As a result, they are both somewhat deaf to certain themes that are very numerous in German philosophy, in which the distinction between mind and soul (*der Geist und die Seele*) is so clear. But since a philosophy of poetry must be given the entire force of the vocabulary, it should not simplify, not harden anything. For such a philosophy, mind and soul are not synonymous, and by taking them as such, we bar translation of certain invaluable texts, we distort documents brought to light thanks to the archeologists of the image. The word "soul" is an immortal word. In certain poems it cannot be effaced, for it is a word born of our breath.[2] The vocal importance alone of a word should arrest the attention of a phenomenologist of poetry. The word "soul" can, in fact, be poetically spoken with such conviction that it constitutes a commitment for the entire poem. The poetic register that corresponds to the soul must therefore remain open to our phenomenological investigations.

In the domain of painting, in which realization seems to imply decisions that derive from the mind, and rejoin obligations of the world of perception, the phenomenology of the soul can reveal the first commitment of an oeuvre. René Huyghe, in his very fine preface for the exhibition of Georges Rouault's works in Albi, wrote: "If we wanted to find out wherein Rouault explodes definitions . . . we should perhaps have to call upon a word that has become rather outmoded, which is the word, soul." He goes on to show that in order to understand, to sense and to love Rouault's work, we must "start from the center, at the very heart of the circle from where the whole thing derives its source and meaning: and here we come back again to that forgotten, outcast word, the soul." Indeed, the soul—as Rouault's painting proves—possesses an inner light, the light that an inner vision knows and expresses in the world of brilliant colors, in the world of sunlight, so that a veritable reversal of psychological perspectives is demanded of those who seek to understand, at the same time that they love Rouault's painting. They must participate in an inner light which is not a reflection of a light from the outside world. No doubt there are many facile claims to the expressions "inner vision" and "inner light." But here it is a painter speaking, a producer of lights. He knows from what heat source the light comes. He experiences the intimate meaning of the passion for red. At the core of such painting, there is a soul in combat—the fauvism, the wildness, is interior. Painting like this is therefore a phenomenon of the soul. The oeuvre must redeem an impassioned soul.

These pages by René Huyghe corroborate my idea that it is reasonable to speak of a phenomenology of the soul. In many circumstances we are obliged to acknowledge that poetry is a commitment of the soul. A consciousness associated with the soul is more relaxed, less intentionalized than a consciousness associated with the phenomena of the mind. Forces are manifested in poems that do not pass through the circuits of knowledge. The dialectics of inspiration and talent become clear if we consider their two poles: the soul and the mind. In my opinion, soul and mind are indispensable for studying the phenomena of the poetic image in their various nuances, above all, for following the evolution of poetic images from the original state of revery to that of execution. In fact, in a future work, I plan to concentrate particularly on poetic revery as a phenomenology of the soul. In itself, revery constitutes a psychic condition that is too frequently confused with dream. But when it is a question of poetic revery, of revery that derives pleasure not only from itself, but also prepares poetic pleasure for other souls, one realizes that one is no longer drifting into somnolence. The mind is able to relax, but in poetic revery the soul keeps watch, with no tension, calmed and active. To compose a finished, well-constructed poem, the mind is obliged to make projects that prefigure it. But for a simple poetic image, there is no project; a flicker of the soul is all that is needed.

And this is how a poet poses the phenomenological problem of the soul in all clarity. Pierre-Jean Jouve writes:[3] "Poetry is a soul inaugurating a form." The soul inaugurates. Here it is the supreme power. It is human dignity. Even if the "form" was already well-known, previously discovered, carved from "commonplaces," before the interior poetic light was turned upon it, it was a mere object for the mind. But the soul comes and inaugurates the form, dwells in it, takes pleasure in it. Pierre-Jean Jouve's statement can therefore be taken as a clear maxim of a phenomenology of the soul.

III

Since a phenomenological inquiry on poetry aspires to go so far and so deep, because of methodological obligations, it must go beyond the sentimental resonances with which we receive (more or less richly—whether this richness be within ourselves or within the poem) a work of art. This is where the phenomeno-logical doublet of resonances and repercussions must be sensi-tized. The resonances are dispersed on the different planes of our life in the world, while the repercussions invite us to give greater depth to our own existence. In the resonance we hear the poem, in the reverberations we speak it, it is our own. The reverberations bring about a change of being. It is as though the poet's being were our being. The multiplicity of resonances then issues from the reverberations' unity of being. Or, to put it more simply, this is an impression that all impassioned poetry-lovers know well: the poem possesses us entirely. This grip that poetry acquires on our very being bears a phenomenological mark that is unmistakable. The exuberance and depth of a poem are always phenomena of the resonance-reverberation doublet. It is as though the poem, through its exuberance, awakened new depths in us. In order to ascertain the psychological action of a poem, we should therefore have to follow the two perspectives of phenomenological analysis, toward the outpourings of the mind and toward the profundities of the soul.

Needless to say, the reverberation, in spite of its derivative name, has a simple phenomenological nature in the domain of poetic imagination. For it involves bringing about a veritable awakening of poetic creation, even in the soul of the reader, through the reverberations of a single poetic image. By its novelty, a poetic image sets in motion the entire linguistic mechanism. The poetic image places us at the origin of the speaking being.

Through this reverberation, by going *immediately* beyond all psychology or psychoanalysis, we feel a poetic power rising naïvely within us. After the original reverberation, we are able to experience resonances, sentimental repercussions, reminders of our past. But the image has touched the depths before it stirs the surface. And this is also true of a simple experience of reading. The image offered us by reading the poem now becomes really our own. It takes root in us. It has been given us by another, but we begin to have the impression that we could have created it, that we should have created it. It becomes a new being in our language, expressing us by making us what it expresses; in other words, it is at once a becoming of expression, and a becoming of our being. Here expression creates being.

This last remark defines the level of the ontology toward which I am working. As a general thesis I believe that everything specifically human in man is *logos*. One would not be able to meditate in a zone that preceded language. But even if this thesis appears to reject an ontological depth, it should be granted, at least as a working hypothesis appropriate to the subject of the poetic imagination.

Thus the poetic image, which stems from the logos, is personally innovating. We cease to consider it as an "object" but feel that the "objective" critical attitude stifles the "reverberation" and rejects on principle the depth at which the original poetic phenomenon starts. As for the psychologist, being deafened by the resonances, he keeps trying to *describe* his feelings. And the psychoanalyst, victim of his method, inevitably intellectualizes the image, losing the reverberations in his effort to untangle the skein of his interpretations. He understands the image more deeply than the psychologist. But that's just the point, he "understands" it. For the psychoanalyst, the poetic image always has a context. When he interprets it, however, he translates it into a language that is different from the poetic logos. Never, in fact, was *"traduttore, traditore"* more justifiably applicable.

When I receive a new poetic image, I experience its quality of inter-subjectivity. I know that I am going to repeat it in order to communicate my enthusiasm. When considered in transmission from one soul to another, it becomes evident that a poetic image eludes causality. Doctrines that are timidly causal, such as psychology, or strongly causal, such as psycho-analysis, can hardly determine the ontology of what is poetic. For nothing prepares a poetic image, especially not culture, in the literary sense, and especially not perception, in the psychological sense.

I always come then to the same conclusion: the essential newness of the poetic image poses the problem of the speaking being's creativeness. Through this creativeness the imagining consciousness proves to be, very simply but very purely, an origin. In a study of the imagination, a phenomenology of the poetic imagination must concentrate on bringing out this quality of origin in various poetic images.

IV

By thus limiting my inquiry to the poetic image at its origin, proceeding from pure imagination, I leave aside the problem of the *composition* of the poem as a grouping together of numerous images. Into this composition enter certain psychologically complex elements that associate earlier cultures with actual literary ideals—components which a complete phenomenology would no doubt be obliged to consider. But so extensive a project might be prejudicial to the purity of the phenomenological observations, however elementary, that I should like to present. The real phenomenologist must make it a point to be systematically modest. This being the case, it seems to me that merely to refer to phenomenological reading powers, which make of the reader a poet on a level with the image he has read, shows already a taint of pride. Indeed, it would be a lack of modesty on my part to assume personally a reading power that could match and re-live the power of organized, complete creation implied by a poem in its entirety.

But there is even less hope of attaining to a synthetic phenomenology which would dominate an entire oeuvre, as certain
psychoanalysts believe they can do. It is therefore on the level
of detached images that I shall succeed in "reverberating" phenomenologically.

Precisely this touch of pride, this lesser pride, this mere reader's pride that thrives in the solitude of reading, bears the unmistakable mark of phenomenology, if its simplicity is maintained.
Here the phenomenologist has nothing in common with the literary critic who, as has frequently been noted, judges a work
that he could not create and, if we are to believe certain facile
condemnations, would not want to create. A literary critic is a
reader who is necessarily severe. By turning inside out like a
glove an overworked complex that has become debased to the
point of being part of the vocabulary of statesmen, we might say
that the literary critic and the professor of rhetoric, who know-
all and judge-all, readily go in for a simplex of superiority. As for
me, being an addict of felicitous reading, I only read and re-read
what I like, with a bit of reader's pride mixed in with much
enthusiasm. But whereas pride usually develops into a massive
sentiment that weighs upon the entire psyche, the touch of pride
that is born of adherence to the felicity of an image remains
secret and unobtrusive. It is within us, mere readers that we are,
it is for us, and for us alone. It is a homely sort of pride. Nobody
knows that in reading we are re-living our temptations to be a
poet. All readers who have a certain passion for reading nurture and repress, through reading, the desire to become a writer.
When the page we have just read is too near perfection, our
modesty suppresses this desire. But it reappears, nevertheless. In
any case, every reader who re-reads a work that he likes knows
that its pages *concern* him. In Jean-Pierre Richard's excellent
collection of essays entitled *Poésie et profondeur* (Poetry and
Depth), there is one devoted to Baudelaire and one to Verlaine.
Emphasis is laid on Baudelaire, however, since, as the author
says, his work "concerns us." There is great difference of tone
between the two essays. Unlike Baudelaire, Verlaine does not
attract complete phenomenological attention. And this is always
the case. In certain types of reading with which we are in deep

sympathy, in the very expression itself, we are the "beneficia-ries." Jean-Paul Richter, in *Le Titan*, gives the following descrip-tion of his hero: "He read eulogies of great men with as much pleasure as though he himself had been the object of these pan-egyrics."[4] In any case, harmony in reading is inseparable from admiration. We can admire more or less, but a sincere impulse, a little impulse toward admiration, is always necessary if we are to receive the phenomenological benefit of a poetic image. The slightest critical consideration arrests this impulse by put-ting the mind in second position, destroying the primitivity of the imagination. In this admiration, which goes beyond the pas-sivity of contemplative attitudes, the joy of reading appears to be the reflection of the joy of writing, as though the reader were the writer's ghost. At least the reader participates in the joy of cre-ation that, for Bergson, is the sign of creation.[5] Here, creation takes place on the tenuous thread of the sentence, in the fleeting life of an expression. But this poetic expression, although it has no vital necessity, has a bracing effect on our lives, for all that. To speak well is part of living well. The poetic image is an emer-gence from language, it is always a little above the language of signification. By living the poems we read, we have then the sal-utary experience of emerging. This, no doubt, is emerging at short range. But these acts of emergence are repeated; poetry puts language in a state of emergence, in which life becomes manifest through its vivacity. These linguistic impulses, which stand out from the ordinary rank of pragmatic language, are miniatures of the vital impulse. A micro-Bergsonism that aban-doned the thesis of language-as-instrument in favor of the thesis of language-as-reality would find in poetry numerous docu-ments on the intense life of language.

Thus, along with considerations on the life of words, as it appears in the evolution of language across the centuries, the poetic image, as a mathematician would say, presents us with a sort of differential of this evolution. A great verse can have a great influence on the soul of a language. It awakens images that had been effaced, at the same time that it confirms the unforeseeable nature of speech. And if we render speech unforeseeable, is this not an apprenticeship to freedom? What

delight the poetic imagination takes in making game of cen-
sors! Time was when the poetic arts codified the licenses to be
permitted. Contemporary poetry, however, has introduced
freedom in the very body of the language. As a result, poetry
appears as a phenomenon of freedom.

V

Even at the level of an isolated poetic image, if only in the progression of expression constituted by the verse, the phenomenological reverberation can appear; and in its extreme
simplicity, it gives us mastery of our tongue. Here we are in the
presence of a minuscule phenomenon of the shimmering consciousness. The poetic image is certainly the psychic event that
has the least importance. To seek justification of it in terms of
perceptible reality, to determine its place and rôle in the poem's
composition, are two tasks that do not need to be undertaken
until later. In the first phenomenological inquiry of the poetic
imagination, the isolated image, the phrase that carries it forward, the verse, or occasionally the stanza in which the poetic
image radiates, form *language areas* that should be studied by
means of topoanalysis. J. B. Pontalis, for instance, presents
Michel Leiris as a "lonely prospector in the galleries of words,"[6]
which describes extremely well this fibered space traversed by
the simple impetus of words that have been experienced. The
atomism of conceptual language demands reasons for fixation,
forces of centralization. But the verse always has a movement,
the image flows into the line of the verse, carrying the imagination along with it, as though the imagination created a nerve
fiber. Pontalis adds the following (p. 932), which deserves to be
remembered as a sure index for a phenomenology of expression: "The speaking subject is the entire subject." And it no
longer seems paradoxical to say that the speaking subject exists
in his entirety in a poetic image, because unless he abandons
himself to it without reservations, he does not enter into the
poetic space of the image. Very clearly, the poetic image furnishes one of the simplest experiences of language that has

been lived. And if, as I propose to do, it is considered as an origin of consciousness, it points to a phenomenology.

Also, if we had to name a "school" of phenomenology, it would no doubt be in connection with the poetic phenomenon that we should find the clearest, the really elementary, lessons. In a recent book, J. H. Van den Berg[7] writes: "Poets and painters are born phenomenonologists." And noting that things "speak" to us and that, as a result of this fact, if we give this language its full value, we have a contact with things, Van den Berg adds: "We are continually living a solution of problems that reflection can not hope to solve." The philosopher whose investigations are centered on the speaking being will find encouragement in these lines by this learned Dutch phenomenologist.

VI

The phenomenological situation with regard to psychoanalytical investigation will perhaps be more precisely stated if, in connection with poetic images, we are able to isolate a sphere of *pure sublimation;* of a sublimation which sublimates nothing, which is relieved of the burden of passion, and freed from the pressure of desire. By thus giving to the poetic image at its peak an absolute of sublimation, I place heavy stakes on a simple nuance. It seems to me, however, that poetry gives abundant proof of this absolute sublimation, as will be seen frequently in the course of this work. When psychologists and psychoanalysts are furnished this proof, they cease to see anything in the poetic image but a simple game, a short-lived, totally vain game. Images, in particular, have no significance for them—neither from the standpoint of the passions, nor from that of psychology or psychoanalysis. It does not occur to them that the significance of such images is precisely a poetic significance. But poetry is there with its countless surging images, images through which the creative imagination comes to live in its own domain.

For a phenomenologist, the attempt to attribute antecedents to an image, when we are in the very existence of the image, is a sign of inveterate psychologism. On the contrary, let us take the poetic image in its being. For the poetic consciousness is so wholly absorbed by the image that appears on the language, above customary language; the language it speaks with the poetic image is so new that correlations between past and present can no longer be usefully considered.

The examples I shall give of breaks in significance, sensation and sentiment will oblige the reader to grant me that the poetic image is under the sign of a new being.

This new being is happy man.

Happy in speech, therefore unhappy in reality, will be the psychoanalyst's immediate objection. Sublimation, for him, is nothing but a vertical compensation, a flight upwards, exactly in the same way that compensation is a lateral flight. And right away, the psychoanalyst will abandon ontological investigation of the image, to dig into the past of man. He sees and points out the poet's secret sufferings. He explains the flower by the fertilizer.

The phenomenologist does not go that far. For him, the image is there, the word speaks, the word of the poet speaks to him. There is no need to have lived through the poet's sufferings in order to seize the felicity of speech offered by the poet—a felicity that dominates tragedy itself. Sublimation in poetry towers above the psychology of the mundanely unhappy soul. For it is a fact that poetry possesses a felicity of its own, however great the tragedy it may be called upon to illustrate.

Pure sublimation, as I see it, poses a serious problem of method, for, needless to say, the phenomenologist cannot disregard the deep psychological reality of the processes of sublimation that have been so lengthily examined by psychoanalysis. His task is that of proceeding phenomenologically to images which have not been experienced, and which life does not prepare, but which the poet creates; of living what has not been lived, and being receptive to an overture of language. There exist a few poems, such as certain poems by Pierre-Jean Jouve, in which experiences of this kind may be found. Indeed, I know of no oeuvre that has been nourished on psychoanalytical meditation more than Jouve's. However, here and there, his poetry passes through flames of such intensity that we no longer need live at its original source. He himself has said:[8] "Poetry constantly surpasses its origins, and because it suffers more deeply in ecstasy or in sorrow, it retains greater freedom." Again, on page 112: "The further I advanced in time, the more the plunge was controlled, removed from the contributory cause, directed toward the pure form of language." I cannot say whether or not Pierre-Jean Jouve would agree to consider the causes divulged by psychoanalysis as "contributory." But in the region of "the pure form of language" the psychoanalyst's causes do not allow us to predict the poetic image in its newness. They are, at the very most, opportunities for liberation. And in the poetic age in which we live, it is in this that poetry is specifically "surprising." Its images are therefore unpredictable. Most literary critics are insufficiently aware of this unpredictability, which is precisely what upsets the plans of the usual psychological explanations. But the poet states clearly: "Poetry, especially in its present endeavors, (can) only correspond to attentive thought that is enamored of something unknown, and essentially receptive to becoming." Later, on page 170: "Consequently, a new definition of a poet is in view, which is: he who knows, that is to say, who transcends, and names what he knows." Lastly (p.10): "There is no poetry without absolute creation."

Such poetry is rare.[9] The great mass of poetry is more mixed with passion, more psychologized. Here, however, rarity and exception do not confirm the rule, but contradict it and set up a new regime. Without the region of absolute sublimation—however restrained and elevated it may be, and even though it may seem to lie beyond the reach of psychologists or psychoanalysts, who, after all, have no reason to examine pure poetry—poetry's exact polarity cannot be revealed.

We may hesitate in determining the exact level of disruption, we may also remain for a long time in the domain of the confusing passions that *perturb* poetry. Moreover, the height at which we encounter pure sublimation is doubtless not the same for all souls. But at least the necessity of separating a sublimation examined by a psychoanalyst from one examined by a phenomenologist of poetry is a necessity of method. A psychoanalyst can of course study the human character of poets but, as a result of his own sojourn in the region of the passions, he is not prepared to study poetic images in their exalting reality. C. J. Jung

said this, in fact, very clearly: by persisting in the habits of judgment inherent in psychoanalysis, "interest is diverted from the
work of art and loses itself in the inextricable chaos of psychological antecedents; the poet becomes a 'clinical case,' an example, to which is given a certain number in the *psychopathia
sexualis*. Thus the psychoanalysis of a work of art moves away
from its object and carries the discussion into a domain of general human interest, which is not in the least peculiar to the artist and, particularly, has no importance for his art."[10] Merely
with a view to summarizing this discussion, I should like to
make a polemical remark, although indulging in polemics is
not one of my habits.

A Roman said to a shoemaker who had directed his gaze
too high:

Ne sutor ultra crepidam.

Every time there is a question of pure sublimation, when the
very being of poetry must be determined, shouldn't the phenomenologist say to the psychoanalyst:

Ne psuchor ultra uterum.

VII

In other words, as soon as an art has become autonomous, it
makes a fresh start. It is therefore salient to consider this start as
a sort of phenomenology. On principle, phenomenology liqui-
dates the past and confronts what is new. Even in an art like
painting, which bears witness to a skill, the important successes
take place independently of skill. In a study of the painting of
Charles Lapicque, by Jean Lescure, we read: "Although his
work gives evidence of wide culture and knowledge of all the
dynamic expressions of space, they are not applied, they are not
made into recipes . . . Knowing must therefore be accompanied
by an equal capacity to forget knowing. Non-knowing is not a
form of ignorance but a difficult transcendence of knowledge.

This is the price that must be paid for an oeuvre to be, at all times, a sort of pure beginning, which makes its creation an exercise in freedom."[11] These lines are of essential importance for us, in that they may be transposed immediately into a phenomenology of the poetic. In poetry, non-knowing is a primal condition; if there exists a skill in the writing of poetry, it is in the minor task of associating images. But the entire life of the image is in its dazzling splendor, in the fact that an image is a transcending of all the premises of sensibility.

It becomes evident, then, that a man's work stands out from life to such an extent that life cannot explain it. Jean Lescure says of the painter (loc. cit., p. 132): "Lapicque demands of the creative act that it should offer him as much surprise as life itself." Art, then, is an increase of life, a sort of competition of surprises that stimulates our consciousness and keeps it from becoming somnolent. In a quotation of Lapicque himself (given by Lescure, p. 132) we read: "If, for instance, I want to paint horses taking the water hurdle at the Auteuil race-course, I expect my painting to give me as much that is unexpected, although of another kind, as the actual race I witnessed gave me. Not for a second can there be any question of reproducing exactly a spectacle that is already in the past. But I have to re-live it entirely, in a manner that is new and, this time, from the standpoint of painting. By doing this, I create for myself the possibility of a fresh impact." And Lescure concludes: "An artist does not create the way he lives, he lives the way he creates."

Thus, contemporary painters no longer consider the image as a simple substitute for a perceptible reality. Proust said already of roses painted by Elstir that they were "a new variety with which this painter, like some clever horticulturist, had enriched the Rose family."[12]

VIII

Academic psychology hardly deals with the subject of the poetic image, which is often mistaken for simple metaphor.

Generally, in fact, the word *image,* in the works of psychologists, is surrounded with confusion: we see images, we reproduce images, we retain images in our memory. The image is everything except a direct product of the imagination. In Bergson's *Matière et mémoire* (Matter and Memory), in which the image concept is very widely treated, there is only one reference (on p. 198) to the *productive* imagination. This production remains, therefore, an act of lesser freedom, that has no relation to the great free acts stressed by Bergsonian philosophy. In this short passage, the philosopher refers to the "play of fantasy" and the various images that derive from it as "so many liberties that the mind takes with nature." But these liberties, in the plural, do not commit our being; they do not add to the language nor do they take it out of its utilitarian rôle. They really are so much "play." Indeed, the imagination hardly lends iridescence to our recollections. In this domain of poeticized memory, Bergson is well this side of Proust. The liberties that the mind takes with nature do not really designate the nature of the mind.

I propose, on the contrary, to consider the imagination as a major power of human nature. To be sure, there is nothing to be gained by saying that the imagination is the faculty of producing images. But this tautology has at least the virtue of putting an end to comparisons of images with memories.

By the swiftness of its actions, the imagination separates us from the past as well as from reality; it faces the future. To the *function of reality,* wise in experience of the past, as it is defined by traditional psychology, should be added a *function of unreality,* which is equally positive, as I tried to show in certain of my earlier works. Any weakness in the function of unreality will hamper the productive psyche. If we cannot imagine, we cannot foresee.

But to touch more simply upon the problems of the poetic imagination, it is impossible to receive the psychic benefit of poetry unless these two functions of the human psyche—the function of the real and the function of the unreal—are made to co-operate. We are offered a veritable cure of rhythmo-analysis through the poem, which interweaves real and unreal, and gives

dynamism to language by means of the dual activity of signification and poetry. And in poetry, the commitment of the imagining being is such that it is no longer merely the subject of the
verb "to adapt oneself." Actual conditions are no longer deter-
minant. With poetry, the imagination takes its place on the
margin, exactly where the function of unreality comes to charm
or to disturb—always to awaken—the sleeping being lost in its
automatisms. The most insidious of these automatisms, the
automatism of language, ceases to function when we enter into
the domain of pure sublimation. Seen from this height of pure
sublimation, reproductive imagination ceases to be of much
importance. To quote Jean-Paul Richter:[13] "Reproductive imagination is the prose of productive imagination."

IX

In this philosophical introduction—doubtless too long—I
have summarized certain general themes that I should like to
put to the test in the work that follows, as also in a few others
which I hope to write. In the present volume, my field of examination has the advantage of being well circumscribed. Indeed,
the images I want to examine are the quite simple images of
felicitous space. In this orientation, these investigations would
deserve to be called topophilia. They seek to determine the
human value of the sorts of space that may be grasped, that
may be defended against adverse forces, the space we love. For
diverse reasons, and with the differences entailed by poetic
shadings, this is eulogized space. Attached to its protective
value, which can be a positive one, are also imagined values,
which soon become dominant. Space that has been seized
upon by the imagination cannot remain indifferent space subject to the measures and estimates of the surveyor. It has been
lived in, not in its positivity, but with all the partiality of the
imagination. Particularly, it nearly always exercises an attraction. For it concentrates being within limits that protect. In the
realm of images, the play between the exterior and intimacy is
not a balanced one. On the other hand, hostile space is hardly

mentioned in these pages. The space of hatred and combat can only be studied in the context of impassioned subject matter and apocalyptic images. For the present, we shall consider the images that *attract*. And with regard to images, it soon becomes clear that to attract and to repulse do not give contrary experiences. The terms are contrary. When we study electricity or magnetism, we can speak symmetrically of repulsion and attraction. All that is needed is a change of algebraic signs. But images do not adapt themselves very well to quiet ideas, or above all, to definitive ideas. The imagination is ceaselessly imagining and enriching itself with new images. It is this wealth of imagined being that I should like to explore.

Here, then, is a rapid account of the chapters that compose this book.

First of all, as is proper in a study of images of intimacy, we shall pose the problem of the poetics of the house. The questions abound: how can secret rooms, rooms that have disappeared, become abodes for an unforgettable past? Where and how does repose find especially conducive situations? How is it that, at times, a provisional refuge or an occasional shelter is endowed in our intimate daydreaming with virtues that have no objective foundation? With the house image we are in possession of a veritable principle of psychological integration. Descriptive psychology, depth psychology, psychoanalysis and phenomenology could constitute, with the house, the corpus of doctrines that I have designated by the name of topoanalysis. On whatever theoretical horizon we examine it, the house image would appear to have become the topography of our intimate being. In order to give an idea of how complex is the task of the psychologist who studies the depths of the human soul, C. G. Jung asks his readers to consider the following comparison: "We have to describe and to explain a building the upper story of which was erected in the nineteenth century; the ground floor dates from the sixteenth century, and a careful examination of the masonry discloses the fact that it was reconstructed from a dwelling-tower of the eleventh century. In the cellar we discover Roman foundation walls, and under the cellar a filled-in cave, in the floor of which stone tools are found and remnants of glacial fauna in the layers below.

That would be a sort of picture of our mental structure."[14] Naturally, Jung was well aware of the limitations of this comparison (cf. p. 120). But from the very fact that it may be so easily developed, there is ground for taking the house as a *tool for analysis* of the human soul. With the help of this tool, can we not find within ourselves, while dreaming in our own modest homes, the consolations of the cave? Are the towers of our souls razed for all time? Are we to remain, to quote Gérard de Nerval's famous line, beings whose "towers have been destroyed"? Not only our memories, but the things we have forgotten are "housed." Our soul is an abode. And by remembering "houses" and "rooms," we learn to "abide" within ourselves. Now everything becomes clear, the house images move in both directions: they are in us as much as we are in them, and the play is so varied that two long chapters are needed to outline the implications of house images.

After these two chapters on the houses of man, I studied a series of images which may be considered the houses of things: drawers, chests and wardrobes. What psychology lies behind their locks and keys! They bear within themselves a kind of esthetics of hidden things. To pave the way now for a phenomenology of what is hidden, one preliminary remark will suffice: an empty drawer is *unimaginable*. It can only be *thought of*. And for us, who must describe what we imagine before what we know, what we dream before what we verify, all wardrobes are full.

At times when we believe we are studying something, we are only being receptive to a kind of daydreaming. The two chapters that I devoted to nests and shells—the two refuges of vertebrates and invertebrates—bear witness to an activity of the imagination which is hardly curbed by the reality of objects. During my lengthy meditation upon the imagination of the four elements, I re-lived countless aerial or aquatic daydreams, according to whether I followed the poets into the nest in the tree, or into the sort of animal cave that is constituted by a shell. Sometimes, even when I touch things, I still dream of an *element*.

After having followed the daydreams of inhabiting these uninhabitable places, I returned to images that, in order for us to live them, require us to become very small, as in nests and shells. Indeed, in our houses we have nooks and corners in which we like to curl up comfortably. To curl up belongs to the phenomenology of the verb "to inhabit," and only those who have learned to do so can inhabit with intensity. In this respect, we have within ourselves an entire assortment of images and recollections that we would not readily disclose. No doubt, a psychoanalyst, who desired to systematize these images of comforting retreat, could furnish numerous documents. All I had at my disposal were literary ones. I thus wrote a short chapter on "nooks and corners," and was surprised myself to see that important writers gave literary dignity to these psychological documents.

After all these chapters devoted to intimate space, I wanted to see what the dialectics of large and small offered for a poetics of space, how, in exterior space, the imagination benefited from the relativity of size, without the help of ideas and, as it were, quite naturally. I have put the dialectics of small and large under the signs of miniature and immensity, but these two chapters are not as antithetical as might be supposed. In both cases, small and large are not to be seized in their objectivity, since, in this present work, I only deal with them as the two poles of a projection of images. In other of my books, particularly with regard to immensity, I have tried to delineate the poet's meditations before the more imposing spectacles of nature.[15] Here, it is a matter of participating more intimately in the movement of the image. For instance, I shall have to prove in following certain poems that the impression of immensity is in us, and not necessarily related to an object.

At this point in my book, I had already collected a sufficient number of images to pose, in my own way, by giving the images their ontological value, the dialectics of within and without, which leads to a dialectics of open and closed.

Directly following this chapter on the dialectics of within and without is a chapter titled "The Phenomenology of Roundness." The difficulty that had to be overcome in writing this chapter was to avoid all geometrical evidence. In other words, I had to start with a sort of intimacy of roundness. I discovered images

of this direct roundness among thinkers and poets, images—
and this, for me, was essential—that were not mere metaphors.
This furnished me with a further opportunity to expose the
intellectualism of metaphor and, consequently, to show once
more the activity that is characteristic of pure imagination.

It was my idea that these two last chapters, which are full of
metaphysical implications, would tie into another book that I
should still like to write. This book would be a condensation
of the many public lectures that I gave at the Sorbonne during
the three last years of my teaching career. But shall I have the
strength to write this book? For there is a great distance
between the words we speak uninhibitedly to a friendly audi-
ence and the discipline needed to write a book. When we are
lecturing, we become animated by the joy of teaching and, at
times, our words think for us. But to write a book requires
really serious reflection.

GASTON BACHELARD

I

THE HOUSE.
FROM CELLAR TO GARRET.
THE SIGNIFICANCE
OF THE HUT

A la porte de la maison qui viendra frapper?
Une porte ouverte on entre
Une porte fermée un antre
Le monde bat de l'autre côté de ma porte.

PIERRE-ALBERT BIROT
Les amusements naturels, p. 217

(At the door of the house who will come knocking?
An open door, we enter
A closed door, a den
The world pulse beats beyond my door.)

The house, quite obviously, is a privileged entity for a phenomenological study of the intimate values of inside space, provided, of course, that we take it in both its unity and its complexity, and endeavor to integrate all the special values in one fundamental value. For the house furnishes us dispersed images and a body of images at the same time. In both cases, I shall prove that imagination augments the values of reality. A sort of attraction for images concentrates them about the house. Transcending our memories of all the houses in which we have found shelter, above and beyond all the houses we have dreamed we lived in, can we isolate an intimate, concrete essence that would be a justification of the uncommon value of all of our images of protected intimacy? This, then, is the main problem.

In order to solve it, it is not enough to consider the house as an "object" on which we can make our judgments and daydreams react. For a phenomenologist, a psychoanalyst, or a psychologist (these three points of view being named in the order of decreasing efficacy), it is not a question of describing houses, or enumerating their picturesque features and analyzing for which reasons they are comfortable. On the contrary, we must go beyond the problems of description—whether this description be objective or subjective, that is, whether it give facts or impressions—in order to attain to the primary virtues, those that reveal an attachment that is native in some way to the primary function of inhabiting. A geographer or an ethnographer can give us descriptions of very varied types of dwellings. In each variety, the phenomenologist makes the effort needed to seize upon the germ of the essential, sure, immediate well-being it encloses. In every dwelling, even the richest, the first task of the phenomenologist is to find the original shell.

But the related problems are many if we want to determine the profound reality of all the subtle shadings of our attachment for a chosen spot. For a phenomenologist, these shadings must be taken as the first rough outlines of a psychological phenomenon. The shading is not an additional, superficial coloring. We should therefore have to say how we inhabit our vital space, in accord with all the dialectics of life, how we take root, day after day, in a "corner of the world."

For our house is our corner of the world. As has often been said, it is our first universe, a real cosmos in every sense of the word. If we look at it intimately, the humblest dwelling has beauty. Authors of books on "the humble home" often mention this feature of the poetics of space. But this mention is much too succinct. Finding little to describe in the humble home, they spend little time there; so they describe it as it actually is, without really experiencing its primitiveness, a primitiveness which belongs to all, rich and poor alike, if they are willing to dream.

But our adult life is so dispossessed of the essential benefits, its anthropocosmic ties have become so slack, that we do not feel their first attachment in the universe of the house. There is no dearth of abstract, "world-conscious" philosophers who discover a universe by means of the dialectical game of the I and the non-I. In fact, they know the universe before they know the house, the far horizon before the resting-place; whereas the real beginnings of images, if we study them phenomenologically, will give concrete evidence of the values of inhabited space, of the non-I that protects the I.

Indeed, here we touch upon a converse whose images we shall have to explore: all really inhabited space bears the essence of the notion of home. In the course of this work, we shall see that the imagination functions in this direction whenever the human being has found the slightest shelter: we shall see the imagination build "walls" of impalpable shadows, comfort itself with the illusion of protection—or, just the contrary, tremble behind thick walls, mistrust the staunchest ramparts. In short, in the most interminable of dialectics, the sheltered being gives perceptible limits to his shelter. He experiences the house in its reality and in its virtuality, by means of thought and dreams. It is no longer in its positive aspects that the house is really "lived," nor is it only in the passing hour that we recognize its benefits. An entire past comes to dwell in a new house. The old saying: "We bring our *lares* with us" has many variations. And the daydream deepens to the point where an immemorial domain opens up for the dreamer of a home beyond man's earliest memory. The house, like fire and water, will permit me, later in this work, to recall flashes of daydreams that illuminate the synthesis of immemorial and recollected. In this remote region, memory and imagination remain associated, each one working for their mutual deepening. In the order of values, they both constitute a community of memory and image. Thus the house is not experienced from day to day only, on the thread of a narrative, or in the telling of our own story. Through dreams, the various dwelling-places in our lives co-penetrate and retain the treasures of former days. And after we are in the new house, when memories of other places we have lived in come back to us, we travel to the land of Motionless Childhood, motionless the way all Immemorial things are. We live fixations, fixations of happiness.[1] We comfort ourselves by reliving memories of protection. Something closed must retain our memories, while leaving them their original value as images. Memories of the outside world will never have the same tonality as those of home and, by recalling these memories, we add to our store of dreams; we are never real historians, but always near poets, and our emotion is perhaps nothing but an expression of a poetry that was lost.

Thus, by approaching the house images with care not to break up the solidarity of memory and imagination, we may hope to make others feel all the psychological elasticity of an image that moves us at an unimaginable depth. Through poems, perhaps more than through recollections, we touch the ultimate poetic depth of the space of the house.

This being the case, if I were asked to name the chief benefit of the house, I should say: the house shelters daydreaming, the house protects the dreamer, the house allows one to dream in peace. Thought and experience are not the only things that sanction human values. The values that belong to daydreaming mark humanity in its depths. Daydreaming even has a privilege of autovalorization. It derives direct pleasure from its own being. Therefore, the places in which we have *experienced daydreaming* reconstitute themselves in a new daydream, and it is because our memories of former dwelling-places are relived as daydreams that these dwelling-places of the past remain in us for all time.

Now my aim is clear: I must show that the house is one of the greatest powers of integration for the thoughts, memories and dreams of mankind. The binding principle in this integration is the daydream. Past, present and future give the house different dynamisms, which often interfere, at times opposing, at others, stimulating one another. In the life of a man, the house thrusts aside contingencies, its councils of continuity are unceasing. Without it, man would be a dispersed being. It maintains him through the storms of the heavens and through those of life. It is body and soul. It is the human being's first world. Before he is "cast into the world," as claimed by certain hasty metaphysics, man is laid in the cradle of the house. And always, in our daydreams, the house is a large cradle. A concrete metaphysics cannot neglect this fact, this simple fact, all the more, since this fact is a value, an important value, to which we return in our daydreaming. Being is already a value. Life begins well, it begins enclosed, protected, all warm in the bosom of the house.

From my viewpoint, from the phenomenologist's viewpoint, the conscious metaphysics that starts from the moment when the being is "cast into the world" is a secondary metaphysics. It passes over the preliminaries, when being is being-well, when the human being is deposited in a being-well, in the well-being originally associated with being. To illustrate the metaphysics of consciousness we should have to wait for the experiences during which being is cast out, that is to say, thrown out, outside the being of the house, a circumstance in which the hostility of men and of the universe accumulates. But a complete metaphysics, englobing both the conscious and the unconscious, would leave the privilege of its values within. Within the being, in the being of within, an enveloping warmth welcomes being. Being reigns in a sort of earthly paradise of matter, dissolved in the comforts of an adequate matter. It is as though in this material paradise, the human being were bathed in nourishment, as though he were gratified with all the essential benefits.

When we dream of the house we were born in, in the utmost depths of revery, we participate in this original warmth, in this well-tempered matter of the material paradise. This is the environment in which the protective beings live. We shall come back to the maternal features of the house. For the moment, I should like to point out the original fullness of the house's being. Our daydreams carry us back to it. And the poet well knows that the house holds childhood motionless "in its arms"[2]:

Maison, pan de prairie, ô lumière du soir
Soudain vous acquérez presque une face humaine
Vous êtes près de nous, embrassants, embrassés.

(House, patch of meadow, oh evening light
Suddenly you acquire an almost human face
You are very near us, embracing and embraced.)

II

Of course, thanks to the house, a great many of our memories are housed, and if the house is a bit elaborate, if it has a cellar and a garret, nooks and corridors, our memories have refuges that are all the more clearly delineated. All our lives we come back to them in our daydreams. A psychoanalyst should, therefore, turn his attention to this simple localization of our memories. I should like to give the name of topoanalysis to this auxiliary of psychoanalysis. Topoanalysis, then, would be the systematic psychological study of the sites of our intimate lives. In the theater of the past that is constituted by memory, the stage setting maintains the characters in their dominant rôles. At times we think we know ourselves in time, when all we know is a sequence of fixations in the spaces of the being's stability—a being who does not want to melt away, and who, even in the past, when he sets out in search of things past, wants time to "suspend" its flight. In its countless alveoli space contains compressed time. That is what space is for.

And if we want to go beyond history, or even, while remaining in history, detach from our own history the always too contingent history of the persons who have encumbered it, we realize that the calendars of our lives can only be established in its imagery. In order to analyze our being in the hierarchy of an ontology, or to psychoanalyze our unconscious entrenched in primitive abodes, it would be necessary, on the margin of normal psychoanalysis, to *desocialize* our important memories, and attain to the plane of the daydreams that we used to have in the places identified with our solitude. For investigations of this kind, daydreams are more useful than dreams. They show moreover that daydreams can be very different from dreams.[3]

And so, faced with these periods of solitude, the topoanalyst starts to ask questions: Was the room a large one? Was the garret cluttered up? Was the nook warm? How was it lighted? How, too, in these fragments of space, did the human being achieve silence? How did he relish the very special silence of the various retreats of solitary daydreaming?

Here space is everything, for time ceases to quicken memory. Memory—what a strange thing it is!—does not record concrete duration, in the Bergsonian sense of the word. We are unable to relive duration that has been destroyed. We can only think of it, in the line of an abstract time that is deprived of all thickness. The finest specimens of fossilized duration concretized as a result of long sojourn, are to be found in and through space. The unconscious abides. Memories are motionless, and the more securely they are fixed in space, the sounder they are. To localize a memory in time is merely a matter for the biographer and only corresponds to a sort of external history, for external use, to be communicated to others. But hermeneutics, which is more profound than biography, must determine the centers of fate by ridding history of its conjunctive temporal tissue, which has no action on our fates. For a knowledge of intimacy, localization in the spaces of our intimacy is more urgent than determination of dates.

Psychoanalysis too often situates the passions "in the century." In reality, however, the passions simmer and resimmer in solitude: the passionate being prepares his explosions and his exploits in this solitude.

And all the spaces of our past moments of solitude, the spaces in which we have suffered from solitude, enjoyed, desired and compromised solitude, remain indelible within us, and precisely because the human being wants them to remain so. He knows instinctively that this space identified with his solitude is creative; that even when it is forever expunged from the present, when, henceforth, it is alien to all the promises of the future, even when we no longer have a garret, when the attic room is lost and gone, there remains the fact that we once loved a garret, once lived in an attic. We return to them in our night dreams. These retreats have the value of a shell. And when we reach the very end of the labyrinths of sleep, when we attain to the regions of deep slumber, we may perhaps experience a type of repose that is pre-human; pre-human, in this case, approaching the immemorial. But in the daydream itself, the recollection of moments of confined, simple, shut-in space are experiences of heartwarming space, of a space that does not seek to become extended, but would like above all still to be possessed. In the past, the attic may have seemed too small, it may have seemed cold in winter and hot in summer. Now, however, in memory recaptured through daydreams, it is hard to say through what syncretism the attic is at once small and large, warm and cool, always comforting.

III

This being the case, we shall have to introduce a slight nuance at the very base of topoanalysis. I pointed out earlier that the unconscious is housed. It should be added that it is well and happily housed, in the space of its happiness. The normal unconscious knows how to make itself at home everywhere, and psychoanalysis comes to the assistance of the ousted unconscious, of the unconscious that has been roughly or insidiously dislodged. But psychoanalysis sets the human being in motion, rather than at rest. It calls on him to live outside the abodes of his unconscious, to enter into life's adventures, to come out of himself. And naturally, its action is a salutary one. Because we must also give an exterior destiny to the interior being. To accompany psychoanalysis in this salutary action, we should have to undertake a topoanalysis of all the space that has invited us to come out of ourselves.

Emmenez-moi, chemins! . . .

(Carry me along, oh roads! . . .)

wrote Marceline Desbordes-Valmore, recalling her native Flanders (*Un ruisseau de la Scarpe*).

And what a dynamic, handsome object is a path! How precise the familiar hill paths remain for our muscular consciousness! A poet has expressed all this dynamism in one single line:

> O, *mes chemins et leur cadence*
> Jean Caubère, *Déserts*

(Oh, my roads and their cadence.)

When I relive dynamically the road that "climbed" the hill, I am quite sure that the road itself had muscles, or rather, countermuscles. In my room in Paris, it is a good exercise for me to think of the road in this way. As I write this page, I feel freed of my duty to take a walk: I am sure of having gone out of my house.

And indeed we should find countless intermediaries between reality and symbols if we gave things all the movements they suggest. George Sand, dreaming beside a path of yellow sand, saw life flowing by. "What is more beautiful than a road?" she wrote. "It is the symbol and the image of an active, varied life" (*Consuelo,* vol. II, p. 116).

Each one of us, then, should speak of his roads, his crossroads, his roadside benches; each one of us should make a surveyor's map of his lost fields and meadows. Thoreau said that he had the map of his fields engraved in his soul. And Jean Wahl once wrote:

> *Le moutonnement des haies*
> *C'est en moi que je l'ai.*
> Poème, p. 46

(The frothing of the hedges
I keep deep inside me.)

Thus we cover the universe with drawings we have lived. These drawings need not be exact. They need only to be tonalized on the mode of our inner space. But what a book would have to be written to decide all these problems! Space calls for action, and before action, the imagination is at work. It mows and ploughs. We should have to speak of the benefits of all these imaginary actions. Psychoanalysis has made numerous observations on the subject of projective behavior, on the willingness of extroverted persons to exteriorize their intimate impressions. An exteriorist topoanalysis would perhaps give added precision to this projective behavior by defining our daydreams of objects. However, in this present work, I shall not be able to undertake, as should be done, the two-fold imaginary geometrical and physical problem of extroversion and introversion. Moreover, I do not believe that these two branches of physics have the same psychic weight. My research is devoted to the domain of intimacy, to the domain in which psychic weight is dominant.

I shall therefore put my trust in the power of attraction of all the domains of intimacy. There does not exist a real intimacy that is repellent. All the spaces of intimacy are designated by an attraction. Their being is well-being. In these conditions, topoanalysis bears the stamp of a topophilia, and shelters and rooms will be studied in the sense of this valorization.

IV

These virtues of shelter are so simple, so deeply rooted in our unconscious that they may be recaptured through mere mention, rather than through minute description. Here the nuance bespeaks the color. A poet's word, because it strikes true, moves the very depths of our being.

Over-picturesqueness in a house can conceal its intimacy. This is also true in life. But it is truer still in daydreams. For the real houses of memory, the houses to which we return in dreams, the houses that are rich in unalterable oneirism, do not readily lend themselves to description. To describe them would be like showing them to visitors. We can perhaps tell everything about the present, but about the past! The first, the oneirically definitive house, must retain its shadows. For it belongs to the literature of depth, that is, to poetry, and not to the fluent type of literature that, in order to analyze intimacy, needs other people's stories. All I ought to say about my childhood home is just barely enough to place me, myself, in an oneiric situation, to set me on the threshold of a daydream in which I shall *find* repose in the past. Then I may hope that my page will possess a sonority that will ring true—a voice so remote within me, that it will be the voice we all hear when we listen as far back as memory reaches, on the very limits of memory, beyond memory perhaps, in the field of the immemorial. All we communicate to others is an *orientation* towards what is secret without ever being able to tell the secret objectively. What is secret never has total objectivity. In this respect, we orient oneirism but we do not accomplish it.[4]

What would be the use, for instance, in giving the plan of the room that was really *my* room, in describing the little room at the *end* of the garret, in saying that from the window, across the indentations of the roofs, one could see the hill. I alone, in my memories of another century, can open the deep cupboard that still retains for me alone that unique odor, the odor of raisins drying on a wicker tray. The odor of raisins! It is an odor that is beyond description, one that it takes a lot of imagination to smell. But I've already said too much. If I said more, the reader, back in his own room, would not open that unique wardrobe, with its unique smell, which is the signature of intimacy. Paradoxically, in order to suggest the values of intimacy, we have to induce in the reader a state of suspended reading. For it is not until his eyes have left the page that recollections of my room can become a threshold of oneirism for him. And when it is a poet speaking, the reader's soul reverberates; it experiences the kind of reverberation that, as Minkowski has shown, gives the energy of an origin to being.

It therefore makes sense from our standpoint of a philosophy of literature and poetry to say that we "write a room," "read a room," or "read a house." Thus, very quickly, at the very first word, at the first poetic overture, the reader who is "reading a room" leaves off reading and starts to think of some place in his own past. You would like to tell everything about your room. You would like to interest the reader in yourself, whereas you have unlocked a door to daydreaming. The values of intimacy are so absorbing that the reader has ceased to read your room: he sees his own again. He is already far off, listening to the recollections of a father or a grandmother, of a mother or a servant, of "the old faithful servant," in short, of the human being who dominates the corner of his most cherished memories.

And the house of memories becomes psychologically complex. Associated with the nooks and corners of solitude are the bedroom and the living room in which the leading characters held sway. The house we were born in is an inhabited house. In it the values of intimacy are scattered, they are not easily stabilized, they are subjected to dialectics. In how many tales of childhood—if tales of childhood were sincere—we should be told of a child that, lacking a room, went and sulked in his corner!

But over and beyond our memories, the house we were born in is physically inscribed in us. It is a group of organic habits. After twenty years, in spite of all the other anonymous stairways, we would recapture the reflexes of the "first stairway," we would not stumble on that rather high step. The house's entire being would open up, faithful to our own being. We would push the door that creaks with the same gesture, we would find our way in the dark to the distant attic. The feel of the tiniest latch has remained in our hands.

The successive houses in which we have lived have no doubt made our gestures commonplace. But we are very surprised, when we return to the old house, after an odyssey of many years, to find that the most delicate gestures, the earliest gestures suddenly come alive, are still faultless. In short, the house we were born in has engraved within us the hierarchy of the various functions of inhabiting. We are the diagram of the functions of inhabiting that particular house, and all the other houses are but variations on a fundamental theme. The word "habit" is too worn a word to express this passionate liaison of our bodies, which do not forget, with an unforgettable house.

But this area of detailed recollections that are easily retained

because of the names of things and people we knew in the first
house can be studied by means of general psychology. Memories of dreams, however, which only poetic meditation can
help us to recapture, are more confused, less clearly drawn.
The great function of poetry is to give us back the situations of
our dreams. The house we were born in is more than an
embodiment of home, it is also an embodiment of dreams.
Each one of its nooks and corners was a resting-place for daydreaming. And often the resting-place particularized the daydream. Our habits of a particular daydream were acquired
there. The house, the bedroom, the garret in which we were
alone, furnished the framework for an interminable dream,
one that poetry alone, through the creation of a poetic work,
could succeed in achieving completely. If we give their function
of shelter for dreams to all of these places of retreat, we may
say, as I pointed out in an earlier work,[5] that there exists for
each one of us an oneiric house, a house of dream-memory,
that is lost in the shadow of a beyond of the real past. I called
this oneiric house the crypt of the house that we were born in.
Here we find ourselves at a pivotal point around which reciprocal interpretations of dreams, through thought and thought
through dreams, keep turning. But the word *interpretation*
hardens this about-face unduly. In point of fact, we are in the
unity of image and memory, in the functional composite of
imagination and memory. The positivity of psychological history and geography cannot serve as a touchstone for determining *the real being* of our childhood, for childhood is certainly
greater than reality. In order to sense, across the years, our
attachment for the house we were born in, dream is more
powerful than thought. It is our unconscious force that crystal-
izes our remotest memories. If a compact center of daydreams
of repose had not existed in this first house, the very different
circumstances that surround actual life would have clouded
our memories. Except for a few medallions stamped with the
likeness of our ancestors, our child-memory contains only
worn coins. It is on the plane of the daydream and not on that
of facts that childhood remains alive and poetically useful
within us. Through this permanent childhood, we maintain

the poetry of the past. To inhabit oneirically the house we were born in means more than to inhabit it in memory; it means living in this house that is gone, the way we used to dream in it.

What special depth there is in a child's daydream! And how happy the child who really possesses his moments of solitude! It is a good thing, it is even salutary, for a child to have periods of boredom, for him to learn to know the dialectics of exaggerated play and causeless, pure boredom. Alexander Dumas tells in his *Mémoires* that, as a child, he was bored, bored to tears. When his mother found him like that, weeping from sheer boredom, she said: "And what is Dumas crying about?" "Dumas is crying because Dumas has tears," replied the six-year-old child. This is the kind of anecdote people tell in their memoirs. But how well it exemplifies absolute boredom, the boredom that is not the equivalent of the absence of playmates. There are children who will leave a game to go and be bored in a corner of the garret. How often have I wished for the attic of my boredom when the complications of life made me lose the very germ of all freedom!

And so, beyond all the positive values of protection, the house we were born in becomes imbued with dream values which remain after the house is gone. Centers of boredom, centers of solitude, centers of daydream group together to constitute the oneiric house which is more lasting than the scattered memories of our birthplace. Long phenomenological research would be needed to determine all these dream values, to plumb the depth of this dream ground in which our memories are rooted.

And we should not forget that these dream values communicate poetically from soul to soul. To read poetry is essentially to daydream.

V

A house constitutes a body of images that give mankind proofs or illusions of stability. We are constantly re-imagining its reality: to distinguish all these images would be to describe the

soul of the house; it would mean developing a veritable psychology of the house.

To bring order into these images, I believe that we should
consider two principal connecting themes: 1) A house is imagined as a vertical being. It rises upward. It differentiates itself
in terms of its verticality. It is one of the appeals to our consciousness of verticality. 2) A house is imagined as a concentrated being. It appeals to our consciousness of centrality.[6]

These themes are no doubt very abstractly stated. But with
examples, it is not hard to recognize their psychologically concrete nature.

Verticality is ensured by the polarity of cellar and attic, the
marks of which are so deep that, in a way, they open up two
very different perspectives for a phenomenology of the imagination. Indeed, it is possible, almost without commentary, to
oppose the rationality of the roof to the irrationality of the cellar. A roof tells its *raison d'être* right away: it gives mankind
shelter from the rain and sun he fears. Geographers are constantly reminding us that, in every country, the slope of the
roofs is one of the surest indications of the climate. We "understand" the slant of a roof. Even a dreamer dreams rationally;
for him, a pointed roof averts rain clouds. Up near the roof all
our thoughts are clear. In the attic it is a pleasure to see the
bare rafters of the strong framework. Here we participate in
the carpenter's solid geometry.

As for the cellar, we shall no doubt find uses for it. It will be
rationalized and its conveniences enumerated. But it is first
and foremost the *dark entity* of the house, the one that par-
takes of subterranean forces. When we dream there, we are in
harmony with the irrationality of the depths.

We become aware of this dual vertical polarity of a house if
we are sufficiently aware of the function of inhabiting to consider it as an imaginary response to the function of constructing. The dreamer constructs and reconstructs the upper stories
and the attic until they are well constructed. And, as I said
before, when we dream of the heights we are in the rational
zone of intellectualized projects. But for the cellar, the

impassioned inhabitant digs and re-digs, making its very depth active. The fact is not enough, the dream is at work. When it comes to excavated ground, dreams have no limit. I shall give later some deep-cellar reveries. But first let us remain in the space that is polarized by the cellar and the attic, to see how this polarized space can serve to illustrate very fine psychological nuances.

Here is how the psychoanalyst, C. G. Jung, has used the dual image of cellar and attic to analyze the fears that inhabit a house. In Jung's *Modern Man in Search of a Soul*[7] we find a comparison which is used to make us understand the conscious being's hope of "destroying the autonomy of complexes by debaptising them." The image is the following: "Here the conscious acts like a man who, hearing a suspicious noise in the cellar, hurries to the attic and, finding no burglars there decides, consequently, that the noise was pure imagination. In reality, this prudent man did not dare venture into the cellar."

To the extent that the explanatory image used by Jung convinces us, we readers relive phenomenologically both fears: fear in the attic and fear in the cellar. Instead of facing the cellar (the unconscious), Jung's "prudent man" seeks alibis for his courage in the attic. In the attic rats and mice can make considerable noise. But let the master of the house arrive unexpectedly and they return to the silence of their holes. The creatures moving about in the cellar are slower, less scampering, more mysterious.

In the attic, fears are easily "rationalized." Whereas in the cellar, even for a more courageous man than the one Jung mentions, "rationalization" is less rapid and less clear; also it is never *definitive*. In the attic, the day's experiences can always efface the fears of night. In the cellar, darkness prevails both day and night, and even when we are carrying a lighted candle, we see shadows dancing on the dark walls.

If we follow the inspiration of Jung's *explanatory* example to a complete grasp of psychological reality, we encounter a co-operation between psychoanalysis and phenomenology which must be stressed if we are to dominate the human phenomenon. As a matter of fact, the image has to be understood

phenomenologically in order to give it psychoanalytical efficacy. The phenomenologist, in this case, will accept the psychoanalyst's image in a spirit of shared trepidation. He will
revive the primitivity and the specificity of the fears. In our
civilization, which has the same light everywhere, and puts
electricity in its cellars, we no longer go to the cellar carrying a
candle. But the unconscious cannot be civilized. It takes a candle when it goes to the cellar. The psychoanalyst cannot cling
to the superficiality of metaphors or comparisons, and the phenomenologist has to pursue every image to the very end. Here,
so far from reducing and explaining, so far from comparing,
the phenomenologist will exaggerate his exaggeration. Then,
when they read Poe's *Tales* together, both the phenomenologist
and the psychoanalyst will understand the value of this achieve-
ment. For these tales are the realization of childhood fears. The
reader who is a "devotee" of reading will hear the accursed cat,
which is a symbol of unredeemed guilt, mewing behind the
wall.[8] The cellar dreamer knows that the walls of the cellar are
buried walls, that they are walls with a single casing, walls that
have the entire earth behind them. And so the situation grows
more dramatic, and fear becomes exaggerated. But where is the
fear that does not become exaggerated? In this spirit of shared
trepidation, the phenomenologist listens intently, as the poet
Thoby Marcelin puts it, "flush with madness." The cellar then
becomes buried madness, walled-in tragedy. Stories of criminal
cellars leave indelible marks on our memory, marks that we
prefer not to deepen; who would like to re-read Poe's "The
Cask of Amontillado"? In this instance, the dramatic element
is too facile, but it exploits natural fears, which are inherent to
the dual nature of both man and house.

Although I have no intention of starting a file on the subject
of human drama, I shall study a few ultra-cellars which prove
that the cellar dream irrefutably increases reality.

If the dreamer's house is in a city it is not unusual that the
dream is one of dominating in depth the surrounding cellars.
His abode wants the undergrounds of legendary fortified
castles, where mysterious passages that run under the enclosing
walls, the ramparts and the moat put the heart of the castle

into communication with the distant forest. The château planted on the hilltop had a cluster of cellars for roots. And what power it gave a simple house to be built on this underground clump!

In the novels of Henri Bosco, who is a great dreamer of houses, we come across ultra-cellars of this kind. Under the house in *L'Antiquaire* (The Antique Dealer, p. 60), there is a "vaulted rotunda into which open four doors." Four corridors lead from the four doors, dominating, as it were, the four cardinal points of an underground horizon. The door to the East opens and "we advance subterraneously far under the house in this neighborhood . . ." There are traces of labyrinthine dreams in these pages. But associated with the labyrinths of the corridor, in which the air is "heavy," are rotundas and chapels that are the sanctuaries of the secret. Thus, the cellar in *L'Antiquaire* is oneirically complex. The reader must explore it through dreams, certain of which refer to the suffering in the corridors, and others to the marvelous nature of underground palaces. He may become quite lost (actually as well as figuratively). At first he does not see very clearly the necessity for such a complicated geometry. Just here, a phenomenological analysis will prove to be effective. But what does the phenomenological attitude advise? It asks us to produce within ourselves a reading pride that will give us the illusion of participating in the work of the author of the book. Such an attitude could hardly be achieved on first reading, which remains too passive. For here the reader is still something of a child, a child who is entertained by reading. But every good book should be re-read as soon as it is finished. After the sketchiness of the first reading comes the creative work of reading. We must then know *the problem* that confronted the author. The second, then the third reading . . . give us, little by little, the solution of this problem. Imperceptibly, we give ourselves the illusion that both the problem and the solution are ours. The psychological nuance: "I should have written that," establishes us as phenomenologists of reading. But so long as we have not acknowledged this nuance, we remain psychologists, or psychoanalysts.

What, then, was Henri Bosco's literary problem in his description of the ultra-cellar? It was to present in one central concrete image a novel which, in its broad lines, is the novel of *underground maneuvers*. This worn-out metaphor is illustrated, in this instance, by countless cellars, a network of passages, and a group of individual cells with frequently padlocked doors. There, secrets are pondered, projects are prepared. And, underneath the earth, action gets under way. We are really in the intimate space of underground maneuvers. It is in a basement such as this that the antique dealers, who carry the novel forward, claim to link people's fates. Henri Bosco's cellar, with its four subdivisions, is a loom on which fates are woven. The hero relating his adventures has himself a ring of fate, a ring carved with signs that date from some remote time. However, the strictly underground, strictly diabolical, activities of the *Antiquaires* fail. For at the very moment when two great destinies of love are about to be joined, one of the loveliest sylphs dies in the vault of the accursed house—a creature of the garden and the tower, the one who was supposed to confer happiness. The reader who is alive to the accompaniment of cosmic poetry that is always active beneath the psychological story in Bosco's novels, will find evidence, in many pages of this book, of the dramatic tension between the aerial and the terrestrial. But to live such drama as this, we must re-read the book, we must be able to displace the interest or carry out our reading in the dual interest of man and things, at the same time that we neglect nothing of the anthropo-cosmic tissue of a human life.

In another dwelling into which this novelist takes us, the ultra-cellar is no longer under the sign of the sinister projects of diabolical men, but is perfectly natural, inherent to the nature of an underground world. By following Henri Bosco, we shall experience a house with cosmic roots.

This house with cosmic roots will appear to us as a stone plant growing out of the rock up to the blue sky of a tower.

The hero of *L'Antiquaire* having been caught on a compromising visit, has been obliged to take to the cellar. Right away, however, interest in the actual story is transferred to the cosmic story. Realities serve here to reveal dreams. At first we are in the labyrinth of corridors carved in the rock. Then, suddenly, we come upon a body of murky water. At this point, description of events in the novel is left in abeyance and we only find compensation for our perseverance if we participate by means of our own night dreams. Indeed, a long dream that has an elemental sincerity is inserted in the story. Here is this poem of the cosmic cellar:[9]

"Just in front of me, water appeared from out of the darkness.

"Water! ... An immense body of water! ... And what water! ... Black, stagnant, so perfectly smooth that not a ripple, not a bubble, marred its surface. No spring, no source. It had been there for thousands of years and remained there, caught unawares by the rock, spread out in a single, impassive sheet. In its stone matrix, it had itself become this black, still rock, a captive of the mineral world. It had been subjected to the crushing mass, the enormous upheavals, of this oppressive world. Under this heavy weight, its very nature appeared to have been changed as it seeped through the thicknesses of the lime slabs that held its secret fast. Thus it had become the densest fluid element of the underground mountain. Its opacity and unwonted[10] consistency made an unknown substance of it, a substance charged with phosphorescences that only appeared on the surface in occasional flashes. These electric tints, which were signs of the dark powers lying on the bottom, manifested the latent life and formidable power of this still dormant element. They made me shiver."

But this shiver, we sense, is no longer human fear; this is cosmic fear, an anthropo-cosmic fear that echoes the great legend of man cast back into primitive situations. From the cavern carved in the rock to the underground, from the underground to stagnant water, we have moved from a constructed to a dreamed world; we have left fiction for poetry. But reality and dream now form a whole. The house, the cellar, the deep earth, achieve totality through depth. The house has become a natural being whose fate is bound to that of mountains and of the waters that plough the land. The enormous stone plant it has become would not flourish if it did not have subterranean water at its base. And so our dreams attain boundless proportions.

The cosmic daydream in this passage of Bosco's book gives the reader a sense of restfulness, in that it invites him to participate in the repose to be derived from all deep oneiric experience. Here the story remains in a suspended time that is favorable to more profound psychological treatment. Now the account of real events may be resumed; it has received its provision of "cosmicity" and daydream. And so, beyond the underground water, Bosco's cellar recovers its stairways. After this poetic pause, description can begin again to unreel its itinerary. "A very narrow, steep stairway, which spiraled as it went higher, had been carved in the rock. I started up it" (p. 155). By means of this gimlet, the dreamer succeeds in getting out of the depths of the earth and begins his adventures in the heights. In fact, at the very end of countless tortuous, narrow passages, the reader emerges into a tower. This is the ideal tower that haunts all dreamers of old houses: it is "perfectly round" and there is "brief light" from "a narrow window." It also has a vaulted ceiling, which is a great principle of the dream of intimacy. For it constantly reflects intimacy at its center. No one will be surprised to learn that the tower room is the abode of a gentle young girl and that she is haunted by memories of an ardent ancestress. The round, vaulted room stands high and alone, keeping watch over the past in the same way that it dominates space.

On this young girl's missal, handed down from her distant ancestress, may be read the following motto:

The flower is always in the almond.

With this excellent motto, both the house and the bedchamber bear the mark of an unforgettable intimacy. For there exists no more compact image of intimacy, none that is more sure of its center, than a flower's dream of the future while it is still enclosed, tightly folded, inside its seed. How we should love to see not happiness, but pre-happiness remain enclosed in the round chamber!

Finally, the house Bosco describes stretches from earth to

sky. It possesses the verticality of the tower rising from the
most earthly, watery depths, to the abode of a soul that
believes in heaven. Such a house, constructed by a writer, illustrates the verticality of the human being. It is also oneirically
complete, in that it dramatizes the two poles of house dreams.
It makes a gift of a tower to those who have perhaps never
even seen a dove-cote. A tower is the creation of another century. Without a past it is nothing. Indeed, a new tower would
be ridiculous. But we still have books, and they give our daydreams countless dwelling-places. Is there one among us who
has not spent romantic moments in the tower of a book he has
read? These moments come back to us. Daydreaming needs
them. For on the keyboard of the vast literature devoted to the
function of inhabiting, the tower sounds a note of immense
dreams. How many times, since reading *L'Antiquaire,* have I
gone to live in Henri Bosco's tower!

This tower and its underground cellars extend the house we
have just been studying in both directions. For us, this house
represents an increase in the verticality of the more modest
houses that, in order to satisfy our daydreams, have to be differentiated in height. If I were the architect of an oneiric house, I
should hesitate between a three-story house and one with four.
A three-story house, which is the simplest as regards essential
height, has a cellar, a ground floor and an attic; while a four-
story house puts a floor between the ground floor and the attic.
One floor more, and our dreams become blurred. In the oneiric
house, topoanalysis only knows how to count to three or four.
   Then there are the stairways: one to three or four of them,
all different. We always *go down* the one that leads to the cellar, and it is this going down that we remember, that characterizes its oneirism. But we go both up and down the stairway
that leads to the bed-chamber. It is more commonly used; we
are familiar with it. Twelve-year-olds even go up it in *ascend-
ing scales,* in thirds and fourths, trying to do fifths, and liking,
above all, to take it in strides of four steps at a time. What joy
for the legs to go up four steps at a time!
   Lastly, we always *go up* the attic stairs, which are steeper

and more primitive. For they bear the mark of ascension to a more tranquil solitude. When I return to dream in the attics of yester-year, I never go down again.

Dreams of stairs have often been encountered in psycho-analysis. But since it requires an all-inclusive symbolism to determine its interpretations, psychoanalysis has paid little attention to the complexity of mixed revery and memory. That is why, on this point, as well as on others, psychoanalysis is better suited to the study of dreams than of daydreams. The phenomenology of the daydream can untangle the complex of memory and imagination; it becomes necessarily sensitive to the differentiations of the symbol. And the poetic daydream, which creates symbols, confers upon our intimate moments an activity that is polysymbolic. Our recollections grow sharper, the oneiric house becomes highly sensitized. At times, a few steps have engraved in our memories a slight difference of level that existed in our childhood home.[11] A certain room was not only a door, but a door plus three steps. When we recall the old house in its longitudinal detail, everything that ascends and descends comes to life again dynamically. We can no longer remain, to quote Joë Bousquet, men with only one story. "He was a man with only one story: he had his cellar in his attic."[12]

By way of antithesis, I shall make a few remarks on dwellings that are oneirically incomplete.

In Paris there are no houses, and the inhabitants of the big city live in superimposed boxes. "One's Paris room, inside its four walls," wrote Paul Claudel, "is a sort of geometrical site, a conventional hole, which we furnish with pictures, objects and wardrobes within a wardrobe."[13] The number of the street and the floor give the location of our "conventional hole," but our abode has neither space around it nor verticality inside it. "The houses are fastened to the ground with asphalt, in order not to sink into the earth."[14] They have no roots and, what is quite unthinkable for a dreamer of houses, sky-scrapers have no cellars. From the street to the roof, the rooms pile up one on top of the other, while the tent of a horizonless sky encloses the entire city. But the height of city buildings is a purely *exterior* one. Elevators do away with the heroism of stair climbing so that there is no longer any virtue in living up near the sky. *Home* has become mere horizontality. The different rooms that compose living quarters jammed into one floor all lack one of the fundamental principles for distinguishing and classifying the values of intimacy.

But in addition to the intimate value of verticality, a house in a big city lacks cosmicity. For here, where houses are no longer set in natural surroundings, the relationship between house and space becomes an artificial one. Everything about it is mechanical and, on every side, intimate living flees. "The streets are like pipes into which men are sucked up" (Max Picard, loc. cit., p. 119).

Moreover, our houses are no longer aware of the storms of the outside universe. Occasionally the wind blows a tile from a roof and kills a passer-by in the street. But this roof crime is only aimed at the belated passer-by. Or lightning may for an instant set fire to the window-panes. The house does not tremble, however, when thunder rolls. It trembles neither with nor through us. In our houses set close one up against the other, we are less afraid. A hurricane in Paris has not the same personal offensiveness towards the dreamer that it has towards the hermit's house. We shall understand this better, in fact, when we have studied, further on, *the house's situation in the world,* which gives us, quite concretely, a variation of the metaphysically summarized situation of man in the world.

Just here the philosopher who believes in the salutary nature of vast daydreams is faced with a problem: how can one help confer greater cosmicity upon the city space that is exterior to one's room? As an example, here is one dreamer's solution to the problem of noise in Paris:

When insomnia, which is the philosopher's ailment, is increased through irritation caused by city noises; or when, late at night, the hum of automobiles and trucks rumbling through the Place Maubert causes me to curse my city-dweller's fate, I can recover my calm by living the metaphors of the ocean. We all know that the big city is a clamorous sea, and it has been said countless times that, in the heart of night in

Paris, one hears the ceaseless murmur of flood and tide. So I make a sincere image out of these hackneyed ones, an image that is as much my own as though I myself had invented it, in line with my gentle mania for always believing that I am the subject of what I am thinking. If the hum of cars becomes more painful, I do my best to discover in it the roll of thunder, of a thunder that speaks to me and scolds me. And I feel sorry for myself. So there you are, unhappy philosopher, caught up again by the storm, by the storms of life! I dream an abstract-concrete daydream. My bed is a small boat lost at sea; that sudden whistling is the wind in the sails. On every side the air is filled with the sound of furious klaxoning. I talk to myself to give myself cheer: there now, your skiff is holding its own, you are safe in your stone boat. Sleep, in spite of the storm. Sleep in the storm. Sleep in your own courage, happy to be a man who is assailed by wind and wave.

And I fall asleep, lulled by the noise of Paris.[15]

In fact, everything corroborates my view that the image of the city's ocean roar is in the very "nature of things," and that it is a true image. It is also a salutary thing to naturalize sound in order to make it less hostile. Just in passing, I have noted the following delicate nuance of the beneficent image in the work of a young contemporary poet, Yvonne Caroutch,[16] for whom dawn in the city is the "murmur of an empty sea shell." Being myself an early riser, this image helps me to wake up gently and naturally. However, any image is a good one, provided we know how to use it.

We could find many other images on the theme of the city-ocean. Here is one that occurred to a painter. The art-critic and historian, Pierre Courthion,[17] tells that when Gustave Courbet was confined in the Sainte Pélagie prison, he wanted to paint a view of Paris, as seen from the top floor of the prison. In a letter to a friend, Courbet wrote that he was planning to paint it "the way I do my marines: with an immensely deep sky, and all its movement, all its houses and domes, imitating the tumultuous waves of the ocean."

Pursuant to my method, I have retained the coalescence of images that refuse an absolute anatomy. I had to mention incidentally the house's "cosmicity." But we shall return later to this characteristic. Now, after having examined the verticality of the oneiric house, we are going to study the centers of condensation of intimacy, in which daydream accumulates.

VI

We must first look for centers of simplicity in houses with many rooms. For as Baudelaire said, in a palace, "there is no place for intimacy."

But simplicity, which at times is too rationally vaunted, is not a source of high-powered oneirism. We must therefore experience the primitiveness of refuge and, beyond situations that have been experienced, discover situations that have been dreamed; beyond positive recollections that are the material for a positive psychology, return to the field of the primitive images that had perhaps been centers of fixation for recollections left in our memories.

A demonstration of imaginary primitive elements may be based upon the entity that is most firmly fixed in our memories: the childhood home.

For instance, in the house itself, in the family sitting-room, a dreamer of refuges dreams of a hut, of a nest, or of nooks and corners in which he would like to hide away, like an animal in its hole. In this way, he lives in a region that is beyond human images. If a phenomenologist could succeed in living the primitiveness of such images, he would locate elsewhere, perhaps, the problems that touch upon the poetry of the house. We find a very clear example of this concentration of the joy of inhabiting in a fragment of Henri Bachelin's life of his father.[18]

Henri Bachelin's childhood home could not have been simpler. Although no different from the other houses in the oversized Morvan village where he was born, it was nevertheless a roomy home with ample outbuildings in which the family lived in security and comfort. The lamplit room where, in the evening, the father read the lives of the saints—he was Church sexton as well as day-laborer—was the scene of the little boy's daydreaming of primitiveness, daydreaming that accentuated solitude to the point of imagining that he lived in a hut in the depth of the forest. For a phenomenologist who is looking for the roots of the function of inhabiting, this passage in Henri Bachelin's book represents a document of great purity. The essential lines are the following (p. 97): "At these moments, I felt very strongly—and I swear to this—that we were cut off from the little town, from the rest of France, and from the entire world. I delighted in imagining (although I kept my feelings to myself) that we were living in the heart of the woods, in the well-heated hut of charcoal burners; I even hoped to hear wolves sharpening their claws on the heavy granite slab that formed our doorstep. But our house replaced the hut for me, it sheltered me from hunger and cold; and if I shivered, it was merely from well-being." Addressing his father—his novel is constantly written in the second person—Bachelin adds: "Comfortably seated in my chair, I basked in the sensation of your strength."

Thus, the author attracts us to the center of the house as though to a center of magnetic force, into a major zone of protection. He goes to the very bottom of the "hut dream," which is well-known to everyone who cherishes the legendary images of primitive houses. But in most hut dreams we hope to live elsewhere, far from the over-crowded house, far from city cares. We flee in thought in search of a real refuge. Bachelin is more fortunate than dreamers of distant escape, in that he finds the root of the hut dream in the house itself. He has only to give a few touches to the spectacle of the family sitting-room, only to listen to the stove roaring in the evening stillness, while an icy wind blows against the house, to know that at the house's center, in the circle of light shed by the lamp, he is living in the round house, the primitive hut, of prehistoric man. How many dwelling places there would be, fitted one into the other, if we were to realize in detail, and in their hierarchical order, all the images by means of which we live our daydreams of intimacy. How many scattered values we should succeed in concentrating, if we lived the images of our daydreams in all sincerity.

In this passage from Bachelin's book, the hut appears to be the tap-root of the function of inhabiting. It is the simplest of human plants, the one that needs no ramifications in order to exist. Indeed, it is so simple that it no longer belongs to our memories—which at times are too full of imagery—but to legend; it is a center of legend. When we are lost in darkness and see a distant glimmer of light, who does not dream of a thatched cottage or, to go more deeply still into legend, of a hermit's hut?

A hermit's hut. What a subject for an engraving! Indeed real images are *engravings*, for it is the imagination that engraves them on our memories. They deepen the recollections we have experienced, which they replace, thus becoming imagined recollections. The hermit's hut is a theme which needs no variations, for at the simplest mention of it, "phenomenological reverberation" obliterates all mediocre resonances. The hermit's hut is an engraving that would suffer from any exaggeration of picturesqueness. Its truth must derive from the intensity of its essence, which is the essence of the verb "to inhabit." The hut immediately becomes centralized solitude, for in the land of legend, there exists no adjoining hut. And although geographers may bring back photographs of hut villages from their travels in distant lands, our legendary past transcends everything that has been seen, even everything that we have experienced personally. The image leads us on towards extreme solitude. The hermit is *alone* before God. His hut, therefore, is just the opposite of the monastery. And there radiates about this centralized solitude a universe of meditation and prayer, a universe outside the universe. The hut can receive none of the riches "of this world." It possesses the felicity of intense poverty; indeed, it is one of the glories of poverty; as destitution increases it gives us access to absolute refuge.

This valorization of a center of concentrated solitude is so strong, so primitive, and so unquestioned, that the image of the distant light serves as a reference for less clearly localized images. When Thoreau heard the sound of a horn in the depths of the woods, this image with its hardly determined center, this sound image that filled the entire nocturnal landscape, suggested repose and confidence to him. That sound, he said, is as friendly as the hermit's distant candle. And for those of us who remember, from what intimate valley do the horns of other days still reach us? Why do we immediately accept the common friendship of this sound world awakened by the horn, or the hermit's world lighted by its distant gleam? How is it that images as rare as these should possess such power over the imagination?

Great images have both a history and a prehistory; they are always a blend of memory and legend, with the result that we never experience an image directly. Indeed, every great image has an unfathomable oneiric depth to which the personal past adds special color. Consequently it is not until late in life that we really revere an image, when we discover that its roots plunge well beyond the history that is fixed in our memories. In the realm of absolute imagination, we remain young late in life. But we must lose our earthly Paradise in order actually to live in it, to experience it in the reality of its images, in the absolute sublimation that transcends all passion. A poet meditating upon the life of a great poet, that is, Victor-Emile Michelet meditating upon the life of Villiers de I'Isle-Adam, wrote: "Alas! we have to grow old to conquer youth, to free it from its fetters and live according to its original impulse."

Poetry gives not so much a nostalgia for youth, which would be vulgar, as a nostalgia for the expressions of youth. It offers us images as we should have imagined them during the "original impulse" of youth. Primal images, simple engravings are but so many invitations to start imagining again. They give us back areas of being, houses in which the human being's certainty of being is concentrated, and we have the impression that, by living in such images as these, in images that are as stabilizing as these are, we could start a new life, a life that would be our own, that would belong to us in our very depths. When we look at images of this kind, when we read the images in Bachelin's book, *we start musing on primitiveness.* And because of this very primitiveness, restored, desired and experienced through simple images, an album of pictures of huts would constitute a textbook of simple exercises for the phenomenology of the imagination.

In line with the distant light in the hermit's hut, symbolic of the man who keeps vigil, a rather large dossier of literary documentation on the poetry of houses could be studied from the single angle of the lamp that glows in the window. This image would have to be placed under one of the greatest of all theorems of the imagination of the world of light: *Tout ce qui brille voit* (All that glows sees). Rimbaud expressed in three syllables the following cosmic theorem: "Nacre voit" (Mother-of-pearl sees).[19] The lamp keeps vigil, therefore it is vigilant. And the narrower the ray of light, the more penetrating its vigilance.

The lamp in the window is the house's eye and, in the kingdom of the imagination, it is never lighted out-of-doors, but is enclosed light, which can only filter to the outside. A poem entitled *Emmuré* (Walled-in), begins as follows:

> *Une lampe allumée derrière la fenêtre*
> *Veille au coeur secret de la nuit.*

> (A lighted lamp in the window
> Watches in the secret heart of night.)

while a few lines above the same poet speaks:

> *Du regard emprisonné*
> *Entre ses quatre murs de pierre*[20]

> (Of a gaze imprisoned
> Between its four stone walls.)

In Henri Bosco's novel *Hyacinthe*, which, together with another story, *Le jardin d'Hyacinthe* (Hyacinth's Garden), constitutes one of the most astounding psychological novels of our time, a lamp *is waiting* in the window, and through it, the house, too, is waiting. The lamp is the symbol of prolonged waiting.

By means of the light in that far-off house, the house sees, keeps vigil, vigilantly waits.

When I let myself drift into the intoxication of inverting

daydreams and reality, that faraway house with its light becomes for me, before me, a house that is looking out—its turn now!—through the keyhole. Yes, there is someone in that house who is keeping watch, a man is working there while I dream away. He leads a dogged existence, whereas I am pursuing futile dreams. Through its light alone, the house becomes human. It sees like a man. It is an eye open to night.

But countless other images come to embellish the poetry of the house in the night. Sometimes it glows like a firefly in the grass, a creature with a solitary light:

> Je verrai vos maisons comme des vers luisants au creux des collines[21]

(I shall see your houses like fireflies in the hollow of the hills.)

Another poet calls houses that shine on earth "stars of grass"; and Christiane Barucoa speaks elsewhere of the lamp in the human house as an

> Etoile prisonnière prise au gel de l'instant

(Imprisoned star caught in the instant's freezing.)

In such images we have the impression that the stars in heaven come to live on earth, that the houses of men form earthly constellations.

With ten villages and their lights, G.-E. Clancier nails a Leviathan constellation to the earth:

> Une nuit, dix villages, une montagne,
> Un léviathan noir clouté d'or.[22]

(A night, ten villages, a mountain,
A black, gold-studded Leviathan.)

Erich Neumann has analyzed the dream of a patient who, while looking at the stars from the top of a tower, saw them rise and shine under the earth; they emerged from the bowels of the earth. In this obsession, the earth was not, however, a mere likeness of the starry sky, but the great life-giving mother of the world, the creator of night and the stars.[23] In his patient's dream, Neumann shows the force of the Mother-Earth (*Mutter-Erde*) archetype. Poetry comes naturally from a daydream, which is less *insistent* than a night-dream; it is only a matter of an "instant's freezing." But the poetic document is none the less indicative. A terrestrial sign is set upon a celestial being. The archeology of images is thus illumined by the poet's swift, instantaneous image.

I have dwelt somewhat at length on this apparently commonplace image, in order to show that images are incapable of repose. Poetic revery, unlike somnolent revery, never falls asleep. Starting with the simplest of images, it must always set the waves of the imagination radiating. But however cosmic the isolated house lighted by the star of its lamp may become, it will always symbolize solitude. I should like to quote one last text which stresses this solitude.

In the *Fragments from an intimate diary* that precede a French collection of Rilke's letters,[24] we find the following scene: one very dark night, Rilke and two friends perceive "the lighted casement of a distant hut, the hut that stands quite alone on the horizon before one comes to fields and marshlands." This image of solitude symbolized by a single light moves the poet's heart in so personal a way that it isolates him from his companions. Speaking of this group of three friends, Rilke adds: "Despite the fact that we were very close to one another, we remained three isolated individuals, seeing night for the first time." This expression can never be meditated upon enough, for here the most commonplace image, one that the poet had certainly seen hundreds of times, is suddenly marked with the sign of "the first time," and it transmits this sign to the familiar night. One might even say that light emanating from a lone watcher, who is also a determined watcher, attains to the power of hypnosis. We are hypnotized by solitude, hypnotized by the gaze of the solitary house; and the tie that binds us to it is so strong that we begin to dream of nothing but a solitary house in the night.

O Licht im schlafenden Haus![25]

(O light in the sleeping house!)

With the example of the hut and the light that keeps vigil on the far horizon, we have shown the concentration of intimacy in the refuge, in its most simplified form. At the beginning of this chapter, on the contrary, I tried to differentiate the house according to its verticality. Now, still with the aid of pertinent literary documents, I shall attempt to give a better account of the house's powers of protection against the forces that besiege it. Then, after having examined this dynamic dialectics of the house and the universe, we shall study a number of poems in which the house is a world in itself.

2

HOUSE AND UNIVERSE

Quand les cimes de notre ciel se rejoindront
Ma maison aura un toit.[1]

(When the peaks of our sky come together
My house will have a roof.)

In the preceding chapter, I pointed out that it was reasonable
to say we "read a house," or "read a room," since both room
and house are psychological diagrams that guide writers and
poets in their analysis of intimacy. We shall now read slowly
several houses and rooms "written" by great writers.

I

Although at heart a city man, Baudelaire sensed the increased
intimacy of a house when it is besieged by winter. In *Les paradis artificiels* (p. 280) he speaks of Thomas de Quincey's joy
when, a prisoner of winter, he read Kant, with the help of the
idealism furnished by opium. The scene takes place in a cottage in Wales. "*Une jolie habitation ne rend-elle pas l'hiver
plus poétique, et l'hiver n'augmente-t-il pas la poésie de
l'habitation? Le blanc cottage était* ASSIS *au fond d'une* PETITE
vallé FERMÉE *de montagnes* SUFFISAMENT HAUTES; *il était
comme emmailloté d'arbustes.*" ("Isn't it true that a pleasant
house makes winter more poetic, and doesn't winter add to
the poetry of a house? The white cottage sat at the end of a

little valley, *shut in* by *rather high* mountains; and it seemed to be *swathed* in shrubs.")

I have underlined the words in this short sentence that belong to the imagination of repose. And what a quiet setting for an opium-eater, reading Kant in the combined solitudes of dream and thought! As for the passage Baudelaire devoted to it, no doubt we can read it the way we can read any easy, too easy, passage. A literary critic might even be surprised by the naturalness with which this great poet has used commonplace images. But if, while reading this over-simplified passage, we accept the daydreams of repose it suggests; if we pause over the underlined words, it soon brings tranquility to body and soul. We feel that we are living in the protective center of the house in the valley. We too are "swathed" in the blanket of winter.

And we feel warm *because* it is cold out-of-doors. Further on in this deep-winter "artificial Paradise" Baudelaire declares that dreamers like a severe winter. "Every year they ask the sky to send down as much snow, hail and frost as it can contain. What they really need are Canadian or Russian winters. Their own nests will be all the warmer, all the downier, all the better beloved . . ."[2] Like Edgar Allan Poe, a great dreamer of curtains, Baudelaire, in order to protect the winter-girt house from cold added "heavy draperies that hung down to the floor." Behind dark curtains, snow seems to be whiter. Indeed, everything comes alive when contradictions accumulate.

Here Baudelaire has furnished us with a centered picture that leads to the heart of a dream which we can then take over for ourselves. No doubt we shall give it certain personal features, such as peopling Thomas de Quincey's cottage with persons from our own past. In this way we receive the benefits of this evocation without its exaggerations; our most personal recollections can come and live here. And through some indefinable current of sympathy, Baudelaire's description has ceased to be commonplace. But it is always like that: well-determined centers of revery are means of communication between men who dream as surely as well-defined concepts are means of communication between men who think.

In *Curiosités esthétiques* (p. 331) Baudelaire also speaks of a canvas by Lavieille which shows "a thatched cottage on the edge of a wood" in winter, "the sad season." "Certain of the effects that Lavieille often got," wrote Baudelaire, "seem to me to constitute the very essence of winter happiness." A reminder of winter strengthens the happiness of inhabiting. In the reign of the imagination alone, a reminder of winter increases the house's value as a place to live in.

If I were asked to make an expert evaluation of the oneirism in De Quincey's cottage, as relived by Baudelaire, I should say that there lingers about it the insipid odor of opium, an atmosphere of drowsiness. But we are told nothing about the strength of the walls, or the fortitude of the roof. The house puts up no struggle. It is as though Baudelaire knew of nothing to shut himself in with but curtains.

This absence of struggle is often the case of the winter houses in literature. The dialectics of the house and the universe are too simple, and snow, especially, reduces the exterior world to nothing rather too easily. It gives a single color to the entire universe which, with the one word, snow, is both expressed and nullified for those who have found shelter. In *Les déserts de l'amour* (p. 104), Rimbaud himself said: "*C'était comme une nuit d'hiver, avec une neige pour étouffer le monde décidément.*" (It was like a winter's night, with snow to stifle the world for certain.)

In any case, outside the occupied house, the winter cosmos is a simplified cosmos. It is a non-house in the same way that metaphysicians speak of a non-I, and between the house and the non-house it is easy to establish all sorts of contradictions. Inside the house, everything may be differentiated and multiplied. The house derives reserves and refinements of intimacy from winter; while in the outside world, snow covers all tracks, blurs the road, muffles every sound, conceals all colors. As a result of this universal whiteness, we feel a form of cosmic negation in action. The dreamer of houses knows and senses this, and because of the diminished entity of the outside world, experiences all the qualities of intimacy with increased intensity.

II

Winter is by far the oldest of the seasons. Not only does it confer age upon our memories, taking us back to a remote past, but, on snowy days, the house too is old. It is as though it were living in the past of centuries gone by. This feeling is described by Bachelin in a passage that presents winter in all its hostility.[3] "Those were evenings when, in old houses exposed to snow and icy winds, the great stories, the beautiful legends that men hand down to one another, take on concrete meaning and, for those who delve into them, become immediately applicable. And thus it was, perhaps, that one of our ancestors, who lay dying in the year one thousand, should have come to believe in the end of the world." For here the stories that were told were not the fireside fairy tales recounted by old women; they were stories about men, stories that reflect upon forces and signs. During these winters, Bachelin writes elsewhere (p. 58), "it seems to me that, under the hood of the great fireplace, the old legends must have been much older then than they are today." What they really had was the immemorial quality of the tragic cataclysms that can presage the end of the world.

Recalling these evenings during the dramatic winters in his father's house, Bachelin writes (p. 104): "When our companions left us, their feet deep in snow and their faces in the teeth of the blizzard, it seemed to me that they were going very far away, to unknown owl-and-wolf-infested lands. I was tempted to call after them, as people did in my early history books: "May God help you!"

And what a striking thing it is that a mere image of the old homestead in the snow-drifts should be able to integrate images of the year one thousand in the mind of a child.

III

We come now to a case which is more complex, and may even appear to be paradoxical. It is taken from a passage in Rilke's correspondence.[4]

Contrary to the general thesis I set forth in the preceding chapter, for Rilke, storms are particularly aggressive in cities, where heaven's ire, too, is most clearly manifested. In the country, apparently, hurricanes are less hostile to us. From my point of view, this is a paradox of cosmic origin. But, needless to say, the Rilke fragment is very fine, and it lends itself to interesting comment.

Here is what Rilke wrote to his fair "musician." "Do you know that when I am in a city I am frightened by hurricanes at night. It is as though, in their elemental pride, they did not see us. But they do see a lonely house in the country; they take it in their powerful arms and, in that way, they inure it, and when you are there, you would like to be out-of-doors, in the roaring garden, or at least, stand at the window and applaud the infuriated old trees that twist and turn as though possessed by the spirits of the prophets."

Photographically speaking, these lines of Rilke seem to me to be a "negative" of the house, the reverse of the function of inhabiting. When the storm rages and lashes the trees, in the shelter of the house, Rilke would like to be out-of-doors, not through any desire to enjoy the wind and the rain, but in order to pursue his own revery. So he shares, we feel, the anger reflex of the tree attacked by the anger of the wind. But he does not share the house's resistance. He puts his trust in the wisdom of the storm, in the clear vision of the lightning, and in all the elements which, even in their rage, see the abodes of men and agree to spare them.

But this "negative" of an image is nonetheless revealing, for it gives evidence of a dynamism in combat that is cosmic in its proportions. Rilke has furnished many proofs—to which we shall often refer—of his cognizance of the drama that attaches to the dwellings of men. At whatever dialectical pole the dreamer stands, whether in the house or in the universe, the dialectics become dynamic. House and space are not merely two juxtaposed elements of space. In the reign of the imagination, they awaken daydreams in each other, that are opposed. Rilke is ready to concede that the old house is "inured" by its trials. The house capitalizes its victories over the hurricanes. And since, in all research concerning the imagination, we must leave the realm of facts behind, we know perfectly that we feel calmer and more confident when in the old home, in the house we were born in, than we do in the houses on streets where we have only lived as transients.

IV

Contrary to the "negative" we have just been considering, let us now take the example of a "positive" that constitutes total adherence to the drama of the house besieged by storms.

In Henri Bosco's *Malicroix,* the house is called La Redousse.[5] It is built on an island in the Camargue region, not far from the great Rhône river. It is a humble house and appears to lack resistance. We shall see what fortitude it possessed.

The author takes many pages to prepare us for the storm that is brewing. A poetic weather forecast goes to the very source from whence the sound and the movement are to come. With what art, to begin with, he achieves absolute silence, the immensity of these silent stretches of space! "There is nothing like silence to suggest a sense of unlimited space. Sounds lend color to space, and confer a sort of sound body upon it. But absence of sound leaves it quite pure and, in the silence, we are seized with the sensation of something vast and deep and boundless. It took complete hold of me and, for several moments, I was overwhelmed by the grandeur of this shadowy peace.

"It asserted itself like a person.

"This peace had a body. It was caught up in the night, made of night. A real, a motionless body."

In this vast prose poem, we come upon passages that

contain the same progression of sounds and fears as is to be found in certain stanzas of Victor Hugo's *Les Djinns*. Only here, the author takes the time to show the narrowing of the space at the center of which the house is to live like an anguished heart. A kind of cosmic anguish precedes the storm. Then the wind starts to howl at the top of its lungs. Soon the entire menagerie of the hurricane lifts its voice. If one had the leisure to analyze the dynamics of storms, what a bestiary of the wind could be found not only in these pages but throughout Bosco's work. For this author knows instinctively that all aggression, whether it come from man or from the world, is of animal origin. However subtle, however indirect, hidden or contrived a human act of aggression may be, it reveals an origin that is unredeemed. In the tiniest of hatreds, there is a little, live, animal filament. And the poet-psychologist—or the psychologist-poet, if such a one exists—cannot go wrong in marking the different types of aggression with an animal cry. It is also a terrible trait of men that they should be incapable of understanding the forces of the universe intuitively, otherwise than in terms of a psychology of wrath.

And faced with this pack, which gradually breaks loose, the house becomes the real being of a pure humanity which defends itself without ever being responsible for an attack. La Redousse is man's Resistance; it is *human virtue,* man's grandeur.

Here is the passage that describes the house's human resistance at the height of the storm (p. 115):

"The house was fighting gallantly. At first it gave voice to its complaints; the most awful gusts were attacking it from every side at once, with evident hatred and such howls of rage that, at times, I trembled with fear. But it stood firm. From the very beginning of the storm, snarling winds had been taking the roof to task, trying to pull it off, to break its back, tear it into shreds, suck it off. But it only hunched over further and clung to the old rafters. Then other winds, rushing along close to the ground, charged against the wall. Everything swayed under the shock of this blow, but the flexible house stood up to the beast. No doubt it was holding firmly to the soil of the island by means of the unbreakable roots from which its thin walls of mud-coated reeds and planks drew their supernatural strength. Though the shutters and doors were insulted, though huge threats were proferred, and there was loud bugling in the chimney, it was of no avail. The already human being in whom I had sought shelter for my body yielded nothing to the storm. The house clung close to me, like a she-wolf, and at times, I could smell her odor penetrating maternally to my very heart. That night she was really my mother.

"She was all I had to keep and sustain me. We were alone."

Discussing maternity in my book, *La terre et les rêveries du repos,*[6] I quoted the following magnificent lines by Milosz,[7] in which the Mother image and the House image are united:

> *Je dis ma Mère. Et c'est à vous que je pense, ô Maison!*
> *Maison des beaux étés obscurs de mon enfance.*
>
> *(Mélancolie)*

> (I say Mother. And my thoughts are of you, oh, House!
> House of the lovely dark summers of my childhood.)
>
> (Melancholy)

It was imperative to find a similar image to express the deep gratitude of the inhabitant of La Redousse. Here, however, the image does not come from a nostalgia for childhood, but is given in its actuality of protection. Here, too, in addition to community of affection, there is community of forces, the concentrated courage and resistance of both house and man. And what an image of concentrated being we are given with this house that "clings" to its inhabitant and becomes the cell of a body with its walls close together. The refuge shrinks in size. And with its protective qualities increased, it grows outwardly stronger. From having been a refuge, it has become a redoubt. The thatched cottage becomes a fortified castle for the recluse, who must learn to conquer fear within its walls. Such a dwelling has an educative value, for in this passage of Bosco's book there is a sort of dovetailing of the reserves of strength with the inner fortresses of courage. In a house that has become for the imagination the very heart of a cyclone, we have to go beyond the mere impressions of consolation that we should feel in any shelter. We have to participate in the dramatic cosmic events sustained by the combatant house. But the real drama of Malicroix is an ordeal by solitude. The inhabitant of La Redousse must dominate solitude in a house on an island where there is no village. He must attain to the dignity of solitude that had been achieved by one of his ancestors, who had become a man of solitude as a result of a deep tragedy in his life. He must live alone in a cosmos which is not that of his childhood. This man, who comes of gentle, happy people, must cultivate courage in order to confront a world that is harsh, indigent and cold. The isolated house furnishes him with strong images, that is, with counsels of resistance.

And so, faced with the bestial hostility of the storm and the hurricane, the house's virtues of protection and resistance are transposed into human virtues. The house acquires the physical and moral energy of a human body. It braces itself to receive the downpour, it girds its loins. When forced to do so, it bends with the blast, confident that it will right itself again in time, while continuing to deny any temporary defeats. Such a house as this invites mankind to heroism of cosmic proportions. It is an instrument with which to confront the cosmos. And the metaphysical systems according to which man is "cast into the world" might meditate concretely upon the house that is cast into the hurricane, defying the anger of heaven itself. Come what may the house helps us to say: I will be an inhabitant of the world, in spite of the world. The problem is not only one of being, it is also a problem of energy and, consequently, of counter-energy.

In this dynamic rivalry between house and universe, we are far removed from any reference to simple geometrical forms. A house that has been experienced is not an inert box. Inhabited space transcends geometrical space.

But can this transposition of the being of a house into human values be considered as an activity of metaphor? Isn't this merely a matter of linguistic imagery? As metaphors, a literary critic would certainly find them exaggerated. On the other hand, a positivist psychologist would immediately reduce this language to the psychological reality of the fear felt by a man immured in his solitude, far from all human assistance. But phenomenology of the imagination cannot be content with a reduction which would make the image a subordinate means of expression: it demands, on the contrary, that images be lived directly, that they be taken as sudden events in life. When the image is new, the world is new.

And in reading applied to life, all passivity disappears if we try to become aware of the creative acts of the poet expressing the world, a world that becomes accessible to our daydreaming. In Bosco's *Malicroix* the world influences solitary man more than the characters are able to do. Indeed, if the many prose-poems the book contains were to be deleted, all that remained would be the story of a legacy, and a duel between the notary and the heir. But much is to be gained for a psychologist of the imagination if to "social" he adds "cosmic" reading. He comes to realize that the cosmos molds mankind, that it can transform a man of the hills into a man of islands and rivers, and that the house remodels man.

With the house that has been experienced by a poet, we come to a delicate point in anthropo-cosmology. The house, then, really is an instrument of topoanalysis; it is even an efficacious instrument, for the very reason that it is hard to use. In short, discussion of our theses takes place on ground that is unfavorable to us. For, in point of fact, a house is first and foremost a geometrical object, one which we are tempted to analyze rationally. Its prime reality is visible and tangible, made of well hewn solids and well fitted framework. It is dominated by straight lines, the plumbline having marked it with its discipline and balance.[8] A geometrical object of this kind ought to resist metaphors that welcome the human body and the human soul. But transposition to the human plane takes place immediately whenever a house is considered as space for cheer and intimacy, space that is supposed to condense and defend intimacy. Independent of all rationality, the dream world beckons. And as I read and re-read *Malicroix,* to quote Pierre-Jean

Jouve, "I hear the iron hooves of dream" on the roof of La Redousse.

But the complex of reality and dream is never definitively resolved. The house itself, when it starts to live humanly, does not lose all its "objectivity." We shall therefore have to examine more closely how houses of the past appear in dream geometry. For these are the houses in which we are going to recapture the intimacy of the past in our daydreams. We shall have to apply ourselves increasingly to studying how, by means of the house, the warm substance of intimacy resumes its form, the same form that it had when it enclosed original warmth.

> *Et l'ancienne maison,*
> *Je sens sa rousse tiédeur*
> *Vient des sens à l'esprit.*[9]

> (And the old house
> I feel its russet warmth
> Comes from the senses to the mind.)

V

First of all, these old houses can be drawn—we can make a representation that has all the characteristics of a copy. An objective drawing of this kind, independent of all daydreaming, is a forceful, reliable document that leaves its mark on a biography.

But let this exteriorist representation manifest an art of drawing, or a talent for representation, and it becomes insistent, inviting. Merely to judge it as a good, well executed likeness leads to contemplation and daydreaming. Daydreams return to inhabit an exact drawing and no dreamer ever remains indifferent for long to a picture of a house.

Long before the time when I began to read poetry every day, I had often said to myself that I should like to live in a house such as one sees in old prints. I was most attracted by the bold outlines of the houses in woodcuts which, it seemed to me, demanded simplicity. Through them, my daydreams inhabited the essential house.

These naïve daydreams, which I thought were my own, were a source of astonishment to me when I found traces of them in my reading.

In 1913, André Lafon had written:

> *Je rêve d'un logis, maison basse à fenêtres*
> *Hautes, aux trois degrés usés, plats et verdis*
>
> *Logis pauvre et secret à l'air d'antique estampe*
> *Qui ne vit qu'en moi-même, où je rentre parfois*
> *M'asseoir pour oublier le jour gris et la pluie*[10]

> (I dream of a house, a low house with high
> Windows, three worn steps, smooth and green
>
> A poor secret house, as in an old print,
> That only lives in me, where sometimes I return
> To sit down and forget the gray day and the rain.)

André Lafon wrote many other poems under the sign of "the poor house." In his literary "prints" the house welcomes the reader like a host. A bit more and he would be ready to seize the chisel and engrave his own reading.

Certain types of prints end by specifying types of houses. Annie Duthil wrote:

> *Je suis dans une maison d'estampes japonaises*
> *Le soleil est partout, car tout est transparent.*[11]

> (I am in a house in a Japanese print
> The sun is everywhere, for everything is transparent.)

There exist sunny houses in which, at all seasons, it is summer, houses that are all windows.

And isn't the poet who wrote the following also an inhabitant of prints?

> Qui n'a pas au fond de son coeur
> Un sombre château d'Elseneur
>
> A l'instar des gens du passé
> On construit en soi-même pierre
> Par pierre un grand chateau hante[12]
>
> (Who has not deep in his heart
> A dark castle of Elsinore
>
> In the manner of men of the past
> We build within ourselves stone
> On stone a vast haunted castle.)

And so I am cheered by the pictures I find in my reading. I go to live in the "literary prints" poets offer me. The more simple the engraved house the more it fires my imagination as an inhabitant. It does not remain a mere "representation." Its lines have *force* and, as a shelter, it is *fortifying*. It asks to be lived in simply with all the *security* that *simplicity* gives. The print house awakens a *feeling for the hut* in me and, through it, I re-experience the *penetrating gaze* of the *little window*. But see now what has happened! When I speak the image sincerely, I suddenly feel a need to underline. And what is *underlining* but *engraving* while we write?

VI

Sometimes the house grows and spreads so that, in order to live in it, greater elasticity of daydreaming, a daydream that is less clearly outlined, are needed. "My house," writes Georges Spyridaki,[13] "is diaphanous, but it is not of glass. It is more of the nature of vapor. Its walls contract and expand as I desire. At times, I draw them close about me like protective armor . . .

But at others, I let the walls of my house blossom out in their own space, which is infinitely extensible."

Spyridaki's house breathes. First it is a coat of armor, then it extends *ad infinitum,* which amounts to saying that we live in it in alternate security and adventure. It is both cell and world. Here, geometry is transcended.

To give unreality to an image attached to a strong reality is in the spirit of poetry. These lines by René Cazelles[14] speak to us of this expansion, if we can inhabit his images. The following was written in the heart of Provence, a country of sharp contours:

"The undiscoverable house, where this lava flower blows, where storms and exhausting bliss are born, when will my search for it cease?

"Symmetry abolished, to serve as fodder for the winds

"I should like my house to be similar to that of the ocean wind, all quivering with gulls."

Thus, an immense cosmic house is a potential of every dream of houses. Winds radiate from its center and gulls fly from its windows. A house that is as dynamic as this allows the poet to inhabit the universe. Or, to put it differently, the universe comes to inhabit his house.

Occasionally, in a moment of repose, the poet returns to the center of his abode (p. 29):

> ... *Tout respire à nouveau*
> *La nappe est blanche*

> (. . . Everything breathes again
> The tablecloth is white.)

This bit of whiteness, this tablecloth suffices to anchor the house to its center. The literary houses described by Georges Spyridaki and René Cazelles are immense dwellings, the walls of which are on vacation. There are moments when it is a salutary thing to go and live in them, as a treatment for claustrophobia.

The image of these houses that integrate the wind, aspire to the lightness of air, and bear on the tree of their impossible growth a nest all ready to fly away, may perhaps be rejected by a positive, realistic mind. But it is of value for a general thesis on the imagination because, without the poet's knowing it apparently, it is touched by the attraction of opposites, which lends dynamism to the great archetypes. In an article[15] in the *Eranos* yearbook, Erich Neumann shows that all strongly terrestrial beings—and a house is strongly terrestrial—are nevertheless subject to the attractions of an aereal, celestial world. The well-rooted house likes to have a branch that is sensitive to the wind, or an attic that can hear the rustle of leaves. The poet who wrote

> *L'escalier des arbres*
> *On y monte*[16]

> (On the stairs of the trees
> We mount.)

was certainly thinking of an attic.

If we compose a poem about a house, it frequently happens that the most flagrant contradictions come to wake us from our doldrums of concepts, as philosophers would say, and free us from our utilitarian geometrical notions. In this fragment by René Cazelles, solidity is achieved by an imaginary dialectics. We inhale in it the impossible odor of lava, here granite has wings. Conversely, the sudden wind is as rigid as a girder. The house conquers its share of sky. It has the entire sky for its terrace.

But my commentary is becoming too precise. Concerning the different characteristics of the house, it is inclined to be hospitable to fragmentary dialectics, and if I were to pursue it, I should destroy the unity of the archetype. However, this is always the case. It is better to leave the ambivalences of the archetypes wrapped in their dominant quality. This is why a poet will always be more suggestive than a philosopher. It is precisely his right to be suggestive. Pursuing the dynamism that belongs to suggestion, then, the reader can go farther, even too far. In reading and re-reading René Cazelles' poem, once we have accepted the burst of the image, we know that we can reside not only in the topmost heights of the house, but in a super-height. There are many images with which I like to make super-height experiments. The image of the house in the solid representation is folded lengthwise. When the poet unfolds it and spreads it out, it presents a very pure phenomenological aspect. Consciousness becomes "uplifted" in contact with an image that, ordinarily, is "in repose." The image is no longer descriptive, but resolutely inspirational.

It is a strange situation. The space we love is unwilling to remain permanently enclosed. It deploys and appears to move elsewhere without difficulty; into other times, and on different planes of dream and memory.

Is there a reader who would fail to take advantage of the ubiquity of a poem like this one:

> Une maison dressée au coeur
> Ma cathédrale de silence
> Chaque matin reprise en rêve
> Et chaque soir abandonnée
> Une maison couverte d'aube
> Ouverte au vent de ma jeunesse[17]

> (A house that stands in my heart
> My cathedral of silence
> Every morning recaptured in dream
> Every evening abandoned
> A house covered with dawn
> Open to the winds of my youth.)

This house, as I see it, is a sort of airy structure that moves about on the breath of time. It really is open to the wind of another time. It seems as though it could greet us every day of our lives in order to give us confidence in life. In my daydreaming, I associate these lines by Jean Laroche with the passage in which René Char[18] dreams in "a room that grew buoyant and, little by little, expanded into the vast stretches of travel." If the Creator listened to poets, He would create a flying turtle that would carry off into the blue the great safeguards of earth.

If further proof of these weightless houses were needed, there is a poem by Louis Guillaume, entitled *"Maison de vent"*[19] (Wind House), in which the poet dreams as follows:

> *Longtemps je t'ai construite, ô maison!*
> *A chaque souvenir je transportais des pierres*
> *Du rivage au sommet de tes murs*
> *Et je voyais, chaume couvé par les saisons*
> *Ton toit changeant comme la mer*
> *Danser sur le fond des nuages*
> *Auxquels il mêlait ses fumées*
>
> *Maison de vent demeure qu'un souffle effaçait.*
>
> (Long did I build you, oh house!
> With each memory I carried stones
> From the bank to your topmost wall
> And I saw your roof mellowed by time
> Changing as the sea
> Dancing against a background of clouds
> With which it mingled its smoke.
>
> Wind house, abode that a breath effaced.)

Some may wonder at this accumulation of examples. For the realist, the matter is settled: "None of that holds water! It is nothing but vain, inconsistent poetry; poetry that has lost all touch with reality." For the positive man, everything that is unreal is alike, the forms being submerged and drowned in unreality; and the only houses that are capable of possessing individuality are real ones.

But a dreamer of houses sees them everywhere, and anything can act as a germ to set him dreaming about them. Jean Laroche has written elsewhere:

Cette pivoine est une maison vague
Où chacun retrouve la nuit

(This peony is an empty house
In which each of us recaptures night.)

The peony encloses a sleeping insect in its red night:

Tout calice est demeure

(Every chalice is a dwelling-place.)

Pivoines et pavots paradis taciturnes!

(Peonies and poppies silent gardens of Paradise!)

writes Jean Bourdeillette[20] in a line that encloses infinity.

When we have dreamed as intensely as this in the hollow of
a flower, the way we recall our lives in the house that is lost
and gone, dissolved in the waters of the past, is no ordinary
way. It is impossible to read the four lines that follow without
entering into a dream that is endless:

La chambre meurt miel et tilleul
Où les tiroirs s'ouvrirent en deuil
La maison se mêle à la mort
Dans un miroir qui se ternit.[21]

(The room is dying honey and linden
Where drawers opened in mourning
The house blends with death
In a mirror whose lustre is dimming.)

VII

If we go from these images, which are all light and shimmer, to
images that insist and force us to remember farther back into our

past, we shall have to take lessons from poets. For how forcefully they prove to us that the houses that were lost forever continue to live on in us; that they insist in us in order to live again,
as though they expected us to give them a supplement of living.
How much better we should live in the old house today! How
suddenly our memories assume a living possibility of being! We
consider the past, and a sort of remorse at not having lived pro-
foundly enough in the old house fills our hearts, comes up from
the past, overwhelms us. Rilke[22] expresses this poignant regret
in unforgettable lines which we painfully make our own, not so
much for their expression as for their dramatic depth of feeling:

> *Ô nostalgie des lieux qui n'étaient point*
> *Assez aimés à l'heure passagère*
> *Que je voudrais leur rendre de loin*
> *Le geste oublié, l'action supplémentaire.*

> (Oh, longing for places that were not
> Cherished enough in that fleeting hour
> How I long to make good from far
> The forgotten gesture, the additional act.)

Why were we so quickly sated with the happiness of living in
the old house? Why did we not prolong those fleeting hours? In
that reality something more than reality was lacking. We did not
dream enough in that house. And since it must be recaptured by
means of daydreams, liaison is hard to establish. Our memories
are encumbered with facts. Beyond the recollections we continually hark back to, we should like to relive our suppressed impressions and the dreams that made us believe in happiness:

> *Où vous ai-je perdue, mon imagerie piétinée?*[23]

> (Where did I lose you, my trampled fantasies?)

If we have retained an element of dream in our memories, if
we have gone beyond merely assembling exact recollections, bit
by bit the house that was lost in the mists of time will appear

from out the shadow. We do nothing to reorganize it; with intimacy it recovers its entity, in the mellowness and imprecision of the inner life. It is as though something fluid had collected our memories and we ourselves were dissolved in this fluid of the past. Rilke, who experienced this intimacy of fusion, speaks of the fusion of being with the lost house: "I never saw this strange dwelling again. Indeed, as I see it now, the way it appeared to my child's eye, it is not a building, but is quite dissolved and distributed inside me: here one room, there another, and here a bit of corridor which, however, does not connect the two rooms, but is conserved in me in fragmentary form. Thus the whole thing is scattered about inside me, the rooms, the stairs that descended with such ceremonious slowness, others, narrow cages that mounted in a spiral movement, in the darkness of which we advanced like the blood in our veins."[24]

Indeed, at times dreams go back so far into an undefined, dateless past that clear memories of our childhood home appear to be detached from us. Such dreams unsettle our daydreaming and we reach a point where we begin to doubt that we ever lived where we lived. Our past is situated elsewhere, and both time and place are impregnated with a sense of unreality. It is as though we sojourned in a limbo of being. And poets and dreamers find themselves writing things upon which metaphysicians would do well to meditate. Here, for instance, is a page of concrete metaphysics which by overlaying our memory of the childhood house with daydreams leads us to the ill-defined, vaguely located areas of being where we are seized with astonishment at being. In his novel *The House of Breath*[25] (p. 40), William Goyen writes: "That people could come into the world in a place they could not at first even name and had never known before; and that out of a nameless and unknown place they could grow and move around in it until its name they knew and called with love, and call it HOME, and put roots there and love others there; so that whenever they left this place they would sing homesick songs about it and write poems of yearning for it, like a lover; . . ." The soil in which chance had sown the human plant was of no importance. And against this background of nothingness human values grow! Inversely, if beyond memories, we pursue our dreams to their very end, in this pre-memory it is as though nothingness caressed and penetrated being, as though it gently unbound the ties of being. We ask ourselves if what has been, was. Have facts really the *value* that memory gives them? Distant memory only recalls them by giving them a value, a halo, of happiness. But let this value be effaced, and the facts cease to exist. Did they ever exist? Something unreal seeps into the reality of the recollections that are on the borderline between our own personal history and an indefinite pre-history, in the exact place where, after us, the childhood home comes to life in us. For before us—Goyen makes us understand this—it was quite anonymous. It was a place that was lost in the world. Thus, on the threshold of our space, before the era of our own time, we hover between awareness of being and loss of being. And the entire reality of memory becomes spectral.

But it would seem that this element of unreality in the dreams of memory affects the dreamer when he is faced with the most concrete things, as with the stone house to which he returns at night, his thoughts on mundane things. William Goyen understands this unreality of reality (loc. cit., p. 56): "So this is why when often as you came home to it, down the road in a mist of rain, it seemed as if the house were founded on the most fragile web of breath and you had blown it. Then you thought it might not exist at all as built by carpenter's hands, nor had ever; and that it was only an idea of breath breathed out by you who, with that same breath that had blown it, could blow it all away." In a passage like this, imagination, memory and perception exchange functions. The image is created through co-operation between real and unreal, with the help of the functions of the real and the unreal. To use the implements of dialectical logic for studying, not this alternative, but this fusion, of opposites, would be quite useless, for they would produce the anatomy of a living thing. But if a house is a living value, it must integrate an element of unreality. All values must remain vulnerable, and those that do not are dead.

When two strange images meet, two images that are the work of two poets pursuing separate dreams, they apparently strengthen each other. In fact, this convergence of two exceptional images furnishes as it were a counter-check for phenomenological analysis. The image loses its gratuitousness; the free play of the imagination ceases to be a form of anarchy. I should like, therefore, to compare Goyen's image in *The House of Breath* with one that I quoted in my book *La terre et les rêveries du repos* (p. 96) and which, at the time, I was unable to relate to any other.[26]

In *Le domaine public* (p. 70) Pierre Seghers writes:

> *Une maison où je vais seul en appelant*
> *Un nom que le silence et les murs me renvoient*
> *Une étrange maison qui se tient dans ma voix*
> *Et qu'habite le vent.*
> *Je l'invente, mes mains dessinent un nuage*
> *Un bateau de grand ciel au-dessus des forêts*
> *Une brume qui se dissipe et disparaît*
> *Comme au jeu des images.*

> (A house where I go alone calling
> A name that silence and the walls give back to me
> A strange house contained in my voice
> Inhabited by the wind
> I invent it, my hands draw a cloud
> A heaven-bound ship above the forests
> Mist that scatters and disappears
> As in the play of images.)

In order to build better this house in the mist and wind, we should need, according to the poet,

> *. . . Une voix plus forte et l'encens*
> *Bleu du coeur et des mots*

> (. . . A more sonorous voice and the blue
> Incense of heart and word.)

Like the house of breath, the house of wind and voice is a value that hovers on the frontier between reality and unreality.

No doubt a realistic mind will remain well this side of this region. But for the poetry lover who reads with joy and imagination, it is a red-letter day when he can hear echoes of the lost house in two registers. The old house, for those who know how to listen, is a sort of geometry of echoes. The voices of the past do not sound the same in the big room as in the little bed chamber, and calls on the stairs have yet another sound. Among the most difficult memories, well beyond any geometry that can be drawn, we must recapture the quality of the light; then come the sweet smells that linger in the empty rooms, setting an aerial seal on each room in the house of memory. Still farther it is possible to recover not merely the timbre of the voices, "the inflections of beloved voices now silent," but also the resonance of each room in the sound house. In this extreme tenuousness of memory, only poets may be expected to furnish us with documents of a subtly psychological nature.

VIII

Sometimes the house of the future is better built, lighter and larger than all the houses of the past, so that the image of *the dream house* is opposed to that of the childhood home. Late in life, with indomitable courage, we continue to say that we are going to do what we have not yet done: we are going to build a house. This dream house may be merely a dream of ownership, the embodiment of everything that is considered convenient, comfortable, healthy, sound, desirable, by other people. It must therefore satisfy both pride and reason, two irreconcilable terms. If these dreams are realized, they no longer belong in the domain of this study, but in that of the psychology of projects. However, as I have said many times, for me, a project is short-range oneirism, and while it gives free play to the mind, the soul does not find in it its vital expression. Maybe it is a good thing for us to keep a few dreams of a house that we shall live in later, always later, so much later, in fact, that we shall not have time to achieve it. For a house that was final, one that stood in symmetrical relation to the house we were born in, would lead to thoughts—serious, sad thoughts—and not to dreams. It is better to live in a state of impermanence than in one of finality.

The following anecdote contains a certain wisdom.

It is told by Campenon, who has been discussing poetry with the poet, Ducis: "When we came to the little poems, indited to *his home, his flower-beds, his kitchen garden, his little wood, or his wine-cellar* . . . I could not help remarking jokingly that, a hundred years hence, he risked obliging his commentators to rack their brains. He began to laugh, and told me that having desired vainly ever since he was young, to have a house in the country, with a small garden, he had made up his mind, at the age of seventy, to give them to himself on his own authority as a poet, and without putting his hand in his pocket. He had begun by acquiring a house, then, as the charm of ownership increased, had added the *garden*, the *little wood*, etc. None of this existed outside his imagination; but it sufficed for these little fancied possessions to take on reality in his eyes. He spoke of them and derived pleasure from them as though they were real; and so powerful was his imagination that I should not be surprised if, on frosty April nights, he didn't show signs of anxiety about his Marly vineyards.

"In this connection, he told me that a decent, honest country fellow, having read in the papers some of his lyrical pieces on the subject of his estate, had written to offer his services as overseer, adding that all he asked was a place to live and whatever wages might be considered fair."

Housed everywhere but nowhere shut in, this is the motto of the dreamer of dwellings. In the last house as well as in the actual house, the daydream of inhabiting is thwarted. A daydream of elsewhere should be left open, therefore, at all times.

An excellent exercise for the function of inhabiting the dream house consists in taking a train trip. Such a voyage unreels a film of houses that are dreamed, accepted and refused, without our ever having been tempted to stop, as we are when motoring. We are sunk deep in daydreaming with all verification healthily forbidden. But lest this manner of travel be merely a

gentle mania of mine, I should like to quote the following passage from Thoreau's Journals, of October 31, 1850:

"I am wont to think that I could spend my days contentedly
in any retired country house that I see; for I see it to advantage
now and without incumbrance; I have not yet imported my
humdrum thoughts, my prosaic habits, into it to mar the landscape." On August 28, 1861, Thoreau addresses in thought the
fortunate owners of the houses he has seen: "Give me but the
eyes to see the things which you possess."

George Sand said that people could be classified according to
whether they aspired to live in a cottage or in a palace. But the
question is more complex than that. When we live in a manor
house we dream of a cottage, and when we live in a cottage we
dream of a palace. Better still, we all have our cottage moments
and our palace moments. We descend to living close to the
ground, on the floor of a cottage, then would like to dominate
the entire horizon from a castle in Spain. And when reading
has given us countless inhabited places, we know how to let the
dialectics of cottage and manor sound inside us. This was experienced by a great poet, Saint-Pol Roux, whose book, *Féeries
intérieurs* (Inner Enchantments), contains two stories that need
only be compared to obtain two quite different pictures of Brit-
tany, and indeed two different worlds. From one world to the
other, from one dwelling to the other, dreams come and go.
The first story is entitled: *Adieux à la chaumière* (Farewell to
the Cottage, p. 205) and the second: *Le châtelain et le paysan*
(Squire and Peasant, p. 359).

The minute they entered the cottage, it opened its heart and
soul: "At dawn, your freshly white-washed being opened its
arms to us: the children felt that they had entered into the
heart of a dove, and we loved the ladder—your stairway—
right away." Elsewhere the poet tells how generously a cottage
radiates peasant humanity and fraternity. This dove-house
was a hospitable ark.

One day, however, Saint-Pol Roux left the cottage for the
manor house. "Before leaving for a life of 'luxury and pride,'"
according to Théophile Briant,[27] "his Franciscan soul lamented,

and he lingered a while longer under the lintel of Roscanvel."
Briant quotes him as follows: "One last time, oh cottage, let me
kiss your humble walls, even in their shadow, which is the color
of my woe . . ."

The Camaret manor, which became Saint-Pol Roux's home,
is undoubtedly a poetic creation, in every sense of the word; it
is the realization of a poet's dream castle. For he first bought a
fisherman's cottage situated right by the sea, on the crest of the
dune that the inhabitants of this Breton peninsula call the Lion
of Toulinguet. With the help of a friend, an artillery officer, he
then drew up plans for a manor house with eight towers, the
center of which was to be the house he had just bought. An
architect modified somewhat this poetic project and the manor
with the cottage heart was built.

"One day," Théophile Briant recalls (loc. cit., p. 37), "to syn-
thesize the little Camaret peninsula for me, Saint-Pol Roux
took a sheet of paper and drew a stone pyramid showing the
hatchings of the wind and the roll of the sea. Underneath it he
wrote: 'Camaret is a stone in the wind on a lyre.'"

A few pages back we discussed poems that sing of breath
and wind houses, poems with which we seemed to have
attained the *ultimate degree of metaphor*. And here we see a
poet who follows the working draft of these metaphors to
build his house!

We should find ourselves indulging in similar daydreams if
we started musing under the cone-shaped roof of a windmill.
We should sense its terrestrial nature, and imagine it to be a
primitive hut stuck together with mud, firmly set on the ground
in order to resist the wind. Then, in an immense synthesis, we
should dream at the same time of a winged house that whines
at the slightest breeze and refines the energies of the wind.
Millers, who are wind thieves, make good flour from storms.

In the second tale in *Féeries intérieures,* Saint-Pol Roux tells
how he lived a peasant's life at the same time that he was lord
of the Camaret manor. Never, perhaps, have the dialectics of
cottage and manor been so simply or so powerfully inverted
as here. "As I stand riveted to the first steps of the perron by
my hob-nailed boots, I hesitate to emerge suddenly from my

rustic's chrysalis in the rôle of lord."[28] And further on (p. 362) he writes: "My flexible nature adapts itself easily to this eagle's well-being, high above town and sea, a well-being in which my imagination loses no time conferring supremacy upon me, over elements and persons. And soon, bound up in my egoism, I forget, upstart peasant that I am, that the original reason for the manor house was, through antithesis, to enable me to really see the cottage."

The word *chrysalis* alone is an unmistakable indication that here two dreams are joined together, dreams that bespeak both the repose and flight of being, evening's crystallization and wings that open to the light. In the body of the winged manor, which dominates both town and sea, man and the universe, he retained a cottage chrysalis in order to be able to hide alone, in complete repose.

Referring to the work of the Brazilian philosopher, Lucio Alberto Pinheiro dos Santos,[29] I once said that by examining the rhythms of life in detail, by descending from the great rhythms forced upon us by the universe to the finer rhythms that play upon man's most exquisite sensibilities, it would be possible to work out a rhythmanalysis that would tend to reconcile and lighten the ambivalences that psychoanalysts find in the disturbed psyche. But if what poets say is true, alternating daydreams cease to be rivals. The two extreme realities of cottage and manor, to be found in the case of Saint-Pol Roux, take into account our need for retreat and expansion, for simplicity and magnificence. For here we experience a rhythmanalysis of the function of inhabiting. To sleep well we do not need to sleep in a large room, and to work well we do not have to work in a den. But to dream of a poem, then write it, we need both. It is the creative psyche that benefits from rhythmanalysis.

Thus the dream house must possess every virtue. However spacious, it must also be a cottage, a dove-cote, a nest, a chrysalis. Intimacy needs the heart of a nest. Erasmus, his biographer tells us, was long "in finding a nook in his fine house in which he could put *his little body* with safety. He ended by confining himself to one room until he could breathe *the parched air* that was necessary to him."[30]

And how many dreamers look everywhere in their house, or in their room, for the garment that suits them!

But I repeat: nest, chrysalis and garment only constitute one moment of a dwelling place. The more concentrated the repose, the more hermetic the chrysalis, the more the being that emerges from it is a being from elsewhere, the greater is his expansion. And, in my opinion, as the reader goes from one poet to the other, he is made more dynamic by his reader's imagination if he listens to Supervielle inviting the entire universe to come back into the house through all the wide-open doors and windows.[31]

Tout ce qui fait les bois, les rivières ou l' air
A place entre ces murs qui croient fermer une chambre
Accourez, cavaliers qui traversez les mers
Je n'ai qu'un toit du ciel, vous aurez de la place.

(All that makes the woods, the rivers or the air
Has its place between these walls which believe they close a room
Make haste, ye gentlemen, who ride across the seas
I've but one roof from heaven, there'll be room for you.)

The house's welcome is so genuine that even what may be seen from the windows belongs to it.

Le corps de la montagne hésite à ma fenêtre:
"Comment peut-on entrer si l'on est la montagne,
Si l'on est en hauteur, avec roches, cailloux,
Un morceau de la Terre altéré par le Ciel?"

(The body of the mountain hesitates before my window:
"How can one enter if one is the mountain,
If one is tall, with boulders and stones,
A piece of Earth, altered by Sky?")

When we have been made aware of a rhythmanalysis by moving from a concentrated to an expanded house, the oscillations reverberate and grow louder. Like Supervielle, great dreamers profess intimacy with the world. They learned this intimacy, however, meditating on the house.

IX

Supervielle's house is a house that is eager to see, one for which seeing is having. It both sees the world and has it. But like a greedy child, its eyes are bigger than its stomach. It has furnished us with one of those exaggerated images that a philosopher of the imagination is obliged to note right away with a reasonably critical smile.

But after this holiday of the imagination we shall have to return to reality, in order to speak of daydreams that accompany household activities. For they keep vigilant watch over the house, they link its immediate past to its immediate future, they are what maintains it in the security of being.

But how can housework be made into a creative activity?

The minute we apply a glimmer of consciousness to a mechanical gesture, or practice phenomenology while polishing a piece of old furniture, we sense new impressions come into being beneath this familiar domestic duty. For consciousness rejuvenates everything, giving a quality of beginning to the most everyday actions. It even dominates memory. How wonderful it is to really become once more the inventor of a mechanical action! And so, when a poet rubs a piece of furniture—even vicariously—when he puts a little fragrant wax on his table with the woolen cloth that lends warmth to everything it touches, he creates a new object; he increases the object's human dignity; he registers this object officially as a member of the human household. Henri Bosco once wrote:[32] "The soft wax entered into the polished substance under the pressure of hands and the effective warmth of a woolen cloth. Slowly the tray took on a dull luster. It was as though the radiance induced by magnetic rubbing emanated from the hundred-year-old sapwood, from the very heart of the dead tree, and spread gradually, in the form of light, over the tray. The old fingers possessed of every virtue, the broad palm, drew from the solid block with its inanimate fibers, the latent powers of life itself. This was creation of an object, a real act of faith, taking place before my enchanted eyes."

Objects that are cherished in this way really are born of an intimate light, and they attain to a higher degree of reality than indifferent objects, or those that are defined by geometric reality. For they produce a new reality of being, and they take their place not only in an order but in a community of order. From one object in a room to another, housewifely care weaves the ties that unite a very ancient past to the new epoch. The housewife awakens furniture that was asleep.

If we attain to the limit at which dream becomes exaggerated, we experience a sort of consciousness of constructing the house, in the very pains we take to keep it alive, to give it all its essential clarity. A house that shines from the care it receives appears to have been rebuilt from the inside; it is as though it were new inside. In the intimate harmony of walls and furniture, it may be said that we become conscious of a house that is built by women, since men only know how to build a house from the outside, and they know little or nothing of the "wax" civilization.

No one has written better of this integration of revery into work, of our vastest dreams into the humblest of occupations, than Henri Bosco, in his description of the old faithful servant, Sidoine (op. cit., p. 173): "This vocation for happiness, so far from prejudicing her practical life, nurtured its action. When she washed a sheet or a tablecloth, when she polished a brass candlestick, little movements of joy mounted from the depths of her heart, enlivening her household tasks. She did not wait to finish these tasks before withdrawing into herself, where she could contemplate to her heart's content the supernatural images that dwelt there. Indeed, figures from this land appeared to her familiarly, however commonplace the work she was doing, and without in the least seeming to dream, she washed, dusted and swept in the company of angels."

I once read an Italian novel in which there was a street sweeper who swung his broom with the majestic gesture of a reaper. In his daydream he was reaping an imaginary field on the asphalt, a wide field in real nature in which he recaptured his youth and the noble calling of reaper under the rising sun.

We should need, then, purer "reagents" than those of psychoanalysis to determine the "composition" of a poetic image. The fine determinations required by poetry bring us into the field of micro-chemistry, and a reagent that had been adulterated by the ready-made interpretations of a psychoanalyst could cloud the solution. No phenomenologist re-living Supervielle's invitation to the mountains to come in through the window would see in it a sexual monstrosity. This is rather the poetic phenomenon of pure liberation, of absolute sublimation. The image is no longer under the domination of things, nor is it subject to the pressures of the unconscious. It floats and soars, immense, in the free atmosphere of a great poem. Through the poet's window the house converses about immensity with the world. And as metaphysicians would say, it too, the house of men, opens its doors to the world.

In the same way, the phenomenologist who follows women's construction of the house through daily polishing must go beyond the psychoanalyst's interpretations. I myself held to these interpretations in some of my earlier books.[33] But I now believe that we can go deeper, that we can sense how a human being can devote himself to things and make them his own by perfecting their beauty. A little more beautiful and we have something quite different.

Here we have the paradox of an incipience of a very customary action. Through housewifely care a house recovers not so much its originality as its origin. And what a great life it would be if, every morning, every object in the house could be made anew by our hands, could "issue" from our hands. In a letter to his brother Theo, Vincent van Gogh tells him that we should "retain something of the original character of a Robinson Crusoe" (p. 25). Make and remake everything oneself, make a "supplementary gesture" toward each object, give another facet to the polished reflections, all of which are so many boons the imagination confers upon us by making us aware of the house's inner growth. To have an active day I keep saying to myself, "Every morning I must give a thought to Saint Robinson."

When a dreamer can reconstruct the world from an object that he transforms magically through his care of it, we become convinced that everything in the life of a poet is germinal. The following long fragment by Rilke, in spite of a certain over-loading (gloves and costumes), gives us a feeling of naïve simplicity.

In *Lettres à une musicienne,* Rilke writes to Benvenuta that in the absence of his cleaning woman, he had been polishing his furniture. "I was, as I said, magnificently alone . . . when suddenly I was seized by my old passion. I should say that this was undoubtedly my greatest childhood passion, as well as my first contact with music, since our little piano fell under my jurisdiction as duster. It was, in fact, one of the few objects that lent itself willingly to this operation and gave no sign of boredom. On the contrary, under my zealous dustcloth, it suddenly started to purr mechanically . . . and its fine, deep black surface became more and more beautiful. When you've been through this there's little you don't know! I was quite proud, if only of my indispensable costume, which consisted of a big apron and little washable suède gloves to protect one's dainty hands. Politeness tinged with mischief was my reaction to the friendliness of these objects, which seemed happy to be so well treated, so meticulously renovated. And even today, I must confess that, while everything about me grew brighter and the immense black surface of my work table, which dominated its surroundings . . . became newly aware, somehow, of the size of the room, reflecting it more and more clearly: pale gray and almost square, . . . well, yes, I felt moved, as though something were happening, something, to tell the truth, which was not purely superficial but immense, and which touched my very soul: I was an emperor washing the feet of the poor, or Saint Bonaventure, washing dishes in his convent."

Benvenuta's comment[34] on these episodes detracts from their charm somewhat when she tells us that Rilke's mother, "while he was still a mere child, forced him to dust the furniture and perform other household tasks." But one cannot help sensing the *nostalgia for work* that emanates from this fragment by Rilke, or realizing that this is an accumulation of psychological documents from different mental ages, since to the joy of helping his mother is added the glory of being one of the great of the earth, washing the feet of the poor. The whole thing is a complex of sentiments, with its association of politeness and mischief, of humility and action. Then, too, there is the striking line with which it opens: "I was magnificently alone"! Alone, as we are at the origin of all real action that we are not "obliged" to perform. And the marvelous thing about easy actions is that they do, in fact, place us at the origin of action.

Removed from its context, this long passage seems to me to be a good test of the reader's interest. Some may disdain it or wonder that it should interest anyone; whereas to others it may seem alive, effective and stimulating, since it offers each one of us a means of becoming aware of our room by strongly synthesizing everything that lives in it, every piece of furniture that wants to be friends.

There is also the courage of the writer who braves the kind of censorship that forbids "insignificant" confidences. But what a joy reading is, when we recognize the importance of these insignificant things, when we can add our own personal daydreams to the "insignificant" recollections of the author! Then insignificance becomes the sign of extreme sensitivity to the intimate meanings that establish spiritual understanding between writer and reader.

And what charm it confers upon our memories to be able to say to ourselves that, except for the suède gloves, we have lived moments similar to those lived by Rilke!

X

All great, simple images reveal a psychic state. The house, even more than the landscape, is a "psychic state," and even when reproduced as it appears from the outside, it bespeaks intimacy. Psychologists generally, and Françoise Minkowska in particular, together with those whom she has succeeded interesting in the subject, have studied the drawings of houses made by children, and even used them for testing. Indeed, the

house-test has the advantage of welcoming spontaneity, for
many children draw a house spontaneously while dreaming
over their paper and pencil. To quote Anne Balif:[35] "Asking a
child to draw his house is asking him to reveal the deepest
dream shelter he has found for his happiness. If he is happy, he
will succeed in drawing a snug, protected house which is well
built on deeply-rooted foundations." It will have the right
shape, and nearly always there will be some indication of its
inner strength. In certain drawings, quite obviously, to quote
Mme. Balif, "it is warm indoors, and there is a fire burning,
such a big fire, in fact, that it can be seen coming out of the
chimney." When the house is happy, soft smoke rises in gay
rings above the roof.

If the child is unhappy, however, the house bears traces of his
distress. In this connection, I recall that Françoise Minkowska
organized an unusually moving exhibition of drawings by Polish and Jewish children who had suffered the cruelties of the
German occupation during the last war. One child, who had
been hidden in a closet every time there was an alert, continued
to draw narrow, cold, closed houses long after those evil times
were over. These are what Mme. Minkowska calls "motionless" houses, houses that have become motionless in their rigidity. "This rigidity and motionlessness are present in the *smoke*
as well as in the window curtains. The surrounding trees are
quite *straight* and give the impression of standing guard over
the house" (loc. cit., p. 55). Mme Minkowska knows that a live
house is not really "motionless," that, particularly, it integrates
the movements by means of which one accedes to the door.
Thus the path that leads to the house is often a climbing one.
At times, even, it is inviting. In any case, it always possesses
certain kinesthetic features. If we were making a Rorschach
test, we should say that the house has "K."

Often a simple detail suffices for Mme. Minkowska, a distinguished psychologist, to recognize the way the house functions. In one house, drawn by an eight-year-old child, she
notes that there is "a knob on the door; people go in the house,
they live there." It is not merely a constructed house, it is also
a house that is "lived-in." Quite obviously the door-knob has a

functional significance. This is the kinesthetic sign, so frequently forgotten in the drawings of "tense" children.

Naturally, too, the door-knob could hardly be drawn in scale with the house, its function taking precedence over any question of size. For it expresses the function of opening, and only a logical mind could object that it is used to close as well as to open the door. In the domain of values, on the other hand, a key closes more often than it opens, whereas the door-knob opens more often than it closes. And the gesture of closing is always sharper, firmer and briefer than that of opening. It is by weighing such fine points as these that, like Françoise Minkowska, one becomes a psychologist of houses.

3

DRAWERS, CHESTS AND WARDROBES

I always feel a slight shock, a certain mild, philological pain, whenever a great writer uses a word in a derogatory sense. To begin with, all words do an honest job in our everyday language, and not even the most ordinary among them, those that are attached to the most commonplace realities, lose their poetic possibilities as a result of this fact. But somehow, when Bergson uses the word "drawer," he does it disdainfully. Indeed, the word always appears in the rôle of a controversial metaphor, giving orders and passing judgment, always in the same way. Our philosopher dislikes compartmented arguments.

This seems to me to be a good example for demonstrating the radical difference between image and metaphor. I shall therefore insist upon this difference before returning to my examination of the images of intimacy that are in harmony with drawers and chests, as also with all the other hiding-places in which human beings, great dreamers of locks, keep or hide their secrets.

Although there is a superabundance of metaphor in Bergson's writings, in the last analysis, his images are rare. It is as though, for him, imagination were entirely metaphorical. Now a metaphor gives concrete substance to an impression that is difficult to express. Metaphor is related to a psychic being from which it differs. An image, on the contrary, product of absolute imagination, owes its entire being to the imagination. Later, when I plan to go more deeply into the comparison between metaphor and image, we shall see that metaphor

could not be studied phenomenologically, and that in fact, it is
not worth the trouble, since it has no phenomenological value.
At the most, it is a *fabricated image*, without deep, true, genuine roots. It is an ephemeral expression. It is, or should be, one
that is used only once, in passing. We must be careful, therefore, not to give it too much thought; nor should the reader
think too much about it. And yet, what a success the drawer
metaphor has had with Bergson's followers!

Contrary to metaphor, we can devote our reading being to
an image, since it confers being upon us. In fact, the image,
which is the pure product of absolute imagination, is a phenomenon of being; it is also one of the specific phenomena of
the speaking creature.

II

As is well known, the drawer metaphor, in addition to certain
others, such as "ready-made garments," is used by Bergson to
convey the inadequacy of a philosophy of concept. Concepts
are drawers in which knowledge may be classified; they are
also ready-made garments which do away with the individuality of knowledge that has been experienced. The concept soon
becomes lifeless thinking since, by definition, it is classified
thinking.

I should like to point out a few passages which show the
polemical nature of the drawer metaphor in Bergsonian philosophy.

In *L'evolution creatrice* (1907, p. 5) we read: "Memory, as I
have tried to prove,[1] is not the faculty for classifying recollections in a drawer, or writing them down in a register. Neither
register nor drawer exists . . ."

Faced with any new object, reason asks (see *L'Evolution
creatrice*, p. 52) "in which of its earlier categories the new
object belongs? In which ready-to-open drawer shall we put it?
With which ready-made garments shall we invest it?" Because,
of course, a ready-made garment suffices to clothe a poor

rationalist. In the second Oxford conference of May 27, 1911 (later included in *La pensée et le mouvant,* p. 172), Bergson shows the indigence of the image according to which there exist "here and there in the brain, keep-sake boxes that preserve fragments of the past."

In the Introduction to Metaphysics (*La pensée et le mouvant,* p. 221) Bergson states that all Kant saw in science was "frames within frames."

He was still haunted by this metaphor when he wrote his essay entitled *La pensée et le mouvant,* 1922, which, in many respects, summarizes his philosophy. On page 80 of the 26th edition, he says again that in memory words are not deposited "in a cerebral or any other kind of drawer."

If this were the occasion to do so, it could be demonstrated that in contemporary science, the active invention of concepts, necessitated by the evolution of scientific thinking, is greater than those determined by simple classifications that "fit into one another," as Bergson expresses it (*La pensée et le mouvant*). In opposition to a philosophy that seeks to discover the conceptualistic features in contemporary science, the "drawer" metaphor remains a crude instrument for polemical discussion. But for our present problem, which is that of distinguishing between metaphor and image, this is an example of a metaphor that hardens and loses even the spontaneousness of the image. This is particularly noticeable in the simplified Bergsonism taught in the classrooms, where the polemical metaphor of the drawer in the filing cabinet comes back time and again in elementary analyses that set out to attack stereotyped ideas. It is even possible, when listening to certain lectures, to foresee that the drawer metaphor is about to appear. And when we sense a metaphor in advance there can be no question of imagination. This metaphor—which, I repeat, is a crude polemical instrument—together with a few others that hardly vary at all, has mechanized the debates that Bergsonians carry on with the philosophies of knowledge, particularly with what Bergson himself, using an epithet that passed quick judgment, called "dry" rationalism.

III

These rapid remarks are intended to show that a metaphor should be no more than an accident of expression, and that it is dangerous to make a thought of it. A metaphor is a false image, since it does not possess the direct virtue of an image formed in spoken revery.

A great novelist has used this Bergsonian metaphor but it was for the purpose of characterizing the psychology of an arrant fool, rather than that of a Kantian rationalist. I refer to Henri Bosco's *Monsieur Carre-Benoit à la campagne,* in which the drawer metaphor is presented in reverse: it is not the intelligence that is a filing cabinet; the filing cabinet is an intelligence.

The only piece of furniture, among all that he possessed, for which Carre-Benoit felt real affection was his solid oak filing cabinet, which he contemplated with satisfaction whenever he passed in front of it. Here, at least, was something that was reliable, that could be counted on. You saw what you were looking at and you touched what you were touching. Its proportions were what they should be, everything about it had been designed and calculated by a meticulous mind for purposes of utility. And what a marvelous tool! It replaced everything, memory as well as intelligence. In this well-fitted cube there was not an iota of haziness or shiftiness. Once you had put something in it, even if you put it a hundred or ten thousand more times, you could find it again in the twinkling of an eye, as it were. Forty-eight drawers! Enough to hold an entire well-classified world of positive knowledge. M. Carre-Benoit attributed a sort of magic power to these drawers concerning which he said that they were "the foundations of the human mind."[2]

It should not be forgotten that in the novel, this is said by a very commonplace man. But the novelist who makes him say it is an unusually gifted one. For with this filing cabinet he has succeeded in embodying the dull administrative spirit. And since stupidity must be turned to ridicule, Henri Bosco's hero has hardly spoken when, as he opens the drawers of the "august cabinet," he finds that the maid has used it as a place to put mustard, salt, rice, coffee, peas and lentils. His reasoning cabinet had become a larder.

Perhaps, after all, this image could be used to illustrate a "philosophy of having," since it may be taken both literally and figuratively. There are many erudite minds that lay in provisions. We shall see later, they say to themselves, whether or not we'll use them.

IV

By way of preamble to our positive study of images of secrecy, we began by examining a hastily formulated metaphor that does not really unite exterior realities with intimate reality. Then, in this passage from Bosco's book, we succeeded in getting a direct, characterological hold, based on a clearly outlined reality. Now we must return to our studies of the imagination, all of them positive. With the theme of drawers, chests, locks and wardrobes, we shall resume contact with the unfathomable store of daydreams of intimacy.

Wardrobes with their shelves, desks with their drawers, and chests with their false bottoms are veritable organs of the secret psychological life. Indeed, without these "objects" and a few others in equally high favor, our intimate life would lack a model of intimacy. They are hybrid objects, subject objects. Like us, through us and for us, they have a quality of intimacy.

Does there exist a single dreamer of words who does not respond to the word wardrobe? . . .

And to fine words correspond fine things, to grave-sounding words, an entity of depth. Every poet of furniture—even if he be a poet in a garret, and therefore has no furniture—knows that the inner space of an old wardrobe is deep. A wardrobe's inner space is also *intimate space,* space that is not open to just anybody.

But words carry with them obligations. Only an indigent

soul would put just anything in a wardrobe. To put just anything, just any way, in just any piece of furniture, is the mark of unusual weakness in the function of inhabiting. In the wardrobe there exists a center of order that protects the entire house against uncurbed disorder. Here order reigns, or rather, this is the reign of order. Order is not merely geometrical; it can also remember the family history. A poet knew this:[3]

> *Ordonnance. Harmonie.*
> *Piles de draps de l'armoire*
> *Lavande dans le linge.*

> (Orderliness. Harmony.
> Piles of sheets in the wardrobe
> Lavender in the linen.)

With the presence of lavender the history of the seasons enters into the wardrobe. Indeed, lavender alone introduces a *Bergsonian durée* into the hierarchy of the sheets. Should we not wait, before using them, for them to be, as they say in France, sufficiently "lavendered"? What dreams are reserved for us if we can recall, if we can return to, the land of tranquility! Memories come crowding when we look back upon the shelf on which the lace-trimmed, batiste and muslin pieces lay on top of the heavier materials: "A wardrobe," writes Milosz,[4] "is filled with the mute tumult of memories."

Bergson did not want the faculty of memory to be taken for a wardrobe of recollections. But images are more demanding than ideas. And the most Bergsonian of his disciples, being a poet, recognized that memory is a wardrobe. The following great line was written by Charles Péguy:

> *Aux rayons de mémoire et aux temples de l'armoire*[5]

> (On the shelves of memory and in the temples of the wardrobe)

But the real wardrobe is not an everyday piece of furniture.

It is not opened every day, and so, like a heart that confides in no one, the key is not on the door.

> —L'armoire était sans clefs! . . . Sans clefs la grande armoire
> On regardait souvent sa porte brune et noire
> Sans clefs! . . . C'était étrange!—On rêvait bien des fois
> Aux mystères dormant entre ses flancs de bois
> Et l'on croyait ouir, au fond de la serrure
> Béante, un bruit lointain, vague et joyeux murmure.[6]

(The wardrobe had no keys! . . . No keys had the big wardrobe
Often we used to look at its brown and black door
No keys! . . . It was strange! Many a time we dreamed
Of the mysteries lying dormant between its wooden flanks
And we thought we heard, deep in the gaping lock
A distant sound, a vague and joyful murmur.)

Here Rimbaud designates a perspective of hope: what good things are being kept in reserve in the locked wardrobe? This time it is filled with promise, it is something more than a family chronicle.

André Breton, with a single word, shows us the marvels of unreality by adding a blessed impossibility to the riddle of the wardrobe. In *Revolver aux cheveux blancs* (p. 110) he writes with typical surrealist imperturbability:[7]

> L'armoire est pleine de linge
> Il y a même des rayons de lune que je peux déplier.

(The wardrobe is filled with linen
There are even moonbeams which I can unfold.)

This carries the image to a point of exaggeration that no reasonable mind would care to attain. But exaggeration is always at the summit of any living image. And to add fantasy linen is to draw a picture, by means of a volute of words, of all the superabundant blessings that lie folded in piles between the flanks of an abandoned wardrobe. How big, how enveloping, is an old sheet when we unfold it. And how white the old tablecloth was, white as the moon on the wintry meadow! If we dream a bit, Breton's image seems perfectly natural.

Nor should we be surprised by the fact that an entity which possesses such great wealth of intimacy should be so affectionately cared for by housewives. Anne de Tourville says of a poor woodcutter's wife: "She had started rubbing, and the high-lights that played on the wardrobe cheered the heart."[8] An armoire radiates a very soft light in the room, a communicative light. It is understandable, therefore, that a poet watching the October light play over the wardrobe should write

> *Le reflet de l'armoire ancienne sous*
> *La braise du crépuscule d'octobre*[9]

> (The reflection on the old wardrobe
> Cast by the live coals of an October twilight.)

If we give objects the friendship they should have, we do not open a wardrobe without a slight start. Beneath its russet wood, a wardrobe is a very white almond. To open it is to experience an event of whiteness.

V

An anthology devoted to small boxes, such as chests and caskets, would constitute an important chapter in psychology. These complex pieces that a craftsman creates are very evident witnesses of the *need for secrecy,* of an intuitive sense of hiding-places. It is not merely a matter of keeping a possession well guarded. The lock doesn't exist that could resist absolute violence, and all locks are an invitation to thieves. A lock is a psychological threshold. And how it defies indiscretion when it is covered with ornaments! What "complexes" are attached to an ornamented lock! Denise Paulme[10] writes that among the

Bambaras, the center of the lock is sculptured "in the form of a crocodile, or a lizard, or a turtle. . . ." The power that opens and shuts must possess the power of life, human power, or the power of a sacred animal. "And among the Dogons, in the Sudan, locks are decorated with two human figures representing the first man and first woman" (loc. cit., p. 35).

But rather than challenge the trespasser, rather than frighten him by signs of power, it is preferable to mislead him. This is where boxes that fit into one another come in. The least important secrets are put in the first box, the idea being that they will suffice to satisfy his curiosity, which can also be fed on false secrets. In other words, there exists a type of cabinet work that is "complexualistic."

For many people, the fact that there should exist a homology between the geometry of the small box and the psychology of secrecy does not call for protracted comment. However, novelists occasionally make note of this homology in a few lines. One of Franz Hellens' characters, wishing to make his daughter a present, hesitates between a silk scarf and a small, Japanese lacquer box. He chooses the box "because it seems to be better suited to her reserved nature."[11] A rapid, simple notation of this kind may well escape the attention of the hurried reader. And yet it is at the very core of a strange tale, in which father and daughter hide the *same* mystery. This same mystery is heading toward the same fate, and the author applies all his talents to making us feel this identity of intimate spirits. Indeed, this is a book that should be added to a dossier on the pent-up soul, with the box for emblem. For it shows us that the psychology of reserved persons is not depicted by listing their negative attitudes, cataloguing their detachments or recounting their moments of silence! Watch them, rather, in the moment of positive joy that accompanies the opening of a new box, like this young girl who receives implicit permission from her father to hide her secrets; that is to say, to conceal her mystery. In this story by Franz Hellens, two human beings "understand" each other without a word, without knowing it, in fact. Two pent-up human beings communicate by means of the same symbol.

VI

In an earlier chapter, I stated that to say one "reads" a house or a room makes sense. We might also say that writers let us read their treasure-boxes, it being understood that a well-calculated geometrical description is not the only way to write "a box." And yet Rilke has spoken of the pleasure he felt when he saw a box that closed well. "A box-top that is in good condition," he wrote, "with its edges unbattered, should have no other desire than to be on its box."[12] A literary critic will probably ask how it was possible, in as well-written a work as the *Cahiers,* for Rilke to have overlooked such a "commonplace" as this. The objection will be overridden, however, if one accepts the germ of daydream contained in the gently closed box. And how far the word *desire* goes! I am reminded of an optimistic proverb according to which: "Every pot has its cover." The world would get along better if pots and covers could always stay together.

Gentle closing calls for gentle opening, and we should want life always to be well oiled.

If we "read" a Rilke box, we shall see how inevitably a secret thought encounters the box image. In a letter to Liliane,[13] Rilke wrote: "Everything that touches upon this ineffable experience must remain quite remote, or only give rise to the most cautious handling at some future time. Yes, I must admit that I imagine it taking place one day the way those heavy, imposing seventeenth-century locks work; the kind that filled the entire top of a chest with all sorts of bolts, clamps, bars and levers, while a single, easily turned key pulled this entire apparatus of defense and deterrence from its most central point. But the key is not alone. You know too that the keyholes of such chests are concealed under a button or under a leather tongue which also only responds to some secret pressure." What concrete images to express the "Open, Sesame" formula! And what secret pressure, what soft words, are needed to gain access to a spirit, to calm a Rilkean heart!

There is no doubt that Rilke liked locks. But who doesn't like both locks and keys? There is an abundant psychoanalytical literature on this theme, so that it would be easy to find documentation on the subject. For our purpose, however, if we emphasized sexual symbols, we should conceal the depth of the dreams of intimacy. Indeed, one is probably never more aware of the monotony of the symbols used in psychoanalysis than in such an example. When a conflict between lock and key appears in a night dream, for psychoanalysis this is a clear sign, so clear, in fact, that it cuts the story short. When we dream of locks and keys there's nothing more to confess. But poetry extends well beyond psychoanalysis on every side. From a dream it always makes a daydream. And the poetic daydream cannot content itself with the rudiments of a story; it cannot be tied to a knotty complex. The poet lives a daydream that is awake, but above all, his daydream remains in the world, facing worldly things. It gathers the universe together around and in an object. We see it open chests, or condense cosmic wealth in a slender casket. If there are jewels and precious stones in the casket, it is the past, a long past, a past that goes back through generations, that will set the poet romancing. The stones will speak of love, of course. But of power too, and fate. All of that is so much greater than a key and its lock!

The casket contains the things that are *unforgettable*, unforgettable for us, but also unforgettable for those to whom we are going to give our treasures. Here the past, the present and a future are condensed. Thus the casket is memory of what is immemorial.

If we take advantage of images to indulge in psychology, we find that every important recollection—Bergson's pure recollection—is set in its little casket. The pure recollection, the image that belongs to us alone, we do not *want* to communicate; we only give its picturesque details. Its very core, however, is our own, and we should never want to tell all there is to tell about it. This in no way resembles unconscious repression, which is an awkward form of dynamism, with symbols that are conspicuous. But every secret has its little casket, and this absolute, well-guarded secret is independent of all dynamism. Here the intimate life achieves a synthesis of Memory and Will. This is *Iron Will*, not against the outside, or against other persons, but beyond all the psychology of being "against." Surrounding certain recollections of our inner self, we have the security of an *absolute casket*.[14]

But with this absolute casket, I too am now talking in metaphors. Let's get back to our images.

VII

Chests, especially small caskets, over which we have more complete mastery, are objects *that may be opened*. When a casket is closed, it is returned to the general community of objects; it takes its place in exterior space. But it opens! For this reason, a philosopher-mathematician would say that it is the first differential of discovery. In a later chapter I plan to study the dialectics of inside and outside. But from the moment the casket is opened, dialectics no longer exist. The outside is effaced with one stroke, an atmosphere of novelty and surprise reigns. The outside has no more meaning. And quite paradoxically, even cubic dimensions have no more meaning, for the reason that a new dimension—the dimension of intimacy— has just opened up.

For someone who is a good judge of values, and who sees things from the angle of the values of intimacy, this dimension can be an infinite one.

As proof, I should like to quote a marvelously perceptive fragment from an article by Jean-Pierre Richard,[15] which offers a veritable theorem of the topoanalysis of intimate space. Jean-Pierre Richard is a writer who analyzes literary works in terms of their dominant images. Here he allows us to relive the moment in Poe's story, *The Gold Bug*, when the casket is opened. To begin with, the jewels found in it are of inestimable value. They could not, of course, be "ordinary" jewels. However, the treasure was not inventoried by a lawyer, but by a poet. It is fraught with "unknown and possible elements, it becomes again an imaginary object, generating hypotheses and dreams, it deepens and escapes from itself toward an infinite number of other treasures." Thus it seems that at the moment when the story reaches its conclusion, a conclusion that is as cold as a police record, it has lost nothing of its oneiric richness. The imagination can never say: was that all, for there is always more than meets the eye. And as I have said several times, an image that issues from the imagination is not subject to verification by reality.

Having achieved valorization of the contents by valorization of the container, Jean-Pierre Richard makes the following penetrating comment: "We shall never reach the bottom of the casket." The infinite quality of the intimate dimension could not be better expressed.

Sometimes, a lovingly fashioned casket has interior perspectives that change constantly as a result of daydream. We open it and discover that it is a dwelling-place, that a house is hidden in it. To illustrate, there exists a marvel of this kind in a prose poem by Charles Cros, in which the poet carries on where the cabinet-maker left off. Beautiful objects created by skillful hands are quite naturally "carried on" by a poet's daydream. And for Charles Cros, imaginary beings are born of the "secret" of a marquetry casket.

"In order to detect its mystery, in order to go beyond the perspectives of marquetry, to reach the imaginary world through the little mirrors," one had to possess a "rapid glance, fine hearing, and be keenly attentive." Indeed, the imagination sharpens all of our senses. The imagining attention prepares our attention for instantaneousness.

And the poet continues: "Finally I caught a glimpse of the clandestine festivity. I heard the tiny minutes, I guessed the complicated web of entanglements that was being woven inside the casket.

"The doors open, and we see what appears to be a parlor for insects, the white, brown and black floors are seen in exaggerated perspective."[16]

But when the poet closes the casket, inside it, he sets a nocturnal world into motion (p. 88).

"When the casket is closed, when the ears of the importunate are stopped with sleep, or filled with outside noises, when the thoughts of men dwell upon some positive object,

"Then strange scenes take place in the casket's parlor, several persons of unwonted size and appearance step forth from the little mirrors."

This time, in the darkness of the casket, it is the enclosed reflections that reproduce objects. The inversion of interior and exterior is experienced so intensely by the poet that it brings about an inversion of objects and reflections.

And once more, after dreaming of this tiny parlor enlivened by the dancing of figurines of another day, the poet opens the casket (p. 90): "The lights go out, the guests, composed of belles and their beaux, and a few aging relatives, disappear pell-mell, into the mirrors and along the corridors and colonnades, without giving a thought to their dignity, while chairs and tables and hangings evaporate into thin air.

"And the parlor remains empty, silent and clean." Serious-minded persons may then say with the poet, "It's a marquetry casket, and that's all." Echoing this reasonable opinion, the reader who is averse to playing with inversions of large and small, exterior and intimacy, may also say: "It's a poem and that's all." "And nothing more."[17]

In reality, however, the poet has given concrete form to a very general psychological theme, namely, that there will always be more things in a closed, than in an open, box. To verify images kills them, and it is always more enriching to *imagine* than to *experience*.

The action of the secret passes continually from the hider of things to the hider of self. A casket is a dungeon for objects. And here is a dreamer who feels that he shares the dungeon of its secret. We should like to open it, and we should also like to open our hearts. The following lines by Jules Supervielle can be read in a dual sense:[18]

> Je cherche dans des coffres qui m'entourent brutalement
> Mettant des ténèbres sens dessus dessous
> Dans des caisses profondes, profondes
> Comme si elles n'étaient plus de ce monde.

(Roughly I search in coffers that surround me
Putting disarray in the darkness
Of cases that are deep, deep
As though they had departed this life.)

He who buries a treasure buries himself with it. A secret is a grave, and it is not for nothing that a man who can be trusted with a secret boasts that he is "like the grave."

All intimacy hides from view, and I recall that the late Joë Bousquet wrote:[19] "No one sees me changing. But who sees me? I am my own hiding-place."

It is not my intention, in this volume, to recall the problem presented by the intimacy of substances, which I have outlined elsewhere.[20] I shall, however, point out the nature of the two dreamers who seek the intimacy of man and the intimacy of matter. Jung has shown very clearly this correspondence between dreamers of alchemy (cf. *Psychologie und Alchemie*). In other words, there is only one *place* for the *superlative* element of what is *hidden*. The hidden in men and the hidden in things belong in the same topoanalysis, as soon as we enter into this strange region of the *superlative,* which is a region that has hardly been touched by psychology. And to tell the truth, all positivity makes the superlative fall back upon the comparative. To enter into the domain of the superlative, we must leave the positive for the imaginary. We must listen to poets.

4

NESTS

Je cueillis un nid dans le squelette du lierre
Un nid doux de mousse champêtre et herbe de songe.
YVAN GOLL, *Tombeau du père*, in *Poètes d'aujourd'hui*, 1950
(Ed. Séghers, p. 156.)

(I found a nest in the skeleton of the ivy
A soft nest of country moss and dream herb.)

Nids blancs vos oiseaux vont fleurir

Vous volerez, sentiers de plume.
ROBERT GANZO, *L'oeuvre poétique*
(Ed. Grasset, p. 63.)

(White nests your birds will flower

You will fly, feather paths.)

In one short sentence, Victor Hugo associates the images and beings of the function of inhabiting. For Quasimodo, he says,[1] the cathedral had been successively "egg, nest, house, country and universe." "One might almost say that he had espoused its form the way a snail does the form of its shell. It was his home, his hole, his envelope . . . He adhered to it, as it were, like a turtle to its carapace. This rugged cathedral was his armor." All of these images were needed to tell how an unfortunate creature assumed the contorted forms of his numerous hiding-places in the corners of this complex structure. In this way, by multiplying his images, the poet makes us aware of the powers of the various refuges. But he immediately adds a sign of moderation to the abundance of images. "It is useless," he continues, "to warn the reader not to take literally the figures of speech that I am obliged to use here to express the strange, symmetrical, immediate, almost consubstantial flexibility of a man and an edifice."

It is striking that even in our homes, where there is light, our consciousness of well-being should call for comparison with animals in their shelters. An example may be found in the following lines by the painter, Vlaminck, who, when he wrote them, was living quietly in the country:[2] "The well-being I feel, seated in front of my fire, while bad weather rages out-of-doors, is entirely animal. A rat in its hole, a rabbit in its burrow, cows in the stable, must all feel the same contentment that I feel." Thus, well-being takes us back to the primitiveness of the refuge. Physically, the creature endowed with a sense of refuge huddles up to itself, takes to cover, hides away, lies snug, concealed. If we were to look among the wealth of our vocabulary for verbs that express the dynamics of retreat, we should find images based on animal movements of withdrawal, movements that are engraved in our muscles. How psychology would deepen if we could know the psychology of each muscle! And what a quantity of animal beings there are in the being of a man! But our research does not go that far. It would already be a good deal if we were able to enhance the value of these images of refuge by showing that by understanding them, in a way, we live them.

With nests and, above all, shells, we shall find a whole series of images that I am going to try to characterize as primal images; images that bring out the primitiveness in us. I shall then show that a human being likes to "withdraw into his corner," and that it gives him physical pleasure to do so.

II

Already, in the world of inanimate objects, extraordinary significance is attached to nests. We want them to be perfect, to bear the mark of a very sure instinct. We ourselves marvel at this instinct, and a nest is generally considered to be one of the marvels of animal life. An example of this much vaunted perfection may be found in one of Ambroise Paré's works:[3] "The enterprise and skill with which animals make their nests is so efficient that it is not possible to do better, so entirely do they surpass all masons, carpenters and builders; for there is not a man who would be able to make a house better suited to himself and to his children than these little animals build for themselves. This is so true, in fact, that we have a proverb according to which men can do everything except build a bird's nest."

A book that is limited to facts soon dampens this enthusiasm, as, for instance, Arthur Landsborough Thomson's book, in which we are told that nests are often barely started, and at times, botched. "When the golden eagle nests in a tree, it sometimes makes an enormous pile of branches to which every year it adds others, until one day the entire thing falls to pieces under its own weight."[4] Between enthusiasm and scientific criticism one could find countless shades of opinion if one followed the history of ornithology. But this is not our subject. Let us note in passing, however, that we have here a controversy over values that often deforms the facts on both sides. And who knows if this fall, not of the eagle, but of the eagle's nest, does not furnish the author with the minor delight of being disrespectful.

III

Positively speaking, there is nothing more absurd than images that attribute *human* qualities to a nest. For a bird, a nest is no doubt a good warm home, it is even a life-giving home, since it continues to shelter the bird that has come out of the egg. It also serves as a sort of downy coverlet for the baby bird until its quite naked skin grows its own down. But why hasten to make a human image, an image for man's use, out of such a paltry thing? The ridiculous nature of this image would become evident if the cosy "little nest," the warm "little nest" that lovers promise each other, were actually compared with the real nest, lost in the foliage. Among birds, need I recall, love is a strictly extracurricular affair, and the nest is not built until later, when the mad love-chase across the fields is over. If we were obliged to reflect upon all this and deduce from it a lesson for human beings, we should have to evolve a dialectics of forest love and love in a city room. But this is not our subject, either. Only someone like André Theuriet would compare a garret to a nest, and accompany the comparison with the following single remark: "Haven't dreams always liked to perch on high?"[5] In short, in literature, the nest image is generally childish.

The "nest" that is "lived" was therefore a poor image to start with. And yet it has certain initial virtues which a phenomenologist who likes simple problems can discover. It offers a fresh opportunity to do away with misunderstandings as to the principal function of philosophical phenomenology. For it is not the task of this phenomenology to describe the nests met with in nature, which is a quite positive task reserved for ornithologists. A beginning of a philosophical phenomenology of nests would consist in our being able to elucidate the interest with which we look through an album containing reproductions of nests, or, even more positively, in our capacity to recapture the naïve wonder we used to feel when we found a nest. This wonder is lasting, and today when we discover a nest it takes us back to our childhood or, rather, to a childhood; to the childhoods we should have had. For not many of us have been endowed by life with the full measure of its cosmic implications.

How many times, in my garden, I have experienced the disappointment of discovering a nest too late. Autumn was there, the leaves had already begun to fall and in the fork of two branches there was an abandoned nest. To think that they had all been there: the father bird, the mother bird and the nestlings. And I had not seen them!

An empty nest found belatedly in the woods in winter mocks the finder. A nest is a hiding-place for winged creatures. How could it have remained invisible? Invisible from above, and yet far from the more dependable hiding-places on the ground? But since, in order to determine the shades of being in an image, we must add a super-impression to it, here is a legend that carries the imagination of an invisible nest to its utmost point. It is taken from Charbonneaux-Lassay's very fine book: *Le bestiaire du Christ.*[6] "People used to think that the hoopoe bird could hide entirely from the sight of all living creatures, which explains the fact that, at the end of the Middle Ages, it was still believed that there was a multicolored herb in the hoopoe's nest which made a man invisible when he wore it."

This may be Yvan Goll's "dream herb."

But the dreams of today do not go this far, and an abandoned nest no longer contains the herb of invisibility. Indeed, the nest we pluck from the hedge like a dead flower is nothing but a "thing." I have the right to take it in my hands and pull it apart. In melancholy mood, I become once more a man of the fields and thickets, and a bit vain at being able to hand on my knowledge to a child, I say: "This is the nest of a titmouse."

And so the old nest enters into the category of objects. The more varied the objects, the simpler the concept. But as our collection of nests grows, our imagination remains idle, and we lose contact with living nests.

And yet it is living nests that could introduce a phenomenology of the actual nest, of the nest found in natural surroundings, and which becomes for a moment the center—the term is no exaggeration—of an entire universe, the evidence of a cosmic situation. Gently I lift a branch. In the nest is a setting bird. But it doesn't fly away, it only quivers a little. I tremble at having caused it to tremble. I am afraid that this setting bird will realize that I am a man, a being that has lost the confidence of birds. I remain motionless. Slowly the bird's fear and my own fear of causing fear are allayed—or so I imagine. I breathe easily again, and let go of the branch. I'll come back tomorrow. Today, I am happy, because some birds have built a nest in my garden.

And the next day when I come back, walking more softly than the day before, I see eight pink-white eggs in the bottom of the nest. But how small they are! How small these thicket eggs are!

This is a living, inhabited nest. A nest is a bird's house. I've known this for a long time, people have told it to me for a long time. In fact, it is such an old story that I hesitate to repeat it, even to myself. And yet, I have just re-experienced it. And I recall very clearly days in my life when I found a live nest. Such genuine recollections as these are rare in life. And how well I understand these lines from Toussenel's *Le monde des oiseaux*:[7] "My recollection of the first bird's nest that I found all by myself has remained more deeply engraved in my memory than that of the first prize I won in grammar school for a Latin version. It was a lovely linnet's nest with four pinkish-gray eggs striated with red lines, like an emblematical map. I was seized with an emotion of such indescribable delight that I stood there for over an hour, glued to one spot, looking. That day, by chance, I found my vocation." What a fine passage for those who are always looking for primal interests! And the fact that from the start, Toussenel reacted with such "emotion" helps us to understand that he should have succeeded in integrating the entire harmonic philosophy of a Fourier in both his life and work, and even added an emblematical life of universal dimensions to the life of a bird.

But in everyday life too, for a man who lives in the woods and fields, the discovery of a nest is always a source of fresh emotion. Fernand Lequenne, the botanist, writes that one day while walking with his wife, Matilda, he saw a warbler's nest in a black hawthorne bush: "Matilda knelt down and, holding out one finger, barely touched the soft moss, then withdrew her finger, only leaving it outstretched. . . .

"Suddenly I began to tremble.

"I had just discovered the feminine significance of a nest set in the fork of two branches. The thicket took on such a human quality that I called out: 'Don't touch it, above all, don't touch it'!"[8]

IV

Toussenel's "emotion" and Lequenne's "trembling" both bear the mark of sincerity. I have recalled them in my reading, since it is in books that we enjoy the surprise of "discovering a nest."

Let us pursue our search for nests in literature. The following is an example in which the author sets the domiciliary value of the nest one tone higher. It is taken from the Journals of Henry David Thoreau, March 17, 1858. Here the entire tree, for the bird, is the vestibule of the nest. Already, a tree that has the honor of sheltering a nest participates in its mystery. For a bird, a tree is already a refuge. Thoreau tells of a green woodpecker that took an entire tree for its home. He compares this taking possession with the joy of a family that returns to live in a house it had long since abandoned.

"It is as when a family, your neighbors, return to an empty house after a long absence, and you hear the cheerful hum of voices and the laughter of children, and see the smoke from the kitchen fire. The doors are thrown open, and children go screaming through the hall. So the flicker dashes through the aisles of the grove, throws up a window here and cackles out it, and then there, airing the house. It makes its voice ring up-stairs and down-stairs, and so, as it were, fits it for its habitation and ours, and takes possession."

In this passage Thoreau gives an expanded version of both nest and house. We are struck too by the fact that the text comes alive in both directions of the metaphor: the happy household is a flourishing nest. The woodpecker's confidence in the shelter of the tree in which it has hidden its nest represents taking possession of a home. Here we leave well behind us the implications of comparisons and allegories. A reasonable critic will no doubt consider that this woodpecker "proprietor," who appears at the window of the tree and sings on its balcony, is an "exaggeration." But a poetic spirit will be grateful to Thoreau for giving it, with this nest that has the dimensions of a tree, a fullness of image. A tree becomes a nest the moment a great dreamer hides in it. In his *Mémoires d'Outretombe,* Chateaubriand made the following confidential note: "I had set up my headquarters, like a nest, in one of these willows, and there, isolated between heaven and earth, I spent hours among the warblers."

And the fact is that, in a garden, we grow more attached to a tree inhabited by birds. However mysterious and invisible among the leaves the green-garbed woodpecker may be at times, he nevertheless becomes familiar to us. For a woodpecker is not a silent dweller. It is not when he sings, however, that we think of him, but when he works. Up and down the tree-trunk, his beak pecks the wood with resounding taps, and although he frequently disappears, we still hear him. He is a garden worker.

And so the woodpecker enters into my sound world and I make a salutary image of him for my own use. In my Paris apartment, when a neighbor drives nails into the wall at an undue hour, I "naturalize" the noise by imagining that I am in my house in Dijon, where I have a garden. And finding everything I hear quite natural, I say to myself: "That's my woodpecker at work in the acacia tree." This is my method for obtaining calm when things disturb me.

V

A nest, like any other image of rest and quiet, is immediately associated with the image of a simple house. When we pass from the image of a nest to the image of a house, and vice versa, it can only be in an atmosphere of *simplicity*. Van Gogh, who painted numerous nests, as well as numerous peasant cottages, wrote to his brother: "The cottage, with its thatched roof, made me think of a wren's nest."[9] For a painter, it is probably *twice* as interesting if, while painting a nest, he dreams of a cottage and, while painting a cottage, he dreams of a nest. It is as though one dreamed twice, in two registers, when one dreams of an image cluster such as this. For the simplest image is doubled; it is itself and something else than itself. Van Gogh's thatched cottages are overladen with thatch. Thick, coarsely plaited straw emphasizes the will to provide shelter by extending well beyond the walls. Indeed, in this instance, among all the shelter virtues, the roof is the dominant evidence. Under the roof's covering the walls are of earth and stone. The openings are low. A thatched cottage is set on the ground like a nest in a field.

And a wren's nest is a thatched cottage, because it is a covered, round nest. The Abbé Vincelot has described it as follows:

"The wren builds its nest in the form of a very round ball, in the bottom of which it makes a small hole to let the water out. Usually this hole is hidden beneath a branch, and I have often examined a nest from every angle before noticing this opening, which also serves as entrance for the female bird."[10] By living Van Gogh's nest-cottage in its obvious liaison, the words suddenly seem to jest. I like to tell myself that a little king lives in that cottage. Here is certainly a fairy-tale image, an image that suggests any number of tales.

VI

A nest-house is never young. Indeed, speaking as a pedant, we might say that it is the natural habitat of the function of inhabiting. For not only do we *come back* to it, but we dream of coming back to it, the way a bird comes back to its nest, or a lamb to the fold. This sign of *return* marks an infinite number of daydreams, for the reason that human returning takes place in the great rhythm of human life, a rhythm that reaches back across the years and, through the dream, combats all absence. An intimate component of faithful loyalty reacts upon the related images of nest and house.

In this domain, everything takes place simply and delicately. The soul is so sensitive to these simple images that it hears all the resonances in a harmonic reading. Reading on the conceptual level, on the other hand, would be insipid and cold; it would be purely linear. For here we are asked to understand the images one after the other. And in this domain of the nest image the lines are so simple that one is surprised at the poet's delight in them. But simplicity brings forgetfulness, and suddenly we feel grateful toward the poet who has the talent to renew it with such rare felicity. No phenomenologist could help reacting to this renewal of such a simple image. We are deeply moved when we read Jean Caubère's simple poem entitled: *Le nid tiède* (The Warm Nest). This poem becomes all the more meaningful when one considers that it appeared in a rather austere volume on the theme of the desert:[11]

Le nid tiède et calme
Où chante l' oiseau

Rappelle les chansons, les charmes
Le seuil pur
De la vieille maison.

(The warm, calm nest
In which a bird sings

Recalls the songs, the charms,
The pure threshold
Of my old home.)

And here the threshold is a hospitable threshold, one that does not intimidate us by its majesty. The two images: the calm nest and the old home, weave the sturdy web of intimacy on the dream loom. And the images are all simple ones, with no attempt at picturesqueness. The poet rightly thought that, at the mention of a nest, a bird's song, and the charms that take us back to the old home, to the first home, a sort of musical chord would sound in the soul of the reader. But in order to make so gentle a comparison between house and nest, one must have lost the house that stood for happiness. So there is also an *alas* in this song of tenderness. If we return to the old home as to a nest, it is because memories are dreams, because the home of other days has become a great image of lost intimacy.

VII

Thus values alter facts. The moment we love an image, it cannot remain the copy of a fact. One of the greatest of dreamers of winged life, Jules Michelet, has given us fresh evidence of this. And yet he only devotes a few pages to "bird architecture." But these are pages that think and dream at the same time.

According to Michelet, a bird is a worker without tools. It has "neither the hand of the squirrel, nor the teeth of the beaver."

"In reality," he writes, "a bird's tool is its own body, that is, its breast, with which it presses and tightens its materials until they have become absolutely pliant, well-blended and adapted to the general plan."[12] And Michelet suggests a house built by and for the body, taking form from the inside, like a shell, in an intimacy that works physically. The form of the nest is commanded by the inside. "On the inside," he continues, "the instrument that prescribes a circular form for the nest is nothing else but the body of the bird. It is by constantly turning round and round and pressing back the walls on every side, that it succeeds in forming this circle." The female, like a living tower, hollows out the house, while the male brings back from the outside all kinds of materials, sturdy twigs and other bits. By exercising an active pressure, the female makes this into a felt-like padding.

Michelet goes on: "The house is a bird's very person; it is its form and its most immediate effort, I shall even say, its suffering. The result is only obtained by constantly repeated pressure of the breast. There is not one of these blades of grass that, in order to make it curve and hold the curve, has not been pressed on countless times by the bird's breast, its heart, surely with difficulty in breathing, perhaps even, with palpitations."

What an incredible inversion of images! Here we have the breast created by the embryo. Everything is a matter of inner pressure, physically dominant intimacy. The nest is a swelling fruit, pressing against its limits.

From the depths of what daydreams do such images arise? They might come, of course, from the dream of the protection that is closest to us, a protection adapted to our bodies. Dreams of a garment-house are not unfamiliar to those who indulge in the imaginary exercise of the function of inhabiting. And if we were to work at our dwelling-places the way Michelet dreams of his nest, we should not be wearing the ready-made clothes, so often viewed with disfavor by Bergson. On the contrary, each one of us would have a personal house of his own, a nest for his body, padded to his measure. In Romain Rolland's novel, *Colas Breugnon*, when, after a life of trials, the leading character is offered a larger, more convenient house, he refuses it as being a garment that would not fit him.

"Either it would hang on me too loosely," he says, "or I should make it burst at the seams."[13]

By following the nest images collected by Michelet to the human level, we realize that, from the start, these were human images. It is even doubtful if an ornithologist would describe the building of a nest the way Michelet does, and a nest built in this way would have to be called a Michelet nest. Phenomenologists will use it to test the dynamisms of a strange sort of withdrawal, which is active and in a state of constant renewal. This is not a dynamics of insomnia, during which we turn and toss in our beds. Michelet points out how the home is modeled by fine touches, which make a surface originally bristling and composite into one that is smooth and soft.

Incidentally, this passage by Michelet constitutes a rare and, for this reason, all the more valuable, document on the subject of the material imagination. Indeed, no one who likes images of matter can forget it, because it describes *dry modeling*. This is the modeling, or shall we say, the marriage, in the dry air and summer sunlight, of moss and down. Michelet's nest is a paean of praise to its felt-like fabric.

It should be noted in closing that few dreamers of nests like a swallow's nest which, they say, is made of saliva and mud. People have even wondered where all the swallows lived before the existence of houses and cities. Swallows, in other words, are not "regular" birds, and Charbonneaux-Lassay wrote of them: "I have heard peasants in the Vendée say that a swallow's nest could frighten the night devils away, even in winter."[14]

VIII

If we go deeper into daydreams of nests, we soon encounter a sort of paradox of sensibility. A nest—and this we *understand* right away—is a precarious thing, and yet it sets us to *daydreaming of security*. Why does this obvious precariousness not arrest daydreams of this kind? The answer to this paradox is simple: when we dream, we are phenomenologists without realizing it. In a sort of naïve way, we relive the instinct of the bird, taking pleasure in accentuating the mimetic features of the green nest in green leaves. We definitely saw it, but we say that it was well hidden. This center of animal life is concealed by the immense volume of vegetable life. The nest is a lyrical bouquet of leaves. It participates in the peace of the vegetable world. It is a point in the atmosphere of happiness that always surrounds large trees.

A poet once wrote:[15]

> *J'ai rêvé d'un nid où les arbres repoussaient la mort.*

> (I dreamed of a nest in which the trees repulsed death.)

And so when we examine a nest, we place ourselves at the origin of confidence in the world, we receive a beginning of confidence, an urge toward cosmic confidence. Would a bird build its nest if it did not have its instinct for confidence in the world? If we heed this call and make an absolute refuge of such a precarious shelter as a nest—paradoxically no doubt, but in the very impetus of the imagination—we return to the sources of the oneiric house. Our house, apprehended in its dream potentiality, becomes a nest in the world, and we shall live there in complete confidence if, in our dreams, we really participate in the sense of security of our first home. In order to experience this confidence, which is deeply graven in our sleep, there is no need to enumerate material reasons for confidence. The nest, quite as much as the oneiric house, and the oneiric house quite as much as the nest—if we ourselves are at the origin of our dreams—knows nothing of the hostility of the world. Human life starts with refreshing sleep, and all the eggs in a nest are kept nicely warm. The experience of the hostility of the world—and consequently, our dreams of defense and aggressiveness—comes much later. In its germinal form, therefore, all of life is well-being. Being starts with well-being. When a philosopher considers a nest, he calms himself by meditating on the subject of his own being in the calm world being. And if we were to translate the absolute naïveté of his daydream into the metaphysical language of today, a dreamer might say that the world is the nest of mankind.

For the world is a nest, and an immense power holds the

inhabitants of the world in this nest. In Herder's history of Hebrew poetry there is an image of the immense sky resting on the immense earth: "The air," he wrote, "is a dove which, as it rests on its nest, keeps its young warm."[16]

I was thinking these thoughts and dreaming these dreams when I read a passage in the Autumn 1954 issue of *Cahiers G.L.M.* that encouraged me to maintain the axiom that identifies the nest with the world and makes it the center of the world. Here Boris Pasternak speaks of "the instinct with the help of which, like the swallow, we construct the world—an enormous nest, an agglomerate of earth and sky, of death and life, and of two sorts of time, one we can dispose of and one that is lacking."[17] Yes, two sorts of time, for what a long time we should need before waves of tranquility, spreading out from the center of our intimacy, reached the ends of the world.

What a concentration of images in Pasternak's swallow's nest! And, in reality, why should we stop building and molding the world's clay about our own shelters? Mankind's nest, like his world, is never finished. And imagination helps us to continue it. A poet cannot leave such a great image as this, nor, to be more exact, can such an image leave its poet. Boris Pasternak also wrote (loc. cit., p. 5): "Man himself is mute, and it is the image that speaks. For it is obvious that the image *alone* can keep pace with nature."

5

SHELLS

The concept that corresponds to a shell is so clear, so hard and so sure that a poet, unable simply to draw it, and reduced rather to speaking of it, is at first at a loss for images. He is arrested in his flight towards dream values by the geometrical reality of the forms. And these forms are so numerous, often so original, that after a positive examination of the shell world, the imagination is defeated by reality. Here it is nature that imagines, and nature is very clever. One has only to look at pictures of ammonites to realize that, as early as the Mesozoic Age, mollusks constructed their shells according to the teachings of a transcendental geometry. Ammonites built their homes around the axis of a logarithmic spiral. (A very clear account of this construction of geometrical forms by life may be read in Monod-Herzen's excellent book.)[1]

A poet naturally understands this esthetic category of life, and Paul Valéry's essay *Les coquillages* (Shells) fairly glows with the spirit of geometry. For Valéry: "A *crystal*, a *flower* or a *shell* stands out from the usual disorder that characterizes most perceptible things. They are privileged forms that are more intelligible for the eye, even though more mysterious for the mind, than all the others we see indistinctly."[2] For this poet, whose thinking was essentially Cartesian, a shell seems to have been a truth of well solidified animal geometry, and therefore "clear and distinct." The created object itself is highly intelligible; and it is the *formation*, not the form, that remains mysterious. As to the form it would eventually assume, a vital decision governed the initial choice that involved knowing whether the shell would coil to the left or to the right. This original vortex has provoked endless commentary. Actually, however, life begins less by reaching upward, than by turning upon itself. But what a marvelously insidious, subtle image of life a coiling vital principle would be! And how many dreams the leftward oriented shell, or one that did not conform to the rotation of its species, would inspire!

Paul Valéry lingered long over the ideal of a modeled, or carved, object that would justify its absolute value by the beauty and solidity of its geometrical form, while remaining unconcerned with the simple matter of protecting its substance. In this case, the mollusk's motto would be: one must live to build one's house, and not build one's house to live in.

However, in a second stage of his meditation, Valéry becomes aware of the fact that a shell carved by a man would be obtained from the outside, through a series of enumerable acts that would bear the mark of touched-up beauty; whereas "the mollusk exudes its shell" (loc. cit., p. 10), it lets the building material "seep through," "distill its marvelous covering as needed." And when the seeping starts, the house is already completed. In this way Valéry returns to the mystery of form-giving life, the mystery of slow, continuous formation.

But this reference to slow formation is only one stage of his meditation, and his book is an introduction to a museum of forms. The collection is illustrated with watercolors by Paul-A. Robert, who, before he started to paint, had prepared the object by polishing all the valves. This delicate polishing laid bare the roots of the colors, which made it possible to participate in a will to color, in the very history of coloration. And at this point the house turns out to be so beautiful, so deeply beautiful, that it would be a sacrilege even to dream of living in it.

II

A phenomenologist who wants to experience the images of the function of inhabiting must not be subject to the charms of external beauty. For generally, beauty exteriorizes and disturbs intimate meditation. Nor can a phenomenologist follow for long the conchologist, whose duty it is to classify the immense variety of shells, and who is looking for diversity. However, a phenomenologist could learn a lot from a conchologist, if the latter were to share with him his own original amazement.

For here too, as with nests, enduring interest should begin with the original amazement of a naïve observer. Is it possible for a creature to remain alive inside stone, inside this piece of stone? Amazement of this kind is rarely felt twice. Life quickly wears it down. And besides, for one "living" shell, how many dead ones there are! For one inhabited shell, how many are empty!

But an empty shell, like an empty nest, invites daydreams of refuge. No doubt we over-refine our daydreams when we follow such simple images as these. But it is my belief that a phenomenologist should go in the direction of maximum simplicity. And therefore I believe that it is worthwhile proposing a phenomenology of the inhabited shell.

III

The surest sign of wonder is exaggeration. And since the inhabitant of a shell can amaze us, the imagination will soon make amazing creatures, more amazing than reality, issue from the shell. In Jurgis Baltrusaitis' fine volume entitled: *Le moyen âge fantastique*, we find reproductions of antique jewels in which "the most unexpected animals: a hare, a bird, a stag, or a dog, come out of a shell, as from out of a magician's hat."[3] This comparison with a magician's hat will be quite useless to anyone who takes up his position in the very center where images develop. When we accept slight amazement, we prepare ourselves to imagine great amazement and, in the world of the imagination, it becomes normal for an elephant, which is an enormous animal, to come out of a snail shell. It would be exceptional, however, if we were to ask him to go back into it. In a later chapter, I shall have an opportunity to show that, in the imagination, to go in and come out are never symmetrical images. "Large, free animals escape mysteriously from some small object," writes Baltrusaitis, and he adds: "Aphrodite was born in these conditions."[4] Beauty and magnitude cause spores to swell. As I shall show later, one of the powers of attraction of smallness lies in the fact that large things can issue from small ones.

Everything about a creature that comes out of a shell is dialectical. And since it does not come out entirely, the part that comes out contradicts the part that remains inside. The creature's rear parts remain imprisoned in the solid geometrical forms. But life is in such haste when it comes out that it does not always take on a designated form, such as that of a young hare or a camel. Certain engravings show strangely mixed creatures, as in the case of the snail shown in this work by Baltrusaitis (p. 58), "with a bearded human head and hare's ears, wearing a bishop's mitre, and with four animal feet." The shell is a witch's cauldron in which bestiality is brewing. According to Baltrusaitis, "*Les heures de Marguerite de Beaujeu* are full of grotesque figures of this kind. Several of them have discarded their shells and remained coiled in the form of the shell. Heads of dogs, wolves and birds, as well as human heads, are attached directly to mollusks." And so, unbridled, bestial daydream produces a diagram for a shortened version of animal evolution. In other words, in order to achieve grotesqueness, it suffices to abridge an evolution.

And the fact is that a creature that comes out of its shell suggests daydreams of a mixed creature that is not only "half fish, half flesh," but also half dead, half alive, and, in extreme cases, half stone, half man. This is just the opposite of the daydream that petrifies us with fear. Man is born of stone. If in C. G. Jung's book *Psychologie und Alchemie*, we examine closely the figures shown on page 86, we see Melusines, not the romantic Melusines that spring from the waters of lakes, but Melusines that are symbols of alchemy, who help us to formulate dreams of the stone from which the principles of life are said to come. Melusine actually comes forth from her scaly, gravelly tail, which reaches back into the distant past, and is slightly spiraled. We have not the impression that this inferior being has retained its energy. The tail-shell does not eject its inhabitant. It is rather a matter of an inferior form of life having been reduced to nothing by a superior one. Here, as elsewhere, life is energetic at its summit. And this summit acquires dynamism in the finished symbol of the human being, for all dreamers of animal evolution have man in mind. In these drawings of alchemical Melusines, the human form issues from a poor, frayed form, to which the artist has devoted little care. But inertness does not incite to daydreaming, and the shell is a covering that will be abandoned. The forces of egress are such, the forces of production and birth are so alive, that two human beings, both wearing diadems, may be seen half emerged from the formless shell, in figure 11 of Jung's book. This is the "Doppelköpfige," or two-headed Melusine.

All of these examples furnish us with phenomenological documents for a phenomenology of the verb "to emerge," and they are all the more purely phenomenological in that they correspond to invented types of "emergence." In this case the animal is merely a pretext for multiplying the images of "emerging." Man lives by images. Like all important verbs, *to emerge from* would demand considerable research in the course of which, besides concrete examples, one would collect the hardly perceptible movements of certain abstractions. We sense little or no more action in grammatical derivations, deductions or inductions. Even verbs become congealed as if they were nouns. Only images can set verbs in motion again.

IV

On the shell theme, in addition to the dialectics of small and large, the imagination is stimulated by the dialectics of creatures that are free and others that are in fetters: and what can we not expect from those that are unfettered!

To be sure, in real life, a mollusk emerges from its shell indolently, so if we were studying the actual phenomena of snail "behavior," this behavior would yield to observations with

no difficulty. If, however, we were able to recapture absolute
naïveté in our observation itself, that is, really to re-experience
our initial observation, we should give fresh impetus to the
complex of fear and curiosity that accompanies all initial
action on the world. We want to see and yet we are afraid to
see. This is the perceptible threshold of all knowledge, the
threshold upon which interest wavers, falters, then returns.
The example at hand for the purpose of indicating the fear
and curiosity complex is not a sizable one. Fear of a snail is
calmed immediately, it is an old story, it is "insignificant." But
then this study is devoted to insignificant things. Occasionally
they reveal strange subtleties. In order to bring them out I shall
place them under the magnifying glass of the imagination.

These undulations of fear and curiosity increase when reality is not there to moderate them, that is, when we are imagining. However, let's not invent, but rather give documents
concerning images which have actually been imagined or
drawn, and which have remained engraved in precious and
other stones. There is a passage in the book by Jurgis Baltrusaitis in which he recalls the *action* of an artist who shows a
dog that "leaps from its shell" and pounces upon a rabbit. One
degree more of aggressiveness and the shell-dog would attack
a man. This is a clear example of the progressing type of action
by means of which imagination surpasses reality. For here the
imagination acts upon not only geometrical dimensions, but
upon elements of power and speed as well—not in an enlarged
space, either, but in a more rapid tempo. When the motion picture camera accelerates the unfolding of a flower, we receive a
sublime image of offering; it is as though the flower we see
opening so quickly and without reservation, sensed the meaning of a gift; as though it were a gift from the world. But if the
cinema showed us a snail emerging from its shell in fast
motion, or pushing its horns toward the sky very rapidly, what
an aggression that would be! What aggressive horns! All our
curiosity would be blocked by fear, and the fear-curiosity
complex would be torn apart.

There is a sign of violence in all these figures in which an
over-excited creature emerges from a lifeless shell. Here the

artist precipitates his animal daydreams. Since they belong to the same type of daydreams, we must associate abbreviations of animals that have their heads and tails fastened together—the artist having neglected to show the intermediary parts of their bodies—with these snail-shells from which emerge quadrupeds, birds and human beings. To do away with what lies between is, of course, an ideal of speed, and thanks to a sort of acceleration of the imagined vital impulse, the creature that emerges from the ground immediately assumes its physiognomy.

But the obvious dynamism of these extravagant figures lies in the fact that they come alive in the dialectics of what is hidden and what is manifest. A creature that hides and "withdraws into its shell" is preparing a "way out." This is true of the entire scale of metaphors, from the resurrection of a man in his grave, to the sudden outburst of one who has long been silent. If we remain at the heart of the image under consideration, we have the impression that, by staying in the motionlessness of its shell, the creature is preparing temporal explosions, not to say whirlwinds, of being. The most dynamic escapes take place in cases of repressed being, and not in the flabby laziness of the lazy creature whose only desire is to go and be lazy elsewhere. If we experience the imaginary paradox of a vigorous mollusk—the engravings in question give us excellent depictions of them—we attain to the most decisive type of aggressiveness, which is postponed aggressiveness, aggressiveness that bides its time. Wolves in shells are crueler than stray ones.

V

By adhering to a method which seems to me decisive in a phenomenology of images, and which consists of designating the image as an excess of the imagination, I have accentuated the dialectics of large and small, hidden and manifest, placid and aggressive, flabby and vigorous. I have also followed the imagination to a point well beyond reality, in its task of enlargement, for in order to surpass, one must first enlarge.

We have seen how freely the imagination acts upon space, time
and elements of power. But the action of the imagination is not
limited to the level of images. On the level of ideas too, it tends
toward extremes, and there are ideas that dream. For instance,
certain theories which were once thought to be scientific are,
in reality, vast, boundless daydreams. I should like to give an
example of a dream-idea of this type, which takes the shell as
the clearest proof of life's ability to constitute forms. According to this theory, which was propounded in the eighteenth
century by J. B. Robinet, everything that has form has a shell
ontogenesis, and life's principal effort is to make shells. It is
my opinion that at the center of Robinet's immense evolution-
ary table there was a vast dream of shells. Indeed the title
alone of one of his books: *Vues philosophiques de la gradation naturelle des formes de l'être, ou les essais de la nature
qui apprend à faire l'homme* (Philosophical Views on the Natural Gradation of Forms of Existence, or the Attempts Made by
Nature While Learning to Create Humanity, Amsterdam, 1768),
describes the orientation of his thinking. Those who have the
patience to read the entire work will discover a veritable commentary, in dogmatic form, on the type of drawings I mentioned earlier. Here too *partial animal forms* appear on every
side. Fossils for Robinet are bits of life, roughcasts of separate
organs, which will find their coherent life at the summit of an
evolution that is preparing the way for man. We might say that
the inside of a man's body is an assemblage of shells. Each
organ has its own causality, that has already been tried out
during the long centuries when nature was teaching herself to
make man, with one shell or another. The function constructs
its form from old models, and life, although only partial, constructs its abode the way the shell-fish constructs its shell.

If one can succeed in reliving this partial life, in the precision of a life that endows itself with a form, the being that possesses form dominates thousands of years. For every form
retains life, and a fossil is not merely a being that once lived,
but one that is still alive, asleep in its form. The shell is the
most obvious example of a universal shell-oriented life.

All of this is firmly stated by Robinet.[5] "I am persuaded that fossils are alive," he writes, "if not from the standpoint of an exterior form of life, for the reason that they lack perhaps certain limbs and senses (I should hesitate to assert this, however), at least from that of an interior, hidden form of life, which is very real of its kind, even though quite inferior to that of a sleeping animal or a plant. But far be it from me to deny them the organs necessary to the functioning of their vital economy. And whatever their form, I consider it as a progress toward the form of their analogues in the vegetable world, among insects, large animals and, lastly, among men."

Robinet's book goes on to give descriptions, accompanied by very fine engravings, of Lithocardites (heart stones), Encephalites (which are a prelude to the brain), stones that imitate a jaw-bone, the foot, the kidney, the ear, the eye, the hand, muscles—then Orchis, Diorchis, Triorchis, the Priapolites, Colites and Phalloïds, which imitate the male organs, and Histerapetia, which imitate the female organs.

It would be a mistake to see nothing in this but a reference to language habits that name new objects by comparing them with other commonplace ones. Here names think and dream, the imagination is active. Lithocardites are heart shells, rough draughts of a heart that one day will beat. Robinet's mineralogical collections are anatomical parts of what man will be when nature learns to make him. A critical mind will object that our eighteenth-century naturalist was a "victim of his imagination." A phenomenologist, however, who avoids all criticism on principle, cannot fail to recognize that in the very extravagance of the being given to words, in the extravagance of his images, is manifested a profound daydream. On all occasions Robinet thinks of form, from the inside out. For him, life originates forms, and it is perfectly natural that life, which is the cause of forms, should create living forms. Once again, for such daydreams as these, form is the habitat of life.

Shells, like fossils, are so many attempts on the part of nature to prepare forms of the different parts of the human body; they are bits of man and bits of woman. In fact Robinet gives a description of the Conch of Venus that represents a woman's vulva. A psychoanalyst would not fail to see a sexual

obsession in these designations and descriptions that enter into
such detail. Nor would he have any difficulty finding, in the
shell museum, such representations of phantasms as that of the
toothed vagina, which is one of the principal themes of Marie
Bonaparte's study of Edgar Allan Poe. Indeed, if we listened to
Robinet, we should be inclined to believe that nature went
mad before man did. And one can imagine the diverting reply
that Robinet would make in defense of his system to the observations of psychoanalysts or psychologists. With simple gravity he wrote: "We should not be surprised at the assiduity with
which Nature has multiplied models of the generative organs,
in view of the importance of these organs" (loc. cit., p. 73).

With a dreamer of scholarly thoughts such as Robinet, who
organized his visionary ideas into a system, a psychoanalyst
accustomed to untangling family complexes would be quite
powerless. We should need a cosmic psychoanalysis, one that
would abandon for a second human considerations and concern
itself with the contradictions of the Cosmos. We should also
need a psychoanalysis of matter which, at the same time that it
accepted the human accompaniment of the imagination of matter, would pay closer attention to the profound play of the images
of matter. Here, in the very limited domain in which we are
studying images, we should have to resolve the contradictions of
the shell, which at times is so rough outside and so soft, so pearly,
in its intimacy. How is it possible to obtain this polish by means
of friction with a creature that is so soft and flabby? And doesn't
the finger that dreams as it strokes the intimate mother-of-pearl
surface surpass our human, all too human, dreams? The simplest things are sometimes psychologically complex.

But if we were to allow ourselves to indulge in all the daydreams of inhabited stone there would be no end to it. Curiously enough, these daydreams are at once long and brief. It is
possible to go on with them forever, and yet reflection can end
them with a single word. At the slightest sign, the shell becomes
human, and yet we know immediately that it is not human.
With a shell, the vital inhabiting impulse comes to a close too
quickly, nature obtains too quickly the security of a shut-in

life. But a dreamer is unable to believe that the work is finished when the walls are built, and thus it is that shell-constructing dreams give life and action to highly geometrically associated molecules. For these dreams, the shell, in the very tissue of its matter, is alive. Proof of this may be found in a great natural legend.

VI

A Jesuit priest, Father Kircher, once asserted that on the coast of Sicily "the shells of shell-fish, after being ground to powder, come to life again and start reproducing, if this powder is sprinkled with salt water." The Abbé de Vallemont[6] cites this fable as a parallel to that of the phoenix that rises from its ashes. Here, then, is a water phoenix. However, the Abbé de Vallemont gives little credence to the fable of either one of these phoenixes. But for me, whose outlook is governed by the imagination, there can be but one conclusion: both phoenixes were products of the imagination. These are *facts of the imagination,* the very positive facts of the imaginary world.

Moreover, these facts of the imagination are related to allegories of very ancient origin. Jurgis Baltrusaitis recalls (loc. cit., p. 57) that "as late as the Carolingian epoch, burial grounds often contained snail shells—an allegory of a grave in which man will awaken." And in *Le bestiaire du Christ,* p. 922, Charbonneaux-Lassay writes: "Taken as a whole, with both its hard covering and its sentient organism, the shell, for the Ancients, was the symbol of the human being in its entirety, body and soul. In fact, ancient symbolics used the shell as a symbol for the human body, which encloses the soul in an outside envelope, while the soul quickens the entire being, represented by the organism of the mollusk. Thus, they said, the body becomes lifeless when the soul has left it, in the same way that the shell becomes incapable of moving when it is separated from the part that gives it life." A wealth of documentation could be assembled on the subject of "resurrection shells."[7] There is no need, however, given the simplicity of the problems treated in this work, for us to insist on very remote traditions. All we have to do is to ask ourselves how, in the case of certain naïve daydreams, the simplest images can nurture a tradition. Charbonneaux-Lassay says these things with all the simplicity and naïveté one could wish. After quoting the Book of Job with its invincible hope of resurrection, he adds (loc. cit., p. 927): "How did it happen that the quiet, earth-bound snail should have been chosen to symbolize this ardent, invincible hope? The explanation is that at the gloomy time of year, when Winter's death holds earth in its grip, the snail plunges deep into the ground, shuts itself up inside its shell, as though in a coffin, by means of a strong, limestone epiphragm, until Spring comes and sings Easter Hallelujahs over its grave . . . Then it tears down its wall and reappears in broad daylight, full of life."

I shall ask readers who may be inclined to smile at such enthusiasm, to try to imagine the amazement of the archeologist who discovered in a grave in the Indre et Loire department "a coffin that contained nearly three hundred snail shells placed about the skeleton from feet to waistline." Such a contact with a belief places us at the origin of all beliefs. A lost symbolism begins to collect dreams again.

All the proofs that we are obliged to present one after the other, of capacity for renewal, of resurrection or reawakening of being, must be taken as coalescence of reveries.

If we add to these allegories and symbols of resurrection the synthesizing nature of dreams of the powers of matter, we understand the fact that profound dreamers are unable to rule out the dream of a water phoenix. The shell itself, in which a resurrection is being prepared in the synthesizing dream, is subject to resurrection. For if the dust in the shell can experience resurrection, there is no reason why the pulverized shell should not recapture its spiraling force.

Of course, a critical mind will scoff at unconditioned images; and a realist would soon demand control experiments. Here, as elsewhere, he would want to verify the images by confronting them with reality. If he were shown a mortar filled with crushed shells, he would say, now make a snail! But a phenomenologist's projects are *more* ambitious: he wants to live *as* the great dreamers of images lived before him. And since I have underlined certain words, I shall ask the reader to note that the word *as* is stronger than the word *like,* which as it happens, would omit a phenomenological nuance. The word *like* imitates, whereas the word *as* implies that one becomes the person who dreams the daydream.

And so, we shall never collect enough daydreams, if we want to *understand phenomenologically* how a snail makes its house; how this flabbiest of creatures constitutes such a hard shell; how, in this creature that is entirely shut in, the great cosmic rhythm of winter and spring vibrates nonetheless. And from the psychological standpoint, this is not a vain problem. It arises automatically, in fact, as soon as we return to the thing itself, as phenomenologists put it, as soon as we start to dream of a house that grows in proportion to the growth of the body that inhabits it. How can the little snail grow in its stone prison? This is a *natural* question, which can be asked quite naturally. (I should prefer not to ask it, however, because it takes me back to the questions of my childhood.) But for the Abbé de Vallemont, it is a question that remains unanswered, and he adds: "When it is a matter of nature, we rarely find ourselves on familiar ground. At every step, there is something that humiliates and mortifies proud minds." In other words, a snail's shell, this house that grows with its inmate, is one of the marvels of the universe. And the Abbé de Vallemont concludes that, in general (loc. cit., p. 255), shells are "sublime subjects of contemplation for the mind."

VII

It is always diverting to see a destroyer of fables become the victim of a fable. At the beginning of the eighteenth century, the Abbé de Vallemont believed no more in the fire phoenix than he did in the water phoenix; but he did believe in palingenesis, that is, in a sort of mixture of both. If we reduce a fern to ashes, which we dissolve in pure water, then allow the water to evaporate, we obtain lovely crystals that have the form of a fern frond. And many other examples could be furnished of dreamers meditating in order to discover what I should call saturated growth salts of formal causality.[8]

But closer to the problems with which we are concerned just now, one feels in the Abbé de Vallemont's book the effect of a contamination of the nest images and those of the shell. At one point, this author speaks of the anatifère plant, or the anatifère shell-fish, that grows on the wood of ships (loc. cit., p. 243). "It is an assemblage of eight shells," he writes, "that looks rather like a bunch of tulips . . . all of the same substance as mussel shells . . . The entrance is at the top, and it is closed by means of little doors that are joined together in a most admirable way. All that remains is to find out how this sea-plant, and the little inmates that occupy these artistically created apartments, are formed."

A few pages on, the contamination of the shell and the nest is presented quite clearly. These shells are nests from which birds have flown (p. 246). "I say that the different shells of my anatifère plant . . . are nests in which the birds of obscure origin that, in France, we call *macreuses* (scoter-ducks), form and hatch."

Here we have a confusion of genres that is quite common to the daydreams of pre-scientific epochs. Scoter-ducks were supposed to be cold-blooded birds. If it was asked how these birds hatched their young, a frequent reply was: Why should their hens set since, by nature, they can warm neither the eggs nor the nestlings? The Abbé de Vallemont adds (p. 250) that "a group of theologians, assembled at the Sorbonne, decided that they would withdraw scoter-ducks from the bird category and put them into the fish category." This being the case, they can be eaten in Lent.

Before it leaves its nest-shell the scoter-duck, which is half-bird, half-fish, is attached to it by a pedunculated beak. Thus a learned dream collects legendary hyphens. Here the great daydreams of nest and shell are presented in two perspectives that could be said to be in reciprocal anamorphosis. Nest and shell are two great images that reflect back their daydreams.

Here forms do not suffice to determine such affinities. Indeed, the principle of the daydreams that welcome such legends goes beyond experience. For here the dreamer has entered into the domain in which convictions that originate beyond what we see and touch are formed. If nests and shells were without significance, their image would not be so easily or so imprudently synthesized. With eyes closed, and without respect to form and color, the dreamer is seized by convictions of a refuge in which life is concentrated, prepared and transformed. Nests and shells cannot unite as strongly as this otherwise than by virtue of their oneirism. Here an entire branch of "dream houses" finds two remote roots that intermingle in the same way that, in human daydreams, everything remote intermingles.

One hesitates to be too explicit about these daydreams, which no memory can either clarify or explain. And if one takes them in the resurgence manifested in the above-mentioned texts, one inclines to think that imagination antedates memory.

VIII

After this long excursion into the more distant regions of daydream, let us return to images that seem closer to reality. Yet I wonder if an image of the imagination is ever close to reality. For often when we think we are describing we merely imagine. We believe that we have achieved a description that is at once instructive and amusing. This false genre overlies an entire literature, as, for instance, in a certain eighteenth-century volume that purports to be a textbook for the instruction of a young knight,[9] and in which we find the following "description" of an open mussel attached to a pebble: "With its cords and stakes it could be mistaken for a tent." Naturally, the author doesn't fail to mention the fact that these tiny cords can be woven into fabric, and it is true that at one time thread actually was made from the mooring-cords of mussels. The author's philosophical conclusion is presented in a very commonplace image: "Snails build a little house which they carry about with them," so "they are always at home in whatever country they travel." I should not repeat such triviality as this if I had not found it hundreds of times in various writings. And here it was offered for meditation to a knight of sixteen!

There is also frequent reference to the perfection of natural dwellings. "They are all built on the same plan," he writes (p. 256), "the object of which is to provide shelter for the animal. But what variety in this very simple plan! Each one has its own perfections, its own charms and conveniences."

Such images as these correspond to a childish, superficial, diffuse type of wonderment. However, a psychology of the imagination must make note of everything, since the most minor interests can prepare the way for major ones.

There also comes a time when one rejects images that are too naïve, and disdains those that have become too hackneyed. Certainly none is more hackneyed than that of the shell-house. It is too simple to be elaborated felicitously and too old to be rejuvenated. It says what it has to say in a single word. But the fact remains that it is a *primal image* as well as an indestructible one. It belongs in the indestructible emporium that deals in cast-offs of the human imagination.

Folklore is filled with ditties inviting the snail to show its horns. Children love to tease it with a blade of grass to make it go back into its shell, and the most unexpected comparisons have been made to explain this retreat. According to one biologist, "a snail withdraws into its kiosk the way a girl who has been teased goes and cries in her room."[10]

Images that are too clear—here we have an example—become generalities, and for that reason block the imagination. We've seen, we've understood, we've spoken. Everything is settled. So we must find a particular image in order to restore life to the general image. Here is one for reviving this paragraph, in which we seem to be victims of the commonplace.

Robinet believed that it was by rolling over and over that the snail built its "staircase." Thus, the snail's entire house would be a stair-well. With each contortion, this limp animal adds a step to its spiral staircase. It contorts itself in order to advance and grow. The bird building its nest was content to turn round and round. Robinet's dynamic shell image may be compared with Michelet's dynamic image of the nest.

IX

Nature has a very simple way of amazing us—through exaggerated size. In the case of the shell commonly known as the *Grand bénitier* (Great Baptismal Font), we see nature dreaming an immense dream, a veritable delirium of protection, that ends in a monstrosity of protection. This mollusk "only weighs 14 pounds, but the weight of each of its valves is between 500 and 600 pounds, and it measures from a yard to a yard and a half in length."[11] The author of this book, which belongs in the famous *Bibliothèque des merveilles* (Collection of Marvels), adds: "In China . . . certain rich mandarins own bathtubs made of one of these shells." A bath taken in the abode of such a mollusk must be very mollifying indeed. And what capacity for relaxation must be felt by a 14-pound animal that occupies this much space! Being myself a mere dreamer of books, I know nothing about biological realities. But when I read this account by Armand Landrin, I sink into a vast dream of cosmicity. And who would not feel cosmically cheered at the thought of taking a bath in the *Grand bénitier*'s shell?

The *Grand bénitier*'s strength is on a par with the height and bulk of its walls. Indeed, according to one observer, it would take two horses hitched to each valve to force the *Grand bénitier* "to yawn, in spite of itself."

I should love to see an engraving that represented this exploit. I can imagine it, however, by recalling an old picture, which I have looked at long and often, of horses hitched to the two hemispheres, between which nothing existed but space. Here this image depicting the "Magdeburg experiment," which is legendary in elementary scientific culture, would have a biological illustration. Four horses to overcome fourteen pounds of limp flesh!

But however exaggerated in size nature's creations may be,

man can easily imagine things that are bigger still. In an engraving by Cork, based on a composition by Hieronymous Bosch, known as: *Shell Navigating on the Water*, we see an enormous mussel shell in which some ten persons are seated, with four children and a dog. There is an excellent reproduction of this mussel shell inhabited by men in the fine book on Hieronymous Bosch, by André Lafon (p. 106).

This hypertrophy of the dream of inhabiting all the hollow objects in the world is accompanied by ludicrous scenes peculiar to Bosch's imagination. In the mussel shell, the travelers are feasting and carousing, with the result that the dream of tranquility we should like to pursue when we "withdraw into our shells" is lost because of the insistence upon frenzied joy that marks the genius of this painter.

But after hypertrophic daydreaming we always have to return to the type of daydreaming that is designated by its original simplicity. We know perfectly well that to inhabit a shell we must be alone. By living this image, one knows that one has accepted solitude.

To live alone; there's a great dream! The most lifeless, the most physically absurd image, such as that of living in a shell, can serve as origin of such a dream. For it is a dream that, in life's moments of great sadness, is shared by everybody, both weak and strong, in revolt against the injustices of men and of fate. As, for instance, Salavin,[12] a weak, sad creature, who takes comfort in his narrow room precisely because it is narrow and permits him to say: "What would I do if I hadn't this little room, this room that is as deep and secret as a shell? Ah! snails don't realize their good fortune."

At times, the image is very unobtrusive, hardly perceptible, but it is effective nonetheless. It expresses the isolation of the human being withdrawn into himself. A poet, at the same time that he dreams of some childhood house, magnified in his memory to become

> *La vieille maison où vont et viennent*
> *L'étoile et la rose*

> (The old house where star and rose
> Come and go)

writes:

> *Mon ombre forme un coquillage sonore*
> *Et le poète écoute son passé*
> *Dans la coquille de l'ombre de son corps*[13]

> (My shadow forms a resonant shell
> And the poet listens to his past
> In the shell of his body's shadow.)

At other times, the image acquires its force through the effect of an isomorphism of all restful space. Then every hospitable hollow is a quiet shell. The poet, Gaston Puel, writes:[14]

> *Ce matin je dirai le simple bonheur d'un homme*
> *   allongé au creux d'une barque.*
> *L'oblongue coquille d'un canot s'est fermée sur lui.*
> *Il dort. C'est une amande. La barque*
> *comme un lit épouse le sommeil.*

> (This morning I shall tell the simple happiness
>   of a man stretched out in the hollow of a boat.
> The oblong shell of a skiff has closed over him.
> He is sleeping. An almond. The boat, like a bed,
>   espouses sleep.)

A man, an animal, an almond, all find maximum repose in a shell. The virtues of repose dominate all of these images.

X

Since it is my endeavor to multiply all the dialectical shadings by which the imagination confers life upon the simplest images, I should like to note a few references to the offensive capacity of shells. In the same way that there are ambush-houses, there exist trap-shells which the imagination makes into fish-nets, perfected with bait and snap. Pliny gives the following account of how the pea-crab's mussel finds its sustenance: "The blind shell-fish opens up, thus exposing its body to all the small fish playing about. When they sense that they can enter with impunity, they become emboldened and fill the shell. At this moment, the crab, which is on the alert, warns the mussel by means of a little bite, upon which the latter closes the shell, crushing everything that is caught between the valves, then divides the prey with its partner."[15]

In the way of animal stories it would be hard to do better. To avoid multiplying examples, therefore, I shall repeat this same fable, since it is borne out by another great name. In Leonardo da Vinci's *Notebooks,* we read: "An oyster opens wide at full moon. When the crabs sees this, it throws a pebble or a twig at the oyster to keep it from closing and thus have it to feed upon." Da Vinci adds the following suitable moral to this fable: "Like the mouth that, in telling its secret, places itself at the mercy of an indiscreet listener."

Extensive psychological research would be needed to determine the value of the moral examples that have always been drawn from animal life. I only point this out in passing, however, since our encounter with the problem is quite accidental. But there are names that tell their own story, such as the name of the *bernard-l'ermite,* or hermit crab. This mollusk does not build its own shell but, as everyone knows, goes to live in an empty shell. It changes when it feels too cramped for space.

The image of the hermit crab that goes to live in abandoned shells is sometimes associated with the habits of the cuckoo, which lays its eggs in other nests. In both cases, Nature seems to enjoy contradicting natural morality. The imagination, whetted by exceptions of all kinds, takes pleasure in adding resources of cunning and ingenuity to the characteristics of this bird squatter. The cuckoo, we are told, after making sure that the setting mother-bird has gone, breaks an egg in the nest in which it plans to lay. If it lays two eggs it breaks two. In

spite of its identifying call, the cuckoo is also past master in
the art of concealment; it loves to play hide and seek. And yet
no one has ever seen it. As often happens in real life, the name
is better known than the bearer. Who, for instance, can distinguish between the russet and the blond cuckoo? According to
Abbé Vincelot (*loc. cit.* p. 101) certain observers have maintained that the russet cuckoo is simply the gray cuckoo when it
is young, and that if some "migrate northward and others
southward, with the result that the two species are not to be
found in the same locality, it is because among migrant birds,
old and young rarely visit the same country."

Is it any wonder, then, that this bird, with its instinct for
secrecy, should have been credited with such powers of meta-
morphosis that, for centuries, according to Abbé Vincelot (p.
102), "the ancients believed that the cuckoo became transformed into a hawk." Musing upon a legend of this kind, and
recalling that the cuckoo is an egg thief, I suggest that the story
of its turning into a hawk might be summarized in a scarcely
altered version of the French proverb: *Qui vole un oeuf, enlève
un boeuf*[16] (He who steals an egg will carry off an ox).

XI

There are minds for which certain images retain absolute pri-
ority. Bernard Palissy's[17] was one of these and, for him, shell
images were of enduring interest. If one had to designate Palissy by the dominating element of his material imagination, he
would fall quite naturally into an "earthly" group. But since
the material imagination is a matter of nuances, Palissy's
imagination would have to be specified as that of an earthly
being in quest of a hard earth that must be further hardened
by fire, but which also has the possibility of attaining natural
hardness through the action of a solidifying, self-containing
salt. Shells manifest this same possibility and, in this respect,
the limp, sticky, "slimy" creatures that inhabit them play a
rôle in their hard consistency. Indeed, the principle of solidifi-
cation is so powerful, the conquest of hardness is carried so

far, that the shell achieves its enamel-like beauty as though it had been helped by fire. Beauty of substance is added to beauty of geometrical form. For a potter or an enamelist, a shell must indeed be a subject for infinite meditation. But there are many animals beneath the enameled glaze of this gifted potter's plates that have made the hardest possible shells of their skins. If we relive Bernard Palissy's passion, in the cosmic drama of different sorts of matter, or in the struggle between clay and fire, we can understand why the humblest snail that secreted its own shell should have provided him with food for infinite dreaming.

Among all these daydreams, I shall note here only those that furnish the most curious images of the house. The following, entitled: "About a fortress city" (*De la ville de forteresse*), is included in Palissy's *Recepte véritable*.[18] In summarizing it I shall try to retain the amplitude of the original.

Faced with "the horrible dangers of war," Bernard Palissy contemplated a design for a "fortress city." He had lost all hope of finding an existing plan "in the cities built today." Vitruvius himself could be of no help in the century of the cannon. So he journeyed through "forests, mountains and valleys to see if he could find some industrious animal that had built some industrious houses." After inquiring everywhere, Palissy began to muse about "a young slug that was building its house and fortress with its own saliva." Indeed, he passed several months dreaming of a construction *from within,* and most of his leisure time was spent walking beside the sea, where he saw "such a variety of houses and fortresses which certain little fishes had made from their own liquor and saliva that, from now on, I began to think that here was something that might be applied to my own project." "The battles and acts of brigandry" that take place in the sea being on a larger scale than those that take place on land, God "had conferred upon each one the diligence and skill needed to build a house that had been surveyed and constructed by means of such geometry and architecture, that Solomon in all his wisdom could never have made anything like it."

With regard to spiralled shells, he wrote that this shape was not at all "for mere beauty, there's much more to it than that. You must understand that there are several fish with such sharply pointed beaks that they would devour most of the above-mentioned fish if the latter's abodes were in a straight line: but when they are attacked by their enemies on the threshold, just as they are about to withdraw inside, they twist and turn in a spiral line and, in this way, the foe can do them no harm."

Meanwhile, someone brought Palissy two large shells from Guinea: "A murex and a whelk." The murex being the weaker must be the best defended, according to Palissy's philosophy. As a matter of fact, the shell having "a number of rather large points around the edges, I decided that these horns had been put there for a purpose, which was for defense of the fortress."

It has seemed necessary to give all these preliminary details, because they show that Palissy was looking for *natural inspiration*. He sought nothing better for constructing his fortress city than to "take the fortress of the above mentioned murex as an example." With this idea in mind, he started work on his plan. In the very center of the fortress city, there was to be an open square on which the governor's house would be located. Starting from this square, a single street would run four times around the square; first, in two circuits that espoused the shape of the square; then, in two octagon-shaped circuits. All doors and windows in this quadruple winding street were to give onto the inside of the fortress, so that the backs of the houses would constitute one continuous wall. The last of the house-walls was to back up against the city wall which, thus, would form a gigantic snail.

Bernard Palissy enlarged at length on the advantages of this *natural* fortress. Even if part of it fell to the enemy there would always remain a possibility of retreat. In fact, it was this spiral movement of retreat that determined the general line of the image. Nor would enemy cannon be able to follow the retreat and "rake" the streets of the coiled city. Enemy artillerymen would be as disappointed as the "pointed-beaked" marauders had been when they tried to attack a coiled shell.

In this summary, which may seem too long to the reader, it has nevertheless been impossible to enter into the detail of mixed images and proof. A psychologist who followed Palis-sy's text line by line would find images used as proof, images that are witnesses of a reasoning imagination. This simple account is psychologically complex. But for us, in this century, the "reasoning" of such images is no longer convincing. We no longer have to believe in natural fortresses. And when military men build "hedgehog" defenses, they know that they are not in the domain of the image, but in that of simple metaphor. It would be a great mistake, however, if we were to confuse the genres and take Palissy's snail-fortress for a simple metaphor. This is an image that has inhabited a great mind.

As for myself, in a leisurely book of this kind, in which I enjoy all the images, I was obliged to linger over this monstrous snail.

And in order to show that, through the simple play of the imagination, any image may be increased in size, I should like to quote the following poem, in which a snail assumes the dimensions of a village:[19]

> *C'est un escargot énorme*
> *Qui descend de la montagne*
> *Et le ruisseau l'accompagne*
> *De sa bave blanche*
> *Très vieux, il n'a plus qu'une corne*
> *C'est son court clocher carré.*

> (It's a giant snail
> Descending the mountain
> With at its side
> The brook's white foam
> Very old, only one horn left
> Which is its short, square belfry.)

And the poet adds:

> *Le château est sa coquille . . .*

> (The manor is its shell . . .)

But there are other passages in Bernard Palissy's works which accentuate this predestined image that we are obliged to recognize in his shell-house experience. As it happens, this potential constructor of a shell-fortress was also an architect and landscape gardener, and to complement his plans for gardens, he added plans for what he called "chambers." These "chambers" were places of retreat that were as rough and rocky on the outside as an oyster shell: "The exterior of the aforementioned chamber," wrote Palissy,[20] "will be of masonry made with large uncut stones, in order that the outside should not seem to have been man-built." Inside, on the contrary, he would like it to be as highly polished as the inside of a shell: "When the masonry is finished, I want to cover it with several layers of enameling, from the top of the vaulted ceiling down to the floor. This done, I should like to build a big fire in it . . . until the aforesaid enameling has melted and coated the aforesaid masonry . . ." In this way, the "inside of the chamber would seem to be made of one piece . . . and would be so highly polished that the lizards and earthworms that come in there would see themselves as in a mirror."

This indoor fire lighted for the purpose of enameling bricks is a far cry from the "blaze" we light in our time to "dry the plaster." Here, perhaps, Palissy recaptured visions of his potter's kiln, in which the fire left brick tears on the walls. In any case, an extraordinary image demands extraordinary means. Here a man wants to live in a shell. He wants the walls that protect him to be as smoothly polished and as firm as if his sensitive flesh had to come in direct contact with them. The shell confers a daydream of purely physical intimacy. Bernard Palissy's daydream expresses the function of inhabiting in terms of touch.

Because dominant images tend to combine, his fourth chamber is a synthesis of house, shell and cave: "The inside masonry will be so skilfully executed," he wrote (loc. cit., p. 82), "that it will appear to be simply a rock that has been hollowed out in order to cut stone from the interior; and the aforesaid chamber will be twisted and humped with several skewed humps and concavities having neither appearance nor form of either the chiseler's art or of work done by human hands; and the ceiling vaults will be so tortuous that they will look as though they are about to fall, for the reason that there will be several pendant humps." Needless to say, the inside of this spiraled house will also be covered with enamel. It will be a cave in the form of a coiled shell. Thus, by means of a great sum of human labor, this cunning architect succeeded in making a *natural* dwelling of it. To accentuate the natural character of the chamber he had it covered with earth "so that, having planted several trees in the aforesaid earth, it would not seem to have been built." In other words, the real home of this man of the earth was subterranean. He wanted to live in the heart of a rock, or, shall we say, in the *shell of a rock*. The pendant humps fill this dwelling with a nightmare dread of being crushed, while the spiral that penetrates deep into the rock gives an impression of anguished depth. But a being who *desires* to live underground is able to dominate commonplace fears. In his daydreams, Bernard Palissy was a hero of subterranean life. In his imagination he derived pleasure—so he said—from the fear manifested by a dog barking at the entrance of a cave; and the same thing was true of the hesitation, on the part of a visitor, to enter further into the tortuous labyrinth. Here the shell-cave is also a "fortress city" for a man alone, a man who loves complete solitude, and who knows how to defend and protect himself with simple images. There's no need of a gate, no need of an iron-trimmed door; people are afraid to come in.

In any case, an important phenomenological investigation remains to be made on the subject of *dark entrance halls*.

XII

With nests, with shells—at the risk of wearying the reader—I have multiplied the images that seem to me to illustrate the function of inhabiting in elementary forms which may be too remotely imagined. Here one senses clearly that this is a mixed problem of imagination and observation. I have simply wanted to show that whenever life seeks to shelter, protect, cover or hide itself, the imagination sympathizes with the being that inhabits the protected space. The imagination experiences protection in all its nuances of security, from life in the most material of shells, to more subtle concealment through imitation of surfaces. As the poet Noël Arnaud expresses it, being seeks dissimulation in similarity.[21] To be in safety under cover of a color is carrying the tranquility of inhabiting to the point of culmination, not to say, imprudence. Shade, too, can be inhabited.

XIII

After this study of shells, we could, of course, tell a number of stories about the turtle which, as the animal with the house that walks, would lend itself to much facile commentary. However, this commentary would only illustrate with new examples themes that have already been treated. I shall therefore forgo writing a chapter on the turtle's house.

But since slight contradictions to primal images can occasionally stimulate the imagination, I should like to comment upon a passage from the Flemish travel notes of the Italian poet, Giuseppe Ungaretti.[22] At the home of the poet Franz Hellens—only poets possess such treasures—Ungaretti saw a woodcut "depicting the fury of a wolf which, having attacked a turtle that had withdrawn into its bony carapace, went mad, without having appeased its hunger."

These three lines keep coming back to my mind, and I tell myself endless stories around them. I see the wolf arriving from a distant, famine-stricken land. It is lean and hungry looking, its tongue hanging out, red and feverish. At that moment, what should come out from under a bush but a turtle, considered by epicures the world over to be a particularly delicate morsel. With one leap, the wolf seizes its prey, but the turtle, which is endowed by nature with unusual alacrity when it wants to withdraw head, limbs and tail into its house, is quicker than the wolf. For the famished wolf, it is now nothing but a stone on the road.

One hardly knows which side to take in this dramatic incident of hunger. I have tried to be impartial. I don't like wolves. But, for once, the turtle might have refrained from action. And Ungaretti, who had thought lengthily about the engraving, said explicitly that the artist had succeeded in making "the wolf likeable and the turtle odious."

A phenomenologist would have many comments to make on this commentary! Of course, the psychological interpretation exceeds the facts, since no drawn line can interpret an "odious" turtle. The animal in its box is sure of its secrets, it has become a monster of impenetrable physiognomy. The phenomenologist, therefore, will have to tell himself the fable of the wolf and the turtle. He will have to elevate the drama to the cosmic level and, from there, meditate upon world-hunger. To put it more simply, the phenomenologist would need to have, for one moment, the entrails of the wolf, faced with a prey that has turned itself into stone.

If I had reproductions of an engraving of this kind, I should use them to differentiate and measure people's views and the depth of their participation in hunger dramas throughout the world. Almost surely, this participation would manifest a certain ambiguity. Some would give in to the drowsiness of the story-telling function and leave the play of the old childish images undisturbed. They would take pleasure in the wicked animal's resentment and laugh up their sleeves at the turtle that withdrew into its shell. Others, however, having been alerted by Ungaretti's interpretation, might reverse the situation. Such a reversal of a fable that has long lain dormant in its traditions, could have a rejuvenating effect on the function of story-telling. For here the imagination makes a fresh start, which could be of advantage to phenomenologists. Reversals of this kind may seem to have only slight documentary interest for the all-of-a-piece school of phenomenologists who take the World as their next-door neighbor. They are immediately conscious of being of and in the world. But the problem becomes more complicated for a phenomenologist of the imagination constantly confronted with the strangeness of the world. And what is more, the imagination, by virtue of its freshness and its own peculiar activity, can make what is familiar into what is strange. With a single poetic detail, the imagination confronts us with a new world. From then on, the detail takes precedence over the panorama, and a simple image, if it is new, will open up an entire world. If looked at through the thousand windows of fancy, the world is in a state of constant change. It therefore gives fresh stimulus to the problem of phenomenology. By solving small problems, we teach ourselves to solve large ones. I have limited myself to proposing exercises conceived for an elementary phenomenology. I am moreover convinced that the human psyche contains nothing that is insignificant.

6

CORNERS

"Fermez l'espace! Fermez la poche du Kangourou! Il y fait chaud."

MAURICE BLANCHARD[1]

(Close space! Close the kangaroo's pouch! It's warm in there.)

I

With nests and shells, I was quite obviously in the presence of transpositions of the function of inhabiting. My aim was to study chimerical or crude types of intimacy, whether light and airy, like the nest in the tree, or symbolic of a life rigidly encrusted in stone, like the mollusk. Now should I like to turn my attention to impressions of intimacy which, however short-lived or imaginary, have nevertheless a more human root, and do not need transposition. They lend themselves to a direct psychology, even if positive minds take them for so much idle musing.

The point of departure of my reflections is the following: every corner in a house, every angle in a room, every inch of secluded space in which we like to hide, or withdraw into ourselves, is a symbol of solitude for the imagination; that is to say, it is the germ of a room, or of a house.

The documents available in literary works are few, for the reason that this purely physical contraction into oneself already bears the mark of a certain negativism. Also, in many respects, a corner that is "lived in" tends to reject and restrain, even to hide, life. The corner becomes a negation of the Universe. In one's corner one does not talk to oneself. When we recall the hours we have spent in our corners, we remember above all silence, the silence of our thoughts. This being the case, why describe the geometry of such indigent solitude? Psychologists and, above all, metaphysicians will find these circuits of topo-analysis quite useless. They know how to observe "uncommunicative" natures directly. They do not need to have a sullen person in a corner described to them as "cornered." But it is not easy to efface the factors of place. And every retreat on the part of the soul possesses, in my opinion, figures of havens. That most sordid of all havens, the corner, deserves to be examined. To withdraw into one's corner is undoubtedly a meager expression. But despite its meagerness, it has numerous images, some, perhaps, of great antiquity, images that are psychologically primitive. At times, the simpler the image, the vaster the dream.

To begin with, the corner is a haven that ensures us one of the things we prize most highly—immobility. It is the sure place, the place next to my immobility. The corner is a sort of half-box, part walls, part door. It will serve as an illustration for the dialectics of inside and outside, which I shall discuss in a later chapter.

Consciousness of being at peace in one's corner produces a sense of immobility, and this, in turn, radiates immobility. An imaginary room rises up around our bodies, which think that they are well hidden when we take refuge in a corner. Already, the shadows are walls, a piece of furniture constitutes a barrier, hangings are a roof. But all of these images are over-imagined. So we have to designate the space of our immobility by making it the space of our being. In *L'état d'ébauche,*[2] Noël Arnaud writes:

> *Je suis l'espace où je suis*
>
> (I am the space where I am.)

This is a great line. But nowhere can it be better appreciated than in a corner.

In *Mein Leben ohne mich* (My Life Without Me), Rilke writes: "Suddenly, a room with its lamp appeared to me, was almost palpable in me. I was already a corner in it, but the shutters sensed me and closed." It would be hard to find a more felicitous way of saying that the corner is the chamber of being.

II

Let us take now an ambiguous text in which being becomes manifest at the very moment when it comes forth from its corner.

Jean-Paul Sartre, writing on Baudelaire, quotes a sentence from Richard Hughes' *A High Wind in Jamaica*[3] that deserves lengthy commentary: "Emily had been playing houses in a nook right in the bows . . ." It is not this line, however, that Sartre discusses, but the following: ". . . and tiring of it (she) was walking rather aimlessly aft . . . when it suddenly flashed into her mind that she was *she* . . ." Before examining these thoughts from various angles, I shall point out that in all probability, in the novel, they correspond to what we are obliged to call *invented childhood,* with which novels abound. For novelists often return to an invented childhood which has not been experienced to recount events whose naïveté is also invented. This unreal past projected through literary means into a time that precedes the story often conceals the actuality of a daydream which would assume all its phenomenological value if it were presented in really actual naïveté. But the verbs *to be* and *to write* are hard to reconcile.

And yet, as it is, the text quoted by Sartre is a valuable one, because it designates topoanalytically, that is, in terms of space and experience of outside and inside, the two directions that psychoanalysts refer to as introvert and extrovert: before life, before the passions, in the very pattern of existence, the novelist encounters this duality. The lightning-like thought that the little girl in the story has found in herself comes to her as she leaves her "house." Here we have a *cogito* of emergence without our having been given the *cogito* of a being withdrawn into itself; the more or less sombre *cogito* of a being who first plays at making itself a "Dutch stove," like Descartes, a sort of chimerical home, in a corner of a boat. The child has just discovered that she is *herself,* in an explosion toward the outside, which is a reaction, perhaps, to certain concentrations in a corner of her being. For the recess in the boat is also a corner of being. But when she has explored the vast universe of the boat in the middle of the ocean, does she return to her little house? Now that she knows that she is *herself,* will she resume her game of "playing houses," will she return home, in other words, withdraw again into herself? One can undoubtedly become aware of existing by escaping from space. Here, however, the figure of being is related to a special concept. Therefore, the novelist should have given us the details of the inversion of a dream that lead from home to the universe, in quest of being. And since this is invented childhood, fictionalized metaphysics, the author holds the key to both domains, he senses their correlation. No doubt he could have illustrated otherwise this sudden awareness of "being." But since the house preceded the universe, we should be told her daydreams in it. As it is, the author has sacrificed—or perhaps suppressed—these "corner" daydreams and placed them in the category of "children's games," by which he more or less admits that the real things of life are the exterior ones.

But life in corners, and the universe itself withdrawn into a corner with the daydreamer, is a subject about which poets will have more to tell us. They will not hesitate to give this daydream all its reality.

III

In the novel *L'amoureuse initiation,* by the Lithuanian poet, O. V. de Milosz, there is a passage in which the leading character, a cynically sincere figure, who has forgotten nothing, is reminiscing (p. 201). But these are not childhood memories. On the contrary, the entire work is set in the experienced present. And we are shown him in his palace, where he leads a fervent existence, setting aside certain corners to which he often repairs. As, for instance, "That little dark corner between the fireplace and the oak chest, where you used to hide," when she went away. It should be noted that he did not wait for her in the vast palace, but in a corner reserved for gloomy waiting, where he could digest his anger at her faithlessness. "With your bottom resting on the hard, cold, marble floor, your blank gaze turned toward the make-believe sky of the ceiling, and in your hands, a book with uncut pages, you spent many a delightfully sad hour there waiting, like the poor blockhead that you were." What a refuge for ambivalence! Here is a dreamer who is happy to be sad, content to be alone, waiting. In his corner he can meditate upon life and death, as befits the heights of passion: "To live and die in this sentimental corner, you told yourself; Yes, indeed, to live and die there; why not, then, Monsieur de Pinamonte, you who so love dark, dusty little corners?"

And all who live in corners will come to confer life upon this image, multiplying the shades of being that characterize the corner dweller. For to great dreamers of corners and holes nothing is ever empty, the dialectics of full and empty only correspond to two geometrical non-realities. The function of inhabiting constitutes the link between full and empty. A living creature fills an empty refuge, images inhabit, and all corners are haunted, if not inhabited. Milosz's corner dreamer, M. de Pinamonte, in his, on the whole, spacious "den," between the chest and the fireplace, resumes his reminiscing: "Here the meditative spider lives powerful and happy; the past shrivels up and all but disappears, like a frightened old lady-bug . . . Ironic, cunning lady-bug, here the past can be recaptured and yet remain hidden from the learned spectacles of collectors of pretty-pretties." Under the poet's magic wand, one cannot help becoming a ladybug, or gathering memories and dreams under the elytra of this round, this roundest of animals. But how well our little earthball of red life hid its ability to fly! It escapes from its sphere as from a hole. Perhaps up in the blue sky it, too, experiences sudden awareness that it is itself, like the little girl in Richard Hughes' novel. And we find it hard to stop dreaming before the spectacle of this little shell that suddenly starts to fly.

Exchanges of animal and human life become frequent in Milosz's novel. His cynical dreamer goes on (p. 242): here, in this corner, between the chest and the fireplace, "you find countless remedies for boredom, and an infinite number of things that deserve to occupy your mind for all time: the musty odor of the minutes of three centuries ago; the secret meaning of the hieroglyphics in fly-dung; the triumphal arch of that mouse-hole; the frayed tapestry against which your round, bony back is lolling; the gnawing noise of your heels on the marble; the powdery sound of your sneeze . . . and finally, the soul of all this old dust from corners forgotten by brooms."

But, except for such "corner readers" as ourselves, who will continue to read about all this dustiness? Someone like Michel Leiris, perhaps, who tells of having picked the dust from the cracks in the floor with a pin.[4] But, I repeat, not everybody will admit to these things.

Yet in such daydreams as these the past is very old indeed. For they reach into the great domain of the undated past. By allowing the imagination to wander through the crypts of memory, without realizing it, we recapture the bemused life of the tiniest burrows in the house, in the almost animal shelter of dreams.

But against this distant background, childhood returns. In his *meditation corner* Milosz's dream questions his conscience. The past rises to the level of the present. And the dreamer finds himself in tears: "Because, already as a child, you liked the eaves of chateaux and corners of dusty old libraries, and you read avidly, without understanding a word, falsely learned volumes on the privileges of the Dutch . . . Ah! you rascal, what delightful hours you used to pass in your rascality in those nostalgia-dredged nooks and corners of the palazzo Merona! The time you squandered there trying to get at the heart of things that had had their day! With what joy you changed yourself into an old shoe, picked out of the gutter, saved from being swept out with the rubbish."

Just here, we can come to an abrupt halt, break up the daydream, and lay aside our reading. For who is prepared to go beyond the spider, the lady-bug and the mouse, to a point of identification with things forgotten in a corner? But what kind of daydream is this that can be broken up? And why break it up for reasons of conscience or good taste, or through disdain for old things? Milosz does not break it up. And when, guided by his book, we ourselves dream beyond it, we share his dream of a corner that is the grave of a "wooden doll forgotten last century, in this corner of the room, by some little girl . . ." No doubt, one would have to sink into profound daydreaming to be moved by the vast museum of insignificant things. It is impossible to dream of an old house that is not the refuge of old things—its own—or that has been filled with old things as a result of the simple craze of a collector of knick-knacks. To restore their soul to corners, it is better to have an old slipper or a doll's head, like those that attract the meditations of Milosz's dreamer. "The mystery of things," the poet continues (p. 243), "little sensations of time, great void of eternity! All infinity can be contained in this stone corner, between the fireplace and the oak chest . . . Where are they now, I ask you! all those marvelous, spidery delights of yours, those profound meditations on poor, dead little things."

Then, from the depths of his corner, the dreamer remembers all the objects identified with solitude, objects that are memories of solitude and which are betrayed by the mere fact of having been forgotten, abandoned in a corner. "Remember the old, old lamp that greeted you from far away, through the window of your thoughts, its panes burned by suns of other years . . ." From the depths of his corner, the dreamer sees an older house, a house in another land, thus making a synthesis of the childhood home and the dream home. The old objects question him: "What will the friendly old lamp think of you, during the lonely winter nights? What will the other objects think of you, the ones that were so kind, so fraternally kind to you? Was not their obscure fate closely united with your own? . . . Motionless, mute things never forget: melancholy and despised as they are, we confide in them that which is humblest and least suspected in the depths of ourselves" (p. 244). What a call to humility this dreamer heard in his corner! For the corner denies the palace, dust denies marble, and worn objects deny splendor and luxury. The dreamer in his corner wrote off the world in a detailed daydream that destroyed, one by one, all the objects in the world. Having crossed the countless little thresholds of the disorder of things that are reduced to dust, these souvenir-objects set the past in order, associating condensed motionlessness with far distant voyages into a world that is no more. With Milosz, the dream penetrates so deeply into the past that it seems to attain to a region beyond memory: "All these things are far, far away, they no longer exist, they never did exist, the Past has lost all recollection of them ... Look, seek and wonder, tremble ... Already you yourself no longer have a past" (p. 245). Meditating upon certain passages of this work, one feels oneself carried away into a sort of antecedence of being, as though into a beyond of dreams.

I V

In quoting this fragment by Milosz, I have sought to present an unusually complete experience of a gloomy daydream, the daydream of a human being who sits motionless in his corner, where he finds a world grown old and worn. Incidentally, I should like to point out the power that an adjective acquires, as soon as it is applied to life. A gloomy life, or a gloomy person, marks an entire universe with more than just a pervading coloration. Even things become crystallizations of sadness, regret or nostalgia. And when a philosopher looks to poets, to a great poet like Milosz, for lessons in how to individualize the world, he soon becomes convinced that the world is not so much a noun as an adjective.

If we were to give the imagination its due in the philosophical systems of the universe, we should find, at their very source, an adjective. Indeed, to those who want to find the essence of a world philosophy, one could give the following advice—look for its adjective.

V

But let us resume contact with shorter daydreams, the kind that are attracted by detail or by features of reality which, at first, seem insignificant. People never tire of recalling that Leonardo da Vinci advised painters who lacked inspiration when faced with nature, to contemplate with a reflective eye the crack in an old wall! For there is a map of the universe in the lines that time draws on these old walls. And each of us has seen a few lines on the ceiling that appeared to chart a new continent. A poet knows all this. But in order to describe in his own way a universe of this kind, created by chance on the confines of sketch and dream, he goes to live in it. He finds a corner where he can abide in this cracked-ceiling world.

Thus we see a poet take the hollow road of a piece of molding in order to reach his hut in the corner of a cornice. In his *Poèmes à l'autre moi* (Poems to My Other Self) Pierre Albert-Birot "espouses," as they say, "the curve that warms." Soon its mild warmth calls upon us to curl up under the covers.

To begin with, Albert-Birot slips into the molding:

> . . . *Je suis tout droit les moulures*
> *qui suivent tout droit le plafond*

> (I follow the line of the moldings
> which follow that of the ceiling.)

But if we "listen" to the design of things, we encounter an angle, a trap detains the dreamer:

> *Mais il y a des angles d'où l'on ne peut plus sortir.*

> (But there are angles from which one cannot escape.)

Yet even in this prison, there is peace. In these angles and corners, the dreamer would appear to enjoy the repose that divides being and non-being. He is the being of an unreality. Only an event can cast him out. And just here the poet adds: "But a klaxon made me come out of the angle where I was beginning to die of an angel's dream."

It is easy for a rhetorician to criticize a text like this. Indeed, the critical mind has every reason to reject such images, such idle musings.

First of all, because they are not "reasonable," because we

do not live in "corners of the ceiling" while lolling in a comfortable bed, because a spider's web is not, as the poet says, drapery—and, to be more personal, because an exaggerated image is bound to seem ridiculous to a philosopher who seeks to concentrate being in its center, and finds in a center of being a sort of unity of time, place and action.

Yes, but even when the criticisms of reason, the scorn of philosophy and poetic traditions unite to turn us from the poet's labyrinthine dreams, it remains nonetheless true that the poet has made a trap for dreamers out of his poem.

As for me, I let myself be caught. I followed the molding.

In an earlier chapter devoted to houses, I said that a house in an engraving may well incite a desire to live in it. We feel that we should like to live there, between the very lines of the engraved drawing. At times, too, the phantasm that impels us to live in corners comes into being by the grace of a mere drawing. But, then, the grace of a curved line is not a simple Bergsonian movement with well placed inflexions. Nor is it merely a time that unreels. It is also habitable space harmoniously constituted. We are again indebted to Pierre Albert-Birot for an engraved "corner," a lovely engraving, in terms of literature:[5]

> *Et voici que je suis devenu un dessin d'ornement*
> *Volutes sentimentales*
> *Enroulement des spirales*
> *Surface organisée en noir et blanc*
> *Et pourtant je viens de m'entendre respirer*
> *Est-ce bien un dessin*
> *Est-ce bien moi.*

> (So now I have become a decorative drawing
> Sentimental scrolls
> Coiling spirals
> An organized surface in black and white
> And yet I just heard myself breathe
> Is it really a drawing
> Is it really I.)

Here it is as though the spiral greeted us with clasped hands. However, the drawing is more effective for what it encloses than for what it exfoliates. The poet feels this when he goes to live in the loop of a scroll to seek warmth and the quiet life in the arms of a curve.

The intellectualist philosopher who wants to hold words to their precise meaning, and uses them as the countless little tools of clear thinking, is bound to be surprised by the poet's daring. And yet a syncretism of sensitivity keeps words from crystallizing into perfect solids. Unexpected adjectives collect about the focal meaning of the noun. A new environment allows the word to enter not only into one's thoughts, but also into one's daydreams. Language dreams.

The critical mind can do nothing about this. For it is a poetic fact that a dreamer can write of a curve that it is *warm*. But does anyone think that Bergson did not exceed *meaning* when he attributed grace to curves and, no doubt, *inflexibility* to straight lines? Why is it worse for us to say that an angle is cold and a curve warm? That the curve welcomes us and the over-sharp angle rejects us? That the angle is masculine and the curve feminine? A modicum of quality changes everything. The grace of a curve is an invitation to remain. We cannot break away from it without hoping to return. For the beloved curve has nest-like powers; it incites us to possession, it is a curved "corner," inhabited geometry. Here we have attained a minimum of refuge, in the highly simplified pattern of a daydream of repose. But only the dreamer who curls up in contemplation of loops understands these simple joys of delineated repose.

No doubt it is very rash on the part of a writer to accumulate, in the final pages of a chapter, disconnected ideas, images that only live in a single detail, and convictions, however sincere, which only last for an instant. But what else can be done by a phenomenologist who wants to brave teeming imagination, and for whom, frequently, a single word is the germ of a dream? When we read the works of a great word dreamer like Michel Leiris (particularly in his *Biffures*), we find ourselves experiencing in words, on the inside of words, secret movements of our own. Like friendship, words sometimes swell, at the dreamer's will, in the loop of a syllable. While in other words, everything is calm, tight. Even as sober a man as Joseph Joubert[6] recognizes the intimate repose of words when he speaks of certain ideas rather curiously as "huts." Words—I often imagine this—are little houses, each with its cellar and garret. Common-sense lives on the ground floor, always ready to engage in "foreign commerce," on the same level as the others, as the passers-by, who are never dreamers. To go upstairs in the word house is to withdraw, step by step; while to go down to the cellar is to dream, it is losing oneself in the distant corridors of an obscure etymology, looking for treasures that cannot be found in words. To mount and descend in the words themselves—this is a poet's life. To mount too high or descend too low is allowed in the case of poets, who bring earth and sky together. Must the philosopher alone be condemned by his peers always to live on the ground floor?

7

MINIATURE

I

Psychologists—and more especially philosophers—pay little attention to the play of miniature frequently introduced into fairy tales. In the eyes of the psychologist, the writer is merely amusing himself when he creates houses that can be set on a pea. But this is a basic absurdity that places the tale on a level with the merest fantasy. And fantasy precludes the writer from entering, really, into the domain of the fantastic. Indeed he himself, when he develops his facile inventions, often quite ponderously, would appear not to believe in a psychological reality that corresponds to these miniature features. He lacks that little particle of dream which could be handed on from writer to reader. To make others believe, we must believe ourselves. Is it worthwhile, then, for a philosopher to raise a phenomenological problem with regard to these literary "miniatures," these objects that are so easily made smaller through literary means? Is it possible for the conscious—of both writer and reader—to play a sincere rôle in the very origin of images of this kind?

Yet we are obliged to grant these images a certain objectivity, from the mere fact that they both attract and interest many dreamers. One might say that these houses in miniature are false objects that possess a true psychological objectivity. Here the process of imagination is typical, and it poses a problem that must be distinguished from the general problem of geometrical similarities. A geometrician sees *exactly the same thing* in two similar figures, drawn to different scales. The plan of a house drawn on a reduced scale implies none of the problems that are inherent to a philosophy of the imagination. There is even no need to consider it from the general standpoint of representation, although it would be important, from this standpoint, to study the phenomenology of similarity. Our study should be specified as belonging definitely under the imagination.

Everything will be clear, for instance, if, in order to enter into the domain where we imagine, we are forced to cross the threshold of absurdity, as in the case of *Trésor des fèves* (Bean Treasure), Charles Nodier's[1] hero, who gets into a fairy's coach the size of a bean. In fact, he gets into it with six "litrons"[2] of beans on his shoulder. There is thus a contradiction in numbers as well as in the size of the space involved. Six thousand beans fit into one. And the same thing is true when Michael—who is oversize—finds himself, to his great surprise, in the house of the *Fée aux miettes* (Beggar Fairy), which is hidden under a tuft of grass. But he feels at home there, and settles down. Happy at being in a small space, he realizes an experience of topophilia; that is, once inside the miniature house, he sees its vast number of rooms; from the interior he discovers *interior* beauty. Here we have an inversion of perspective, which is either fleeting or captivating, according to the talent of the narrator, or the reader's capacity for dream. Nodier, who was often too eager to be "agreeable," and too much amused to give full rein to his imagination, allows certain badly camouflaged rationalizations to subsist. In order to explain psychologically this entry into the tiny house, he recalls the little cardboard houses that children play with. In other words, the tiny things we imagine simply take us back to childhood, to familiarity with toys and *the reality of toys*.

But the imagination deserves better than that. In point of fact, imagination in miniature is natural imagination which appears at all ages in the daydreams of born dreamers. Indeed, the element of amusement must be removed, if we are to find its true psychological roots. For instance, one might devote a *serious* reading to this fragment by Hermann Hesse, which appeared in *Fontaine*[3] (No. 57, p. 725). A prisoner paints a landscape on the wall of his cell showing a miniature train entering a tunnel. When his jailers come to get him, he asks them "politely to wait a moment, to allow me to verify something in the little train in my picture. As usual, they started to laugh, because they considered me to be weak-minded. I made myself very tiny, entered into my picture and climbed into the little train, which started moving, then disappeared into the darkness of the tunnel. For a few seconds longer, a bit of flaky smoke could be seen coming out of the round hole. Then this smoke blew away, and with it the picture, and with the picture, my person . . ." How many times poet-painters, in their prisons, have broken through walls, by way of a tunnel! How many times, as they painted their dreams, they have escaped through a crack in the wall! And to get out of prison all means are good ones. If need be, mere absurdity can be a source of freedom.

And so, if we follow the poets of miniature sympathetically, if we take the imprisoned painter's little train, geometrical contradiction is redeemed, and Representation is dominated by Imagination. Representation becomes nothing but a body of expressions with which to communicate our own images to others. In line with a philosophy that accepts the imagination as a basic faculty, one could say, in the manner of Schopenhauer: "The world is my imagination." The cleverer I am at miniaturizing the world, the better I possess it. But in doing this, it must be understood that values become condensed and enriched in miniature. Platonic dialectics of large and small do not suffice for us to become cognizant of the dynamic virtues of miniature thinking. One must go beyond logic in order to experience what is large in what is small.

By analyzing several examples, I shall show that miniature literature—that is to say, the aggregate of literary images that are commentaries on inversions in the perspective of size—stimulates profound values.

II

I shall first take a fragment from Cyrano de Bergerac, which is quoted in a very fine article by Pierre-Maxime Schuhl, entitled

Le thème de Gulliver et le postulat de Laplace. Here the author is led to accentuate the intellectualist nature of Cyrano de Bergerac's amused images in order to compare them with this astronomer-mathematician's ideas.[4]

The Cyrano text is the following: "This apple is a little universe in itself, the seed of which, being hotter than the other parts, gives out the conserving heat of its globe; and this germ, in my opinion, is the little sun of this little world, that warms and feeds the vegetative salt of this little mass."

In this text, nothing stands out, but everything is imagined, and the imaginary miniature is proposed to enclose an imaginary value. At the center is the seed, which is *hotter* than the entire apple. This condensed heat, this warm well-being that men love, takes the image out of the class of images one can see into that of images that are lived. The imagination feels cheered by this germ which is fed by a vegetable salt.[5] The apple itself, the fruit, is no longer the principal thing, but the seed, which becomes the real dynamic value. Paradoxically, it is the seed that creates the apple, to which it transmits its aromatic saps and conserving strength. The seed is not only born in a tender cradle, protected by the fruit's mass. It is the generator of vital heat.

In such imagination as this, there exists total inversion as regards the spirit of observation. Here the mind that imagines follows the opposite path of the mind that observes, the imagination does not want to end in a diagram that summarizes acquired learning. It seeks a pretext to multiply images, and as soon as the imagination is interested by an image, this increases its value. From the moment when Cyrano imagined the Seed-Sun, he had the conviction that the seed was a source of life and heat, in short, that it was a value.

Naturally, this is an exaggerated image. The jesting element in Cyrano, as in many writers, as for instance Nodier, whom we mentioned a few pages back, is prejudicial to imaginary meditation. The images go too fast, and too far. But a psychologist who reads slowly and examines images in slow motion, lingering as long as is needed over each image, will experience a sort of coalescence of unlimited values. Values become engulfed in miniature, and miniature causes men to dream.

Pierre-Maxime Schuhl concludes his analysis by underlining in the case of this particularly felicitous example, the dangers of the imagination, which is master of error and falsehood. I think as he does, but I dream differently or, to be more exact, I am willing to react to my reading the way a dreamer does. Here we have the entire problem of the oneiric attitude toward oneiric values. Already, when we describe a daydream *objectively* this diminishes and interrupts it. How many dreams told objectively have become nothing but oneirism reduced to dust! In the presence of an image that dreams, it must be taken as an invitation to continue the daydream that created it.

The psychologist of the imagination who defines the positivity of the image by the dynamism of daydream must justify the invention of the image. In the present example, the problem posed: is the seed of an apple its sun? is an absurd one. If we dream enough—and undoubtedly a lot is needed—we end by giving this question oneiric value. Cyrano de Bergerac did not wait for Surrealism to delight in tackling absurd questions. From the standpoint of the imagination, he was not "wrong"; the imagination is never wrong, since it does not have to confront an image with an objective reality. But we must go further: Cyrano did not mean to deceive his readers. He knew quite well that readers would not mistake it. He had always hoped to find readers worthy of his imagination. Indeed, there is a sort of innate optimism in all works of the imagination. Gérard de Nerval wrote, in *Aurélia* (p. 41): "I believe that the human imagination never invented anything that was not true, in this world or any other."

When we have experienced an image like the planetary image of Cyrano's apple, we understand that it was not prepared by thought. It has nothing in common with images that illustrate or sustain scientific ideas. On the other hand, the planetary image of Bohr's atom—in scientific thinking, if not in a few indigent, harmful evaluations of popular philosophy—is a pure synthetic construct of mathematical thoughts. In Bohr's planetary atom, the little central sun *is not hot*.

This brief remark is to underline the essential difference

between an absolute image that is self-accomplishing, and a post-ideated image that is content to summarize existing thoughts.

III

Our second example of valorized literary miniature will be a botanist's daydream. Botanists delight in the miniature of being exemplified by a flower, and they even ingenuously use words that correspond to things of ordinary size to describe the intimacy of flowers. The following description of the flower of the German stachys may be read under *Herbs* in the *Dictionnaire de botanique chrétienne,* which is a large volume of the *Nouvelle encyclopédie théologique,* published in 1851:

"These flowers, which are grown in cotton cradles, are pink and white in color, and small and delicate. I take off the little chalice by means of the web of long silk threads that covers it . . . The lower lip of the flower is straight and a bit folded under; it is a deep pink on the inside, and on the outside is covered with thick fur. The entire plant causes smarting when touched. It wears a typically northern costume with four little stamens that are like little yellow brushes." Thus far, this account may pass for objective. But it soon becomes psychological, and, gradually, the description is accompanied by a daydream: "The four stamens stand erect and on excellent terms with one another in the sort of little niche formed by the lower lip, where they remain snug and warm in little padded case-mates. The little pistil remains respectfully at their feet, but since it is very small, in order to speak to it, they, in turn, must bend their knees. These little women are very important, and those that appear to be the humblest often assume great authority in their homes. The four seeds remain at the bottom of the chalice, where they are grown, the way, in India, children swing in a hammock. Each stamen recognizes its own handiwork, and there can be no jealousy."

Here our learned botanist has found wedded life in miniature, in a flower; he has felt the gentle warmth preserved by fur, he has seen the hammock that rocks the seed. From the harmony of the forms, he has deduced the well-being of the home. Need one point out that, as in the Cyrano text, the gentle warmth of enclosed regions is the first indication of intimacy? This warm intimacy is the root of all images. Here—quite obviously—the images no longer correspond to any sort of reality. Under a magnifying glass we could probably recognize the little yellow brushes of the stamens. But no *observer* could see the slightest real feature that would justify the psychological images accumulated by the narrator in this Dictionary of Christian Botany. We are inclined to think that the narrator would have been more cautious had he had to describe an object with ordinary dimensions. But he *entered* into a miniature world and right away images began to abound, then grow, then escape. Large issues from small, not through the logical law of a dialectics of contraries, but thanks to liberation from all obligations of dimensions, a liberation that is a special characteristic of the activity of the imagination. Under *Periwinkle,* in this same dictionary of Christian Botany, we find: "Reader, study the periwinkle in detail, and you will see how detail increases an object's stature."

In two lines, this man with a magnifying glass expresses an important psychological law. He situates us at a sensitive point of objectivity, at the moment when we have to accept unnoticed detail, and dominate it. The magnifying glass in this experience conditions an entry into the world. Here the man with the magnifying glass is not an old man still trying to read his newspaper, in spite of eyes that are weary of looking. The man with the magnifying glass takes the world as though it were quite new to him. If he were to tell us of the discoveries he has made, he would furnish us with documents of pure phenomenology, in which discovery of the world, or entry into the world, would be more than just a worn-out word, more than a word that has become tarnished through over-frequent philosophical use. A philosopher often describes his "entry into the world," his "being in the world," using a familiar object as symbol. He will describe his ink-bottle phenomenologically, and a paltry thing becomes the janitor of the wide world.

The man with the magnifying glass—quite simply—bars

the every-day world. He is a fresh eye before a new object. The botanist's magnifying glass is youth recaptured. It gives him back the enlarging gaze of a child. With this glass in his hand, he returns to the garden,

où les enfants regardent grand[6]

(where children see enlarged)

Thus the minuscule, a narrow gate, opens up an entire world. The details of a thing can be the sign of a new world which, like all worlds, contains the attributes of greatness.

Miniature is one of the refuges of greatness.

IV

Of course, in describing a phenomenology of the man with the magnifying glass, I was not thinking of the laboratory worker. A scientific worker has a discipline of objectivity that precludes all daydreams of the imagination. He has already seen what he observes in the microscope and, paradoxically, one might say that he never sees anything for the first time. In any case, in the domain of scientific observation that is absolutely objective, the "first time" doesn't count. Observation, then, belongs in the domain of "several times." In scientific work, we have first to digest our surprise psychologically. What scholars observe is well defined in a body of thoughts and experiments. It is not, then, on the level of problems of scientific experiment that I shall make my comments when we study the imagination. When we have forgotten all our habits of scientific objectivity, we look for the *images of the first time*. If we were to consult psychological documents in the history of science—since the objection may well be raised that, in this history, there is quite a store of "first times"—we should find that the first microscopic observations were legends about small objects, and when the object was endowed with life, legends of life. Indeed, one observer, still in the domain of naïveté, saw human forms in " 'spermatazoic' animals!"[7]

Here I am again, then, obliged to pose the problems of the Imagination in terms of "first time," which justifies my having chosen examples in realms of the most exaggerated fantasy. And by way of a surprising variation on the theme of the man with the magnifying glass, I shall study a prose poem by André Pieyre de Mandiargues, entitled "The Egg in the Landscape."[8]

Like countless others, our poet is sitting dreaming at the window. But he discovers in the glass itself a slight deformation, which spreads deformation throughout the universe. "Come nearer the window," Mandiargues tells his reader, "while you force yourself not to allow your attention to be too much attracted by the out-of-doors. Until you have seen one of these kernels that are like cysts in the glass, at times transparent little knucklebones, but more often, befogged or very vaguely translucent, and so long in shape that they make you think of the pupils of a cat's eyes." But what happens to the outside world, when it is seen through this little glazed lune, this pupil of a cat's eye? "Does the nature of the world change [p. 106], or is it real nature that triumphs over appearances? In any event, the experimental fact is that the introduction of the nucleus into the landscape sufficed to make it look limp . . . Walls, rocks, tree-trunks, metal constructions, lost all rigidity in the area surrounding the mobile nucleus." Here the poet makes images surge up on all sides, he presents us with an atom universe in the process of multiplication. Under his guidance, the dreamer can renew his own world, merely by moving his face. From the miniature of the glass cyst, he can call forth an entire world and oblige it to make "the most unwonted contortions" (p. 107). The dreamer sends waves of unreality over what was formerly the real world. "The outside world in its entirety is transformed into a milieu as malleable as could be desired, by the presence of this single, hard, piercing object, this veritable philosophical ovum which the slightest twitch of my face sets moving all through space."

Here the poet did not look far for his dream instrument. And yet with what art he nucleized the landscape! With what fantasy he conferred multiple curvature on space! This is really a fantasy on Riemann's curved space. Because every universe is enclosed in curves, every universe is concentrated in a nucleus, a spore, a dynamized center. And this center is powerful, because it is an imagined center. One step further into the world of images offered us by Pieyre de Mandiargues, and we see the center that imagines; then we can read the landscape in the glass nucleus. We no longer look at it while looking through it. This nucleizing nucleus is a world in itself. The miniature deploys to the dimensions of a universe. Once more, large is contained in small.

To use a magnifying glass is to pay attention, but isn't paying attention already having a magnifying glass? Attention by itself is an enlarging glass. Elsewhere,[9] Pieyre de Mandiargues meditates upon the flower of the euphorbia: "Like the crosscut of a flea under the lens of a microscope, the euphorbia had grown mysteriously under his overattentive scrutiny: it was now a pentagonal fortress, looming stupendously high above him, in a desert of white rocks, and the pink spires of the five towers that studded the castle set in the front line of the flora on the arid countryside appeared inaccessible."

A reasonable philosopher—and the species is not uncommon—will object, perhaps, that these documents are exaggerated, and that, with words, they make the large, even the immense, issue too gratuitously from the small. For him they are nothing but verbal prestidigitation, which is a poor thing compared to the feat of the real prestidigitator who makes an alarm-clock come out of a thimble. I shall nevertheless defend "literary" prestidigitation. The prestidigitator's action amazes and amuses us, while that of the poet sets us to dreaming. I cannot live and relive what is done by the former. But the poet's creation is mine if only I like to daydream.

This reasonable philosopher would excuse our images if they could be presented as the effect of a drug, such as mescaline. Then they would have physiological reality for him; and he could use them to elucidate his problems of the union of soul and body. I myself consider literary documents as *realities of the imagination,* pure products of the imagination. And why should the actions of the imagination not be as real as those of perception?

Is there any reason, either, why these "extreme" images, which we should be unable to form ourselves, but which readers can receive sincerely from poets, should not be virtual "drugs"—if we must keep to this notion—that procure the seeds of daydreams for us? This virtual drug, moreover, possesses very pure efficacy. For with an "exaggerated" image we are sure to be in the direct line of an autonomous imagination.

V

I felt a certain scruple when, a few pages back, I introduced that long description by the botanist in the *Nouvelle encyclopédie théologique*. This fragment abandons the seed of daydream too quickly. But because of its gossipy nature, we accept it when we have time for pleasantry. We must dismiss it, however, when we are trying to find the living seed of products of the imagination. If one may say this, it is a miniature made with big pieces and I shall have to look for a better contact with the miniaturizing imagination. Unfortunately, being, as I am, a philosopher who plies his trade at home, I haven't the advantage of actually seeing the works of the miniaturists of the Middle Ages, which was the great age of solitary patience. But I can well imagine this patience, which brings peace to one's fingers. Indeed, we have only to imagine it for our souls to be bathed in peace. All small things must evolve slowly, and certainly a long period of leisure, in a quiet room, was needed to miniaturize the world. Also one must love space to describe it as minutely as though there were world molecules, to enclose an entire spectacle in a molecule of drawing. In this feat there is an important dialectics of the intuition—which always sees big—and work, which is hostile to flights of fancy. Intuitionists, in fact, take in everything at one glance, while details reveal themselves and patiently take their places, one after the other, with the discursive impishness of the clever miniaturist. It is as though the miniaturist challenged the intuitionist philosopher's lazy contemplation, as though he said to him: "You would not have seen that! Take the time needed to see all these little things that cannot be seen all together." In looking at a miniature, unflagging attention is required to integrate all the detail.

Naturally, miniature is easier to tell than to do, and it is not hard to find literary descriptions that put the world in the diminutive. But because these descriptions tell things in tiny detail, they are automatically verbose. This is true of the following passage by Victor Hugo (I have cut it somewhat), in whose name I shall request the reader's attention for examination of a type of daydream that may seem insignificant.

Although Hugo is generally thought to have had a magnifying vision of things, he also knew how to describe them in miniature, as in this passage from *Le Rhin*:[10] "In Freiburg I forgot for a long time the vast landscape spread out before me, in my preoccupation with the plot of grass on which I was seated, atop a wild little knoll on the hill. Here, too, was an entire world. Beetles were advancing slowly under deep fibres of vegetation; parasol-shaped hemlock flowers imitated the pines of Italy . . . , a poor, wet bumble-bee, in black and yellow velvet, was laboriously climbing up a thorny branch, while thick clouds of gnats kept the daylight from him; a blue-bell trembled in the wind, and an entire nation of aphids had taken to shelter under its enormous tent . . . I watched an earthworm that resembled an antediluvian python come out of the mud and writhe heavenward, breathing in the air. Who knows, perhaps it, too, in this microscopic universe, has its Hercules to kill it and its Cuvier[11] to describe it. In short, this universe is as large as the other one." The account continues, to the poet's evident amusement. Having mentioned Micromégas, he goes on to pursue a facile theory. But the unhurried reader—I personally hope for no others—undoubtedly enters into this miniaturizing daydream. Indeed, this leisurely reader has often indulged in daydreams of this kind himself, but he would never have dared to write them down. Now the poet has given them literary dignity. It is my ambition to give them philo-

sophical dignity. For in fact, the poet is right, he has just discovered an entire world. "Here, too, was an entire world."
Why should a metaphysician not confront this world? It would
permit him to renew, at little cost, his experiences of "an opening onto the world," of "entrance into the world." Too often
the world designated by philosophy is merely a non-I, its vastness an accumulation of negativities. But the philosopher pro-
ceeds too quickly to what is positive, and appropriates for
himself the World, a World that is unique of its kind. Such formulas as: being-in-the-world and world-being are too majestic
for me and I do not succeed in experiencing them. In fact, I
feel more at home in miniature worlds, which, for me, are
dominated worlds. And when I live them I feel waves that gen-
erate world-consciousness emanating from my dreaming self.
For me, the vastness of the world has become merely the jam-
ming of these waves. To have experienced miniature sincerely
detaches me from the surrounding world, and helps me to
resist dissolution of the surrounding atmosphere.

Miniature is an exercise that has metaphysical freshness; it
allows us to be world-conscious at slight risk. And how restful
this exercise on a dominated world can be! For miniature rests
us without ever putting us to sleep. Here the imagination is
both vigilant and content.

But in order to devote myself to this miniaturized metaphysics with a clear conscience, I should need the increased support
of additional texts. Otherwise, by confessing my love of miniature, I should be afraid of confirming the diagnosis suggested,
some twenty-five years ago, by my old friend Mme. Favez-
Boutonier, who told me that my Lilliputian hallucinations
were characteristic of alcoholism.

There exist numerous texts in which a meadow is a forest,
and a tuft of grass a thicket. In one of Thomas Hardy's novels,
a handful of moss is a pine wood; and in *Niels Lyne*,[12]
J. P. Jacobsen's novel of subtle passions, the author, describing
the Forest of Happiness, with its autumn leaves and the shadbush
"weighted down with red berries," completes his picture with
"vigorous, thick moss that looked like pine trees, or like palms."

Also, "there was in addition, a thin moss that covered the tree-trunks and reminded one of the wheat-fields of elves" (p. 255 of the French translation). For a writer whose task it is to follow a highly intense human drama—as was the case with Jacobsen—to interrupt his passionate story, in order to "write this minia-ture," presents a paradox that would need elucidating if we wanted to take an exact measure of literary interests. By follow-ing the text closely, it is as though something human gained in delicacy in this effort to see this delicate forest set in the forest of big trees. From one forest to the other, from the forest in dias-tole to the forest in systole, there is the breathing of a cosmicity. And paradoxically, it seems that by living in the world of minia-ture, one relaxes in a small space.

This is one of the many daydreams that take us out of this world into another, and the novelist needed it to transport us into the region beyond the world that is the world of new love. People who are hurried by the affairs of men will not enter there. Indeed the reader of a book that follows the undulations of a great love may be surprised at this interruption through cosmicity. But he only gives the book a linear reading that fol-lows the thread of the human events. For this reader, events do not need a picture. And linear reading deprives us of countless daydreams.

Daydreams of this sort are invitations to verticality, pauses in the narrative during which the reader is invited to dream. They are very pure, since they have no use. They must also be distinguished from the fairy-tale convention in which a dwarf hides behind a head of lettuce to lay traps for the hero, as in *Le nain jaune* (The Yellow Dwarf) by Countess d'Aulnoy.[13] Cos-mic poetry is independent of the plots that characterize stories for children. In the examples given, it demands participation in a really intimate vegetism that has none of the torpor to which Bergsonian philosophy condemned it. Indeed, through its attachment to miniaturized forces, the vegetal world is great in smallness, sharp in gentleness, vividly alive in its greenness.

At times, a poet seizes upon some tiny dramatic incident, as for instance, Jacques Audiberti, who, in his amazing *Abraxas*, makes us sense the dramatic moment at which "the climbing

nettle raises the gray scale" in its struggle with a stone wall.
What a vegetal Atlas! In *Abraxas* Audiberti weaves a closely-
knit fabric of dream and reality. He knows the daydreams that
put intuition at the *punctum maximum.* One would like to
help the nettle root make one more blister on the old wall.

But we haven't time, in this world of ours, to love things and
see them at close range, in the plenitude of their smallness. Only
once in my life I saw a young lichen come into being and spread
out on a wall. What youth and vigor to honor the surface!

Of course, we should lose all sense of real values if we inter-
preted miniatures from the standpoint of the simple relativism
of large and small. A bit of moss may well be a pine, but a pine
will never be a bit of moss. The imagination does not function
with the same conviction in both directions.

Poets learn to know the primal germ of flowers in the gardens of tininess. And I should like to be able to say with André
Breton:

> *J'ai des mains pour te cueillir,*
> *thym minuscule de mes rêves,*
> *romarin de mon extrême pâleur.*[14]

> (I have hands to pluck you,
> wee thyme of my dreams,
> rosemary of my excessive pallor.)

VI

A fairy tale is a reasoning image. It tends to associate extraordinary images as though they could be coherent images,
imparting the conviction of a primal image to an entire ensem-
ble of derivative images. But the tie is so facile, and the reasoning so fluid that soon we no longer know where the germ of
the tale lies.

In the case of a story told in miniature such as *Petit Poucet*
(Tom Thumb), we seem to have no difficulty in finding the
principle of the primal image: mere tininess paves the way for

everything that happens. But when we examine it more closely, the phenomenological situation of this narrated miniature is precarious. And the fact is that it is subject to the dialectics of wonder and jest. A single overdrawn feature suffices sometimes to interrupt participation in wonderment. In a drawing, we might continue to admire it, but the commentary exceeds the limits: in one version, quoted by Gaston Paris,[15] Poucet is so small "that he splits a grain of dust with his head, and passes through it with his entire body." In another, he is killed by a kick from an ant. But in this last, there is no oneiric value. Our animalized oneirism, which is so powerful as regards large animals, has not recorded the doings and gestures of tiny animals. In fact, in the domain of tininess, animalized oneirism is less developed than vegetal oneirism.[16]

Gaston Paris notes that this direction, in which Poucet is killed by a kick from an ant, leads inevitably to the epigram, and a sort of insult through the image that expresses contempt for lowly creatures. Here we are faced with counter participation. "These witty games may be found among the Romans," he writes, "who, at the period of the decadence, addressed a dwarf with the following epigram: 'A flea's skin would be too big for you.'" "Today still," adds Gaston Paris, "the same jokes are to be found in the song about Le petit mari"[17] (The Little Husband). Gaston Paris describes this song, moreover, as a "children's song," which will no doubt astonish our psychoanalysts. Fortunately, in the last seventy-five years, we have acquired new means of psychological explanation.

In any case, Gaston Paris clearly designated the weak point of the legend (loc. cit., p. 23): the passages that jeer at tininess deform the original story, the pure miniature. In the original tale, which the phenomenologist must always reinstate, "smallness is not ridiculous, but wonderful. In fact, the most interesting features of the story are the extraordinary things that Poucet accomplishes, thanks to his smallness; he is witty and clever on all occasions, and always extricates himself triumphantly from the awkward situations in which he happens to be."

But then, in order to participate in the story really, this subtlety of wit should be accompanied by material subtlety. The tale invites us to "slip" between the difficulties. In other words, in addition to the design, we must seize the dynamism of the miniature, this being a supplementary phenomenological instance. And what a thrill we get from the story if we trace the source of this smallness, the nascent movement of this tiny creature, exerting influence upon the large one. As an example, the dynamism of miniature is often evidenced by the stories in which, seated in the horse's ear, Poucet is master of the forces that pull the plough. "This, in my opinion," writes Paris (p. 23), "is the original basis of his story; for this is a feature that is found among the legends of all peoples, whereas the other stories that are attributed to him, and which are creations of the imagination, once it has been stirred by this amusing little creature, usually differ among different peoples."

Naturally, when he is in the horse's ear, Poucet orders it to turn right or left. He is the *center of decision*, that the daydreams of our will advise us to set up in any small space. I said earlier that tininess is the habitat of greatness. But if we sympathize dynamically with this lively little Poucet, tininess soon appears to be the habitat of primitive strength. A Cartesian philosopher—if a Cartesian could indulge in pleasantry—would say that, in this story, Petit Poucet is the pineal gland of the plough. In any case, the infinitesimal is master of energies, small commands large. When Poucet has spoken, horse, ploughshare and man have only to follow. The better these three subordinates obey, the greater the certainty that the furrow will be straight.

Petit Poucet is at home in the space of an ear, at the entrance of the natural sound cavity. He is an ear within an ear. Thus the tale figured by visual representations is duplicated by what, in the next paragraph, I shall call a miniature of sound. As a matter of fact, as we follow the tale, we are invited to go beyond the auditory threshold, to hear with our imagination. Poucet climbed into the horse's ear in order to speak softly, that is to say, to command loudly, with a voice that none could hear except he who should "listen." Here the word "listen" takes on the double meaning of to hear and to obey. It is moreover in the minimum of sound, in a sound miniature like the one that illustrates this legend, that the play of this double meaning is most delicate.

This Poucet, who guides the farmer's team with his intelligence and will, seems rather remote from the Poucet of my youth. And yet it is in line with the fables that will lead us to primitive legend, in the footsteps of Gaston Paris, who was the great dispenser of primitivity.

For Paris, the key to the legend of Petit Poucet—as in so many legends!—is in the sky; in other words, it is Poucet who drives the constellation of the Grand Chariot.[18] And as a matter of fact, in many lands, according to this author, a little star just above the chariot is designated by the name of Poucet.

We need not follow all the convergent proofs that the reader can find in this work by Gaston Paris. However, I should like to insist upon a Swiss legend which will give us our full of an ear that knows how to dream. In this legend, also recounted by Paris (p. 11), the chariot turns over at midnight with a frightful noise. Such a legend teaches us to listen to the night. The time of night? The time of the starry sky? I once read somewhere that a hermit who was watching his hour-glass without praying heard noises that split his eardrums. He suddenly heard the catastrophe of time, in the hour-glass. The tick tock of our watches is so mechanically jerky that we no longer have ears subtle enough to hear the passage of time.

VII

The tale of Petit Poucet, transposed into the sky, shows that images move easily from small to large and from large to small. The Gulliver type of daydream is natural, and a great dreamer sees his images doubly, on earth and in the sky. But in this poetic life of images there is more than a mere game of dimensions. Daydream is not geometrical. The dreamer commits himself absolutely. In an appendix to C. A. Hackett's thesis on *Le lyrisme de Rimbaud,* under the title *Rimbaud et Gulliver,* there is an excellent passage in which Rimbaud is represented as small beside his mother, and great in the dominated world. Whereas in the presence of his mother he is nothing but "a little man in Brobdingnag's country," at school, little "Arthur imagines that he is Gulliver among the Lilliputians." And C. A. Hackett quotes Victor Hugo, who, in *Les contemplations (Souvenirs paternels)*, shows children who laugh

> *De voir d'affreux géants très bêtes*
> *Vaincus par des nains d'esprit.*

> (When they see frightful, very stupid giants
> Overpowered by witty dwarfs.)

Here Hackett has given an indication of all the elements of a psychoanalysis of Rimbaud. But although psychoanalysis, as I have often observed, can furnish us valuable information with regard to the deeper nature of a writer, occasionally it can divert us from the study of the direct virtue of an image. There are images that are so immense, their power of communication lures us so far from life, from our own life, that psychoanalytical commentary can only develop on the margin of values. There is immense daydreaming in these two lines by Rimbaud:

> *Petit Poucet rêveur, j'égrenais dans ma course*
> *Des rimes. Mon auberge était à la Grande Ourse.*

> (Dreamy Petit Poucet, on my way, as though in prayer,
> I said rhymes, my inn was under the sign of the Great Bear.)

It is of course possible to admit that, for Rimbaud, the Great Bear was an "image of Mme. Rimbaud" (Hackett, p. 69). But additional psychological insight does not give us the dynamism of this outburst of image that led the poet to recapture the legend of the Walloon Poucet. In fact I shall have to leave aside my psychoanalytical knowledge if I want to be touched by the phenomenological grace of the dreamer's image, of the image of this fifteen-year-old prophet. If the Great Bear Inn is merely the harsh home of an ill-handled adolescent, it awakens no positive memory in me, no active daydream. Here I can only dream in Rimbaud's sky. The particular origin that psychoanalysis finds in the writer's life, even though it may be psychologically correct, has little chance of recapturing an influence over anyone. And yet I receive the message of this extraordinary image, and for a brief instant, by detaching me from my life, it transforms me into an imagining being. It is in such moments of reading as this that, little by little, I have come to doubt not only the psychoanalytical origin of the image, but all psychological causality of the poetic image as well. Poetry, in its paradoxes, may be counter-causal, which is yet another way of being of the world, of being engaged in the dialectics of the passions. But when poetry attains its autonomy, we can say that it is a-causal. In order to receive *directly* the virtue of an isolated image—and an image in isolation has all its virtue—phenomenology now seems to me to be more favorable than psychoanalysis, for the precise reason that phenomenology requires us to assume this image ourselves, uncritically and with enthusiasm.

Consequently, in its *direct revery* aspect, "The Great Bear Inn" is not a maternal prison any more than it is a village sign. It is a "house in the sky." If we dream intensely at the sight of a square, we sense its stability, we know that it is a very safe refuge. Between the four stars of the Great Bear, a great dreamer can go and live. Perhaps he is fleeing the earth, and a psychoanalyst can enumerate the reasons for his flight. But the dreamer is sure to find a resting place proportionate to his dreams. And this house in the sky keeps turning round and round! The other stars, lost in the heavenly tides, turn ineptly. But the Grand Chariot does not lose its way. To watch it turning so smoothly is already to be master of the voyage. And, while dreaming, the poet undoubtedly experiences a coalescence of legends, all of which are given new life through the image. They are not an ancient wisdom. The poet does not repeat old-wives' tales. He has no past, but lives in a world that is new. As regards the past and the affairs of this world, he has realized absolute sublimation. The phenomenologist must follow the poet. The psychoanalyst is only interested in the negativity of sublimation.

VIII

On the theme of Petit Poucet, in folklore as well as among poets, we have just seen transpositions of size that give a double life to poetic space. Two lines suffice sometimes for this transposition, as, for instance, these lines by Noël Bureau:[19]

> *Il se couchait derrière le brin d'herbe*
> *Pour agrandir le ciei.*

> (He lay down behind the blade of grass
> To enlarge the sky.)

But sometimes the transactions between small and large multiply, have repercussions. Then, when a familiar image grows to the dimensions of the sky, one is suddenly struck by the impression that, correlatively, familiar objects become the miniatures of a world. Macrocosm and microcosm are correlated.

This correlation, which can become operative in both directions, has served as basis for certain poems by Jules Supervielle, especially those collected under the revealing title *Gravitations*. Here every poetic center of interest, whether in the sky or on the earth, is a center of active gravity. For the poet, this center of gravity is soon, if one can say this, both in heaven and on earth. For instance, with what freedom of movement in the images, the family table becomes an aerial table, with the sun for its lamp.[20]

> *L'homme, la femme, les enfants*
> *A la table aérienne*
> *Appuyée sur un miracle*
> *Qui cherche à se dèfinir.*

> (The man, the woman, the children
> At the aerial table
> Resting on a miracle
> That seeks its definition.)

Then, after this "explosion of unreality," the poet comes down to earth again:

> *Je me retrouve à ma table habituelle*
> *Sur la terre cultivée*
> *Celle qui donne le maïs et les troupeaux*
>
> *Je retrouvais les visages autour de moi*
> *Avec les pleins et les creux de la vèrité.*
>
> (I am back again at my usual table
> On the cultivated earth
> The one that yields corn and flocks
>
> I recognized the faces about me
> With their lights and shades of truth.)

The image that serves as pivot for this transforming day-dream, which is by turns earthly and aerial, familiar and cosmic, is the image of the lamp-sun or the sun-lamp. One could find innumerable literary documents on the subject of this very ancient image. But Jules Supervielle contributes an important variation by making it active in both directions. Thus he restores its entire suppleness to the imagination, a suppleness so miraculous that the image can be said to represent the sum of the direction that enlarges and the direction that concentrates. The poet keeps the image from becoming motionless.

If we are alive to Supervielle's cosmic allusions, under this title *Gravitations,* which is filled with scientific significance for the modern mind, may be found ideas that have a distinguished past. When the history of science is not over-modernized, and Copernicus, for instance, is taken as he was, with all his dreams and ideas, it becomes evident that the stars gravitate about light, and that the sun is, primarily, the great Light of the World. Later, mathematicians decided that it was a magnetic mass. Upper light, being the principle of centrality, is a very important value in the hierarchy of images. For the imagination, therefore, the world gravitates about a *value.*

The evening lamp on the family table is also the center of a world. In fact, the lamp-lighted table is a little world in itself, and a dreamer-philosopher may well fear lest our indirect lighting cause us to lose the center of the evening room. If this happens, will memory retain the faces of other days,

> *With their lights and shades of truth?*

When we have followed Supervielle's entire poem, both in its astral ascensions and its return to the world of human beings, we perceive that the familiar world assumes the new relief of a dazzling cosmic miniature. We did not know that the familiar world was so large. The poet has shown us that large is not incompatible with small. And we are reminded of Baudelaire's comments on certain Goya lithographs, which he called "vast pictures in miniature."[21] He also said of Marc Baud,[22] an enamelist, "he knows how to create large in small."

In reality, as we shall see later, especially when we examine images of immenseness, tiny and immense are compatible. A poet is always ready to see large and small. For instance, thanks to the image, a man like Paul Claudel, in his cosmogony was quick to assimilate the vocabulary—if not the thinking—of contemporary science. The following lines are from his *Cinq grandes odes* (p.180): "Just as we see little spiders or certain insect larvae hidden like precious stones in their cotton and satin pouches,

"In the same way, I was shown an entire nestful of still embarrassed suns in the cold folds of the nebula."

If a poet looks through a microscope or a telescope, he always sees the same thing.

IX

Distance, too, creates miniatures at all points on the horizon, and the dreamer, faced with these spectacles of distant nature, picks out these miniatures as so many nests of solitude in which he dreams of living.

In this connection, Joë Bousquet[23] writes: "I plunge into the tiny dimensions that distance confers, for I am anxious to measure the immobility in which I am confined with this reduction." A permanent invalid, this great dreamer bestrode the intervening space in order to "plunge" into tininess. The isolated villages on the horizon become homelands for the eyes. Distance disperses nothing but, on the contrary, composes a miniature of a country in which we should like to live. In distant miniatures, disparate things become reconciled. They then offer themselves for our "possession," while denying the distance that created them. We possess from afar, and how peacefully!

These miniature pictures on the horizon may be compared with the sights that characterize belfry daydreams, and which are so numerous that they are considered commonplace. Writers note them in passing but vary them hardly at all. And yet what a lesson in solitude! From the solitude of a belfry-tower, a man watches other men "running about" on the distant square bleached white by the summer sun. The men look "the size of flies," and move about irrationally "like ants." These comparisons, which are so hackneyed that one no longer dares to use them, appear as though inadvertently in numerous passages that recount a belfry daydream. It remains true, nevertheless, that a phenomenologist of images must take note of the extreme simplicity of these reflections which so successfully separate the daydreamer from the restless world, and give him an impression of domination at little cost. But once its commonplace nature has been pointed out, we realize that this is specifically the dream of high solitude. Enclosed solitude would think other thoughts. It would deny the world otherwise, and would not have a concrete image with which to dominate it. From the top of his tower, a philosopher of domination sees the universe in miniature. Everything is small because he is so high. And since he is high, he is great, the height of his station is proof of his own greatness.

Many a theorem of topoanalysis would have to be elucidated to determine the action of space upon us. For images cannot be measured. And even when they speak of space, they change in size. The slightest value extends, heightens, or multiplies them. Either the dreamer becomes the being of his image, absorbing all its space, or he confines himself in a miniature version of his images. What metaphysicians call our being-in-the-world (*être-là*) should be determined as regards each image, lest, occasionally, we find nothing but a miniature of being. I shall return to these aspects of this problem in a later chapter.

X

Since I have centered all my considerations on the problems of experienced space, miniature, for me, is solely a visual image. But the *causality of smallness* stirs all our senses, and an interesting study could be undertaken of the "miniatures" that appeal to each sense. For the sense of taste or smell, the problem might be even more interesting than for the sense of vision, since sight curtails the dramas it witnesses. But a whiff of perfume, or even the slightest odor, can create an entire environment in the world of the imagination.

Naturally, the problems of causality of smallness have been analyzed by sensory psychology. In a perfectly positive way, the psychologist carefully determines the different *thresholds* at which the various sense organs go into action. These thresholds may differ with different persons, but there is no contesting their reality. In fact, the idea of threshold is one of the most clearly objective ideas in modern psychology.

In this paragraph I should like to see if the imagination does not attract us to an area beyond these thresholds; if a poet who is hyper-alert to the inner word, by making form and color speak, doesn't hear in a region beyond perception. There exist too many paradoxical metaphors in this connection, for us not to examine them systematically, since they must conceal a certain reality, a certain truth of the imagination. I shall give some examples of what, for the sake of brevity, I shall call sound miniatures.

First of all, we must dismiss the usual references to problems of hallucination. For they refer to objective phenomena detectable in actual behavior that can be recorded thanks to photographs of faces in anguish at hearing imaginary voices. They would therefore not allow us to really enter into the domains of pure imagination. Nor do I believe that we can apprehend the autonomous activity of the creative imagination through a mixture of true sensations and hallucinations that may be either true or false. The problem for me, I repeat, is not to examine men, but images. And the only images that can be examined phenomenologically are transmissible ones; they are those we receive in a successful transmission. And even if the creator of an image were the victim of an hallucination, the image can very well fulfill our desire to imagine as readers, who are not hallucinated.

It must be recognized that a veritable ontological change took place when what psychiatrists designate as auditory hallucinations were given literary dignity by a great writer like Edgar Allan Poe. In such a case, psychological or psychoanalytical explanations concerning the author of the work of art can lead to a situation where problems of the creative imagination would be posed wrongly, or not at all. In general, too, *facts* do not explain *values*. And in works of the poetic imagination, values bear the mark of such novelty that everything related to the past is lifeless beside them. All memory has to be reimagined. For we have in our memories micro-films that can only be read if they are lighted by the bright light of the imagination.

Naturally, it can still be affirmed that Poe wrote "The Fall of the House of Usher" because he *suffered* from auditory hallucinations. But "suffer" runs counter to "create," and we may be sure that it was not while he was "suffering" that he wrote this tale, in which the images are brilliantly associated and the shades and silences have very delicately corresponding features. "Terrestrial objects were glowing" in the darkness, words were "murmurs." A sensitive ear knows that this is a poet writing in prose, and that, at a certain point, poetry dominates meaning. In short, in the auditory category, we have here an immense sound miniature, the miniature of an entire cosmos that speaks softly.

Faced with such a miniature of world sounds as this, a phenomenologist must systematically point out all that goes beyond perception, organically as well as objectively. This is not a matter of ears burning or of wall lizards growing bigger. There's a dead woman in a vault, who doesn't want to die. On a shelf in the library are very old books that tell of another past than the one the dreamer has known. Dreams, thoughts and memories weave a single fabric. The soul dreams and thinks, then it imagines. The poet has brought us to an extreme situation beyond which we are afraid to venture, a situation that lies between mental disorder and reason, between the living and a woman who is dead. The slightest sound prepares a catastrophe, while mad winds prepare general chaos. Murmur and clangor go hand in hand. We are taught the ontology of presentiment. In this tense state of fore-hearing, we are asked to become aware of the slightest indications, and in this cosmos of extremes, things are indications before they are phenomena; the weaker the indication, the greater the significance, since it indicates an origin. Taken as origins, it seems as though all these indications occur and reoccur without the tale coming to an end. Here genius teaches us some quite simple things. The tale ends by taking root in our consciousness and, for this reason, becomes the possession of the phenomenologist.

Meanwhile, consciousness increases; not, however, in relations between human beings, upon which psychoanalysis generally bases its observations. For it is not possible to concentrate on human problems in the face of a cosmos in danger. Everything lives in a sort of pre-quake, in a house about to collapse beneath the weight of walls which, when they too collapse, will have achieved definitive burial for a dead woman.

But this cosmos is not real. As Poe himself said, it is a *sulphurous* ideality, created by the dreamer with each new wave of his images. Man and the World, man and *his* world, are at their closest, it being in the power of the poet to designate them to us in their moments of greatest proximity. Man and the world are in a community of dangers. They are dangerous for each other. All this can be heard and pre-heard in the subrumbling murmur of the poem.

But my demonstration of the reality of poetic sound miniatures will be simpler, no doubt, if I take miniatures that are less composed. I shall therefore choose examples that may be contained in a few lines.

Poets often introduce us into a world of *impossible* sounds, so impossible, in fact, that their authors may be charged with creating fantasy that has no interest. One smiles and goes one's way. And yet, most often, the poet did not take his poem lightly, and a certain tenderness presided over these images.

René-Guy Cadou, who lived in the Village of Happy Homes, was moved to write:[24]

> *On entend gazouiller les fleurs du paravent*

> (You can hear the prattle of the flowers on the screen.)

Because all flowers speak and sing, even those we draw, and it is impossible to remain unsociable when we draw a flower or a bird. Another poet writes:

> *Son secret c'était*

> *D'écouter la fleur*
> *User sa couleur.*[25]

> (Her secret was
> Listening to flowers

> Wear out their color.)

Like so many poets, Claude Vigée hears the grass grow:[26]

> *J'ecoute*
> *Un jeune noisetier*
> *Verdir.*

> (I hear
> A young nut-tree
> grow green.)

Such images as these must be taken, at the least, in their existence as a *reality of expression*. For they owe their entire being to poetic expression, and this being would be diminished if we tried to refer them to a reality, even to a psychological reality. Indeed, they dominate psychology and correspond to no psychological impulse, save the simple need for self-expression, in one of those leisurely moments when we listen to everything in nature that is unable to speak.

It would be quite superfluous for such images to be true. They exist. They possess the absoluteness of the image, and they have passed beyond the limit that separates conditioned from absolute sublimation.

But even when they start from psychology, the turning away from psychological impressions to poetic expression is sometimes so subtle that one is tempted to attribute a basis of psychological reality to what is pure expression. The Touraine writer, J. Moreau, could "not resist the pleasure of quoting Théophile Gautier, when he gives poetic form to the impressions he had while smoking hashish."[27] "My hearing," Gautier wrote, "became enormously keen; I heard the noises of colors; green, red, blue, yellow sounds came to me in perfectly distinct waves." But Moreau was not taken in, and he notes that he quoted the poet's words "in spite of the poetic exaggeration that marks them, and which it is useless to point out." But then, for whom is this document intended? For the psychologist, or for the philosopher, who is interested in the poetic human being? In other words, is it the hashish or the poet that exaggerates? Alone, the hashish would not have succeeded in exaggerating so well. And we quiet readers, whose knowledge of hashish impressions has been acquired through literary proxy, would not hear colors shudder if a poet had not known how to make us listen, not to say, super-listen.

Then how shall we see without hearing? There exist complicated forms which, even when they are at rest, make a noise. Twisted things continue to make creaking contortions. And Rimbaud knew this when

Il ecoutait grouiller les galeux espaliers
(Les poètes de sept ans)

(He listened to mangy trellises crawling.)

The form of the mandrake maintains its legend. Indeed, this root in human form must cry out when it is pulled up from the ground. And for ears that dream, what a noise of syllables there is in its name![28] Words are clamor-filled shells. There's many a story in the miniature of a single word!

There are also great waves of silence that vibrate in poems, as in the little selection of poems by Pericle Patocchi, prefaced by Marcel Raymond. Here we have the silence of the distant world concentrated in one line:

Au loin j'entendais prier les sources de la terre
(Vingt poèmes)

(Far off I heard the springs of earth praying.)

Some poems move toward silence the way we descend in memory. As, for instance, in this great poem by Milosz:

Tandis que le grand vent glapit des noms de mortes
Ou bruit de vieille pluie aigre sur quelque route

Ecoute—plus rien—seul le grand silence—écoute.
(O. W. De L. Milosz)[29]

(While the high wind yelps the names of women long dead
Or the sound of bitter old rain on a road

Listen—now there's nothing—but complete silence—listen.)

Here there is nothing that would require the kind of poetic imitation to be found in Victor Hugo's great play, *Les Djinns*. It is the silence, rather, that obliges the poet to listen, and gives the dream greater intimacy. We hardly know where to situate this silence, whether in the vast world or in the immense past. But we do know that it comes from beyond a wind that dies down or a rain that grows gentle. In another poem (loc. cit., p. 372) we find this unforgettable line by Milosz:

> *L'odeur du silence est si vieille*

> (The odor of silence is so old . . .)

As life grows older, we are besieged by many a silence!

XI

How hard it is to situate the values of being and non-being! And where is the root of silence? Is it a distinction of non-being, or a domination of being? It is "deep." But where is the root of its depth? In the universe where sources about to be born are praying, or in the heart of a man who has suffered? And at what height of being should listening ears become aware?

Being myself a philosopher of adjectives, I am caught up in the perplexing dialectics of deep and large; of the infinitely diminished that deepens, or the large that extends beyond all limits. In Claudel's *L'annonce faite à Marie,* the dialogue between Violaine and Mara reaches down to unplumbed depths, establishing in a few words the ontological link between invisible and inaudible.

VIOLAINE (*who is blind*)—I hear . . .
MARA—What do you hear?
VIOLAINE—Things existing with me.

Here the touch goes so deep that one would have to meditate at length upon a world that exists in depth by virtue of its sonority, a world the entire existence of which would be the existence of voices. This frail, ephemeral thing, a voice, can bear witness to the most forceful realities. In Claudel's dialogues—abundant proof of this would be easy to find—the voice assumes the certainties of a reality that unites man and the world. But before speaking, one must listen. Claudel was a great listener.

XII

We have just seen united in grandeur of being, the transcendency of what is seen and what is heard. The following bit of daring, however, will serve as a simpler indication of this dual transcendency:[30]

> *Je m'entendais fermer les yeux, les rouvrir.*

> (I heard myself close my eyes, then open them.)

All solitary dreamers know that they hear differently when they close their eyes. And when we want to think hard, to listen to the inner voice, or compose the tightly constructed key sentence that will express the very core of our thinking, is there one of us who hasn't his thumb and forefinger pressed firmly against his lids? The ear knows then that the eyes are closed, it knows that it is responsible for the being who is thinking and writing. Relaxation will come when the eyes are reopened.

But who will tell us the daydreams of closed, half-closed, or even wide-open eyes? How much of the world must one retain in order to be accessible to transcendency? On page 247 of the above-mentioned book written over a century ago, by J. J. Moreau, we read: "With certain patients, merely to lower their eye-lids, while still awake, suffices to produce visual hallucinations." Moreau quotes Baillarger, adding: "Lowering the eyelids does not produce visual hallucinations only, but auditory hallucinations as well."

By associating the observations of these doctors of the old school, with a gentle poet like Loys Masson, I provide myself with countless daydreams. What a fine ear this poet has! And what mastery in directing the play of the dream devices known to us as seeing and hearing, ultra-seeing and ultra-hearing, hearing oneself seeing.

Another poet teaches us, if one may say this, to hear ourselves listen:

> *Ecoute bien pourtant. Non pas*
> *mes paroles, mais le tumulte qui*
> *s'élève en ton corps lorsque tu t'écoutes.*[31]
>
> (Yet listen well. Not to my words,
> but to the tumult that rages in
> your body when you listen to yourself.)

Here René Daumal has seized upon a point of departure for a phenomenology of the verb "to listen."

The fact that I have made use of all the documents of fantasy and daydreams that like to play with words and the most ephemeral sort of impressions is another admission on my part of my intention of remaining in the domain of the superficial. I have only explored the thin layer of nascent images. No doubt, the frailest, most inconsistent image can reveal profound vibrations. But to determine the metaphysics of all that transcends our perceptive life would require a different type of research. Particularly, if we were to describe how silence affects not only man's time and speech, but also his very being, it would fill a large volume. Fortunately, this volume exists. I recommend Max Picard's *The World of Silence.*[32]

8

INTIMATE IMMENSITY

> *Le monde est grand, mais en nous*
> *il est profond comme la mer.*
>
> R. M. RILKE
>
> (The world is large, but in us
> it is deep as the sea.)

> *L'espace m'a toujours rendu silencieux*
>
> JULES VALLÈS, *L'enfant*, p. 238
>
> (Space has always reduced me to silence.)

I

One might say that immensity is a philosophical category of daydream. Daydream undoubtedly feeds on all kinds of sights, but through a sort of natural inclination, it contemplates grandeur. And this contemplation produces an attitude that is so special, an inner state that is so unlike any other, that the daydream transports the dreamer outside the immediate world to a world that bears the mark of infinity.

Far from the immensities of sea and land, merely through memory, we can recapture, by means of meditation, the resonances of this contemplation of grandeur. But is this really memory? Isn't imagination alone able to enlarge indefinitely the images of immensity? In point of fact, daydreaming, from the very first second, is an entirely constituted state. We do not see it start, and yet it always starts the same way, that is, it flees the object nearby and right away it is far off, elsewhere, in the space of *elsewhere*.[1]

When this *elsewhere* is in *natural* surroundings, that is, when it is not lodged in the houses of the past, it is immense. And one might say that daydream is *original contemplation*.

If we could analyze impressions and images of immensity, or what immensity contributes to an image, we should soon enter into a region of the purest sort of phenomenology—a phenomenology without phenomena; or, stated less paradoxically, one that, in order to know the productive flow of images, need not wait for the phenomena of the imagination to take form and become stabilized in completed images. In other words, since immense is not an object, a phenomenology of immense would refer us directly to our imagining consciousness. In analyzing images of immensity, we should realize within ourselves the pure being of pure imagination. It then becomes clear that works of art are the *by-products* of this existentialism of the imagining being. In this direction of daydreams of immensity, the real *product* is consciousness of enlargement. We feel that we have been promoted to the dignity of the admiring being.

This being the case, in this meditation, we are not "cast into the world," since we open the world, as it were, by transcending the world seen as it is, or as it was, before we started dreaming. And even if we are aware of our own paltry selves—through the effects of harsh dialectics—we become aware of grandeur. We then return to the natural activity of our magnifying being.

Immensity is within ourselves. It is attached to a sort of expansion of being that life curbs and caution arrests, but which starts again when we are alone. As soon as we become motionless, we are elsewhere; we are dreaming in a world that is immense. Indeed, immensity is the movement of motionless man. It is one of the dynamic characteristics of quiet daydreaming.

And since we are learning philosophy from poets, here is a lesson in three lines, by Pierre Albert-Bireau:[2]

> *Et je me crée d'un trait de plume*
> *Maître du Monde*
> *Homme illimité.*

(And with a stroke of the pen I name myself
Master of the World
Unlimited man.)

II

However paradoxical this may seem, it is often this *inner immensity* that gives their real meaning to certain expressions concerning the visible world. To take a precise example, we might make a detailed examination of what is meant by the *immensity of the forest*. For this "immensity" originates in a body of impressions which, in reality, have little connection with geographical information. We do not have to be long in the woods to experience the always rather anxious impression of "going deeper and deeper" into a limitless world. Soon, if we do not know where we are going, we no longer know where we are. It would be easy to furnish literary documents that would be so many variations on the theme of this limitless world, which is a primary attribute of the forest. But the following passage, marked with rare psychological depth, from Marcault and Thérèse Brosse's excellent work,[3] will help us to determine the main theme: "Forests, especially, with the mystery of their space prolonged indefinitely beyond the veil of tree-trunks and leaves, space that is veiled for our eyes, but transparent to action, are veritable psychological transcendents."[4] I myself should have hesitated to use the term "psychological transcendents." But at least it is a good indicator for directing phenomenological research toward the transcendencies of present-day psychology. It would be difficult to express better that here the functions of description—psychological as well as objective—are ineffective. One feels that there is *something else* to be expressed besides what is offered for objective expression. What should be expressed is

hidden grandeur, depth. And so far from indulging in prolix-
ity of expression, or losing oneself in the detail of light and
shade, one feels that one is in the presence of an "essential"
impression seeking expression; in short, in line with what our
authors call a "psychological transcendent." If one wants to
"experience the forest," this is an excellent way of saying that
one is in the presence of *immediate immensity*, of the immediate immensity of its depth. Poets feel this immediate immensity of old forests:[5]

> *Forêt pieuse, forêt brisée où l'on n'enlève pas les morts*
> *Infiniment fermée, serrée de vieilles tiges droites roses*
> *Infiniment resserrée en plus vieux et gris fardés*
> *Sur la couche de mousse énorme et profonde en cri de velours*

> (Pious forest, shattered forest, where the dead are left lying
> Infinitely closed, dense with pinkish straight old stems
> Infinitely serried, older and grayed
> On the vast, deep, mossy bed, a velvet cry.)

Here the poet does not describe. He knows that his is a
greater task. The pious forest is shattered, closed, serried. It
accumulates its infinity within its own boundaries. Farther on
in the poem he will speak of the symphony of an "eternal"
wind that lives in the movement of the tree-tops.

Thus, Pierre-Jean Jouve's "forest" is *immediately sacred*,
sacred by virtue of the tradition of its nature, far from all history of men. Before the gods existed, the woods were sacred,
and the gods came to dwell in these sacred woods. All they did
was to add human, all too human, characteristics to the great
law of forest revery.

But even when a poet gives a geographical dimension, he
knows instinctively that this dimension can be determined on
the spot, for the reason that it is rooted in a particular oneiric
value. Thus, when Pierre Guéguen speaks of "the deep forest"
(the forest of Broceliande),[6] he adds a dimension; but it is not
the dimension that gives the image its intensity. And when he
says that the deep forest is also called "the quiet earth, because

of its immense silence curdled in thirty leagues of green," Gué-guen bids us participate in transcendent quiet and silence. Because the forest rustles, the "curdled" quiet trembles and shudders, it comes to life with countless lives. But these sounds and these movements do not disturb the silence and quietude of the forest. When we read this passage of Guéguen's book we sense that this poet has calmed all anxiety. Forest peace for him is inner peace. It is an inner state.

Poets know this, and some reveal it in one line as, for instance, Jules Supervielle, who knows that in our peaceful moments we are

> *Habitants délicats des forêts de nous-mêmes.*

> (Sensitive inhabitants of the forests of ourselves.)

Others, who are more logical, such as René Ménard, present us with a beautiful album devoted to trees, in which each tree is associated with a poet. Here is Ménard's own *intimate forest:* "Now I am traversed by bridle paths, under the seal of sun and shade . . . I live in great density . . . Shelter lures me. I slump down into the thick foliage . . . In the forest, I am my entire self. Everything is possible in my heart just as it is in the hiding places in ravines. Thickly wooded distance separates me from moral codes and cities."[7] But one should read this whole prose poem which, as the poet says, is actuated by "reverent apprehension of the Imagination of Creation."

In the domains of poetic phenomenology under consideration, there is one adjective of which a metaphysician of the imagination must beware, and that is, the adjective *ancestral.* For there is a corresponding valorization to this adjective which is too rapid, often entirely verbal, and never well supervised, with the result that the direct nature of depth imagination and of depth psychology, generally, is lacking. Here the "ancestral" forest becomes a "psychological transcendent" at small cost, it is an image suited to children's books. And if there exists a phenomenological problem with regard to this image, it is to find out for what *actual* reason, by virtue of what active value of the imagination, such an image charms and speaks to us. The hypothesis, according to which it is due to remote permeation from infinite ages, is a psychologically gratuitous one. Indeed, if it were to be taken into consideration by a phenomenologist, such a hypothesis would be an invitation to lazy thinking. And, for myself, I feel obliged to establish the actuality of archetypes. In any event, the word "ancestral," as a value of the imagination, is one that needs explaining; it is not a word that explains.

But who knows the temporal dimensions of the forest? History is not enough. We should have to know how the forest experiences its great age; why, in the reign of the imagination, there are no young forests. I myself can only meditate upon things in my own country, having learned the dialectics of fields and woods from my unforgettable friend, Gaston Roupnel.[8] In the vast world of the non-I, the non-I of fields is not the same as the non-I of forests. The forest is a before-me, before-us, whereas for fields and meadows, my dreams and recollections accompany all the different phases of tilling and harvesting. When the dialectics of the I and the non-I grow more flexible, I feel that fields and meadows are with me, in the with-me, with-us. But forests reign in the past. I know, for instance, that my grandfather got lost in a certain wood. I was told this, and I have not forgotten it. It happened in a past before I was born. My oldest memories, therefore, are a hundred years old, or perhaps a bit more.

This, then, is my ancestral forest. And all the rest is fiction.

III

When such daydreams as these take hold of meditating man, details grow dim and all picturesqueness fades. The very hours pass unnoticed and space stretches out interminably. Indeed, daydreams of this kind may well be called daydreams of infinity. With these images of the "deep" forest, I have just outlined the power of immensity that is revealed in a value. But one can follow the opposite course. In the presence of such obvious

immensity as the immensity of night, a poet can point the way
to intimate depth. A passage in Milosz's *L'amoureuse initiation* (p. 64) will serve as a center where we can sense the concordance of world immensity with intimate depth of being.

"As I stood in contemplation of the garden of the wonders of
space," Milosz writes, "I had the feeling that I was looking into
the ultimate depths, the most secret regions of my own being;
and I smiled, because it had never occurred to me that I could
be so pure, so great, so fair! My heart burst into singing with
the song of grace of the universe. All these constellations are
yours, they exist in you; outside your love they have no reality!
How terrible the world seems to those who do not know themselves! When you felt so alone and abandoned in the presence of
the sea, imagine what solitude the waters must have felt in the
night, or the night's own solitude in a universe without end!"
And the poet continues this love duet between dreamer and
world, making man and the world into two wedded creatures
that are paradoxically united in the dialogue of their solitude.

Elsewhere in this same work (p. 151), in a sort of meditation-
exaltation which unites the two movements that concentrate
and dilate, Milosz writes: "Oh, space, you who separate the
waters; my joyful friend, with what love I sense you! Here I am
like the flowering nettle in the gentle sunlight of ruins, like the
pebble on the spring's edge, or the serpent in the warm grass!
Is this instant really eternity? Is eternity really this instant?"
And the passage goes on, linking infinitesimal with immense,
the white nettle with the blue sky. All these sharp contradictions, the thin edge of the pebble and the clear spring, are now
assimilated and destroyed, the dreaming being having transcended the contradiction of small and large. This exaltation
of space goes beyond all frontiers (p. 155). "Away with boundaries, those enemies of horizons! Let genuine distance appear!"
And further (p. 168): "Everything was bathed in light, gentleness and wisdom; in the unreal air, distance beckoned to distance. My love enveloped the universe."

Of course, if it were my aim to study images of immensity
objectively, I should have to start a voluminous file, for immensity is an inexhaustible poetic theme. I touched on this in an

earlier work,[9] in which I insisted upon the desire for confronta-
tion that exists in man meditating upon an infinite universe. I
also spoke of a spectacle complex in which pride of seeing is the
core of the consciousness of a being in contemplation. But the
problem under consideration in this present work is that of a
more relaxed participation in images of immensity, a more intimate relationship between small and large. I should like to liq-
uidate, as it were, the spectacle complex, which could harden
certain values of poetic contemplation.

IV

When a relaxed spirit meditates and dreams, immensity seems
to expect images of immensity. The mind sees and continues
to see objects, while the spirit finds the nest of immensity in an
object. We shall have various proofs of this if we follow the
daydreams that the single word *vast* inspired in Baudelaire.
Indeed, "vast" is one of the most Baudelairian of words, the
word that marks most naturally, for this poet, infinity of intimate space.

No doubt, pages could be found in his work in which the
word "vast" has merely its ordinary geometrically objective
meaning: "Around a vast oval table . . ." is from a description
in *Curiosités esthétiques* (p. 390). But when one has become
hypersensitive to this word, one sees that it denotes attraction
for felicitous amplitude. Moreover, if we were to count the different usages of the word "vast" in Baudelaire's writings, we
should be struck by the fact that examples of its positive,
objective use are rare compared with the instances when the
word has more intimate resonances.[10]

Despite the fact that Baudelaire consciously avoided words
used by force of habit, and took particular pains not to let his
adjectives be dictated by his nouns, he did not keep a close eye
on his use of the word *vast*. Whenever a thing, a thought or a
daydream was touched by grandeur, this word became indispensable to him. I should like to give a few examples of the
astonishing variety of uses to which he put it.

The opium-eater must have "a vast amount of leisure"[11] to derive benefit from his soothing daydreams. Daydreaming is encouraged by "the vast silence of the country."[12] The "moral world opens up vast perspectives filled with new clarities."[13] Certain dreams are laid "on the vast canvas of memory." And elsewhere, Baudelaire speaks of a man who was "the prey of great projects, oppressed by vast thoughts."

Describing a nation, he wrote, "Nations . . . (are) vast animals whose organization is adequate to their environment"; and returning later to the same subject,[14] "Nations (are) vast collective creatures." Here there is no doubt that the word *vast* increases the tonality of the metaphor; in fact, without this word, to which he attached importance, he would have perhaps hesitated because of the indigence of the image. But the word *vast* saves everything and Baudelaire adds that readers will understand this comparison if they are at all familiar with "these vast subjects of contemplation."

It is no exaggeration to say that, for Baudelaire, the word "vast" is a metaphysical argument by means of which the vast world and vast thoughts are united. But actually this grandeur is most active in the realm of intimate space. For this grandeur does not come from the spectacle witnessed, but from the unfathomable depths of vast thoughts. In his *Journaux intimes* (loc. cit., p. 29) Baudelaire writes: "In certain almost supernatural inner states, the depth of life is entirely revealed in the spectacle, however ordinary, that we have before our eyes, and which becomes the symbol of it." Here we have a passage that designates the phenomenological direction I myself pursue. The exterior spectacle helps intimate grandeur unfold.

The word "vast," for Baudelaire, is also the word that expresses the highest degree of synthesis. In order to learn the difference between the discursive ventures of the mind and the powers of the spirit, we must meditate upon the following thought:[15] "the lyrical spirit takes strides that are as vast as synthesis while the novelist's mind delights in analysis."

Thus, under the banner of the word *vast*, the spirit finds its synthetic being. The word *vast* reconciles contraries.

"As vast as night and light." In a poem about hashish,[16] we find some elements of this famous line that haunts the memory of all Baudelaire's admirers: "The moral world opens up vast perspectives, filled with new clarities." And so it is the "moral" nature, the "moral" temple that conveys grandeur in its pristine state. Throughout this poet's work, one can follow the action of a "vast unity" that is always ready to unite dislocated riches. The philosophical mind goes in for endless discussion on the relation of the one to the many, while Baudelaire's meditations, which are very typically poetic, find a deep, somber unity in the very power of the synthesis through which the different impressions of the senses enter into correspondence. Often these "correspondences" have been examined too empirically as being the effects of sensibility. However, the range of sensibility from one dreamer to the other rarely coincides. Except for the delight that it affords every reader's ear, myrrh is not given to all of us. But from the very first chords of the sonnet "*Correspondances,*" the synthesizing action of the lyrical spirit is at work. Even though poetic sensibility enjoys countless variations on the theme of "correspondences," we must acknowledge that the theme itself is also eminently enjoyable. And Baudelaire says, in fact, that at such moments "the sense of existence is immensely increased."[17] Here we discover that immensity in the intimate domain is intensity, an intensity of being, the intensity of a being evolving in a vast perspective of intimate immensity. It is the principle of "correspondences" to receive the immensity of the world, which they transform into intensity of our intimate being. They institute transactions between two kinds of grandeur. We cannot forget that Baudelaire experienced these transactions.

Movement itself has, so to speak, a favorable volume, and because of its harmony, Baudelaire included it in the esthetic category of vastness. Writing about the movement of a ship, he said, "The poetic idea that emanates from this operation of movement inside the lines is the hypothesis of a vast, immense creature, complicated but eurhythmic, an animal endowed with genius, suffering and sighing every sigh and every human ambition." Thus, the ship, beautiful volume resting on the waters, contains the infinite of the word *vast,* which is a word that does not describe, but gives

primal being to everything that must be described. For Baudelaire, the word *vast* contains a complex of images that deepen one
another because they grow on a vast being.

At the risk of my demonstration becoming diffuse, I have
tried to indicate the places in Baudelaire's work where this
strange adjective appears; strange because it confers grandeur
upon impressions that have nothing in common.

But in order to give my demonstration greater unity, I shall
follow a line of images, or values, which will show that, for
Baudelaire, immensity is an intimate dimension.

A rarely felicitous expression of the intimate nature of the
notion of immensity may be found in the pages Baudelaire
devoted to Richard Wagner,[18] and in which he lists, so to speak,
three states of this impression of immensity. He begins by quoting the program of the concert at which the Prelude to *Lohen-
grin* was played (loc. cit., p. 212). "From the very first measures,
the spirit of the pious recluse who awaits the sacred cup is
plunged into infinite space. Little by little, he sees a strange
apparition assuming form. As this apparition becomes clearer,
the *marvelous band of angels*, bearing in their midst the sacred
goblet, passes. The holy procession approaches, little by little
the heart of God's elect is uplifted; it swells and expands,
stirred by ineffable aspirations; *it yields to increasing bliss*, and
as it comes nearer the *luminous apparition*, when at last the
Holy Grail itself appears in the midst of the procession, *it sinks
into ecstatic adoration as though the whole world had suddenly disappeared*." All the underlinings in this passage were
made by Baudelaire himself. They make us sense clearly the
progressive expansion of the daydream up to the ultimate point
when immensity that is born intimately, in a feeling of ecstasy,
dissolves and absorbs, as it were, the perceptible world.

The second state of what we might call an increase of being is
furnished by a few lines by Liszt. These lines permit us to participate in mystic space (loc. cit., p. 213) born of musical meditation. "Vaporous ether . . . overspreads a broad dormant sheet
of melody." In the rest of this text by Liszt, metaphors of light
help us to grasp this extension of a transparent musical world.

But these texts only prepare Baudelaire's own note on the

subject, in which the "correspondences" appear to be intensifi-
cation of the senses, each enlargement of an image enlarging
the grandeur of another image, as immensity develops. Here
Baudelaire, who is now entirely immersed in the oneirism of
the music, has, as he says, "one of those impressions of happiness that nearly all imaginative men have experienced in their
sleeping dreams. I felt freed from *the powers of gravity,* and,
through memory, succeeded in recapturing the extraordinary
voluptuousness that pervades *high places.* Involuntarily I pic-
tured to myself the delightful state of a man in the grip of a
long daydream, in absolute solitude, but a solitude with an
immense horizon and widely diffused light; in other words,
immensity with no other setting than itself."

In the text that follows, any number of factors may be found
that could be used for a phenomenology of extension, expansion and ecstasy. But after having been lengthily prepared by
Baudelaire, we have now come upon the formula that must be
put in the center of our phenomenological observations:
"immensity with no other setting than itself." Concerning this
immensity, Baudelaire has just told us in detail, that it is a conquest of intimacy. Grandeur progresses in the world in proportion to the deepening of intimacy. Baudelaire's daydream does
not take shape in contemplation of a universe. He pursues it—
as he tells us—with closed eyes. He does not live on memories,
and his poetic ecstasy has become, little by little, an eventless
life. The angels whose wings had once shown blue in the sky
have blended into a universal blue. Slowly, immensity becomes
a primal value, a primal, intimate value. When the dreamer
really experiences the word "immense," he sees himself liber-
ated from his cares and thoughts, even from his dreams. He is
no longer shut up in his weight, the prisoner of his own being.

If we were to study these fragments by Baudelaire according
to the normal methods of psychology, we might conclude that
when the poet left behind him the settings of the world, to
experience the single "setting" of immensity, he could only
have knowledge of an "abstraction come true." Intimate space
elaborated in this way by a poet would be merely the pendant
of the outside space of geometricians, who seek infinite space

with no other sign than infinity itself. But such a conclusion would fail to recognize the concrete ventures of long daydreaming. Here every time daydream abandons a too picturesque feature, it gains further extension of intimate being. Without even having the privilege of hearing *Tannhäuser,* the reader who reflects on these pages by Baudelaire, while recalling the successive states of the poet's daydream, cannot fail to realize that in rejecting metaphors that are too facile he is marked for an ontology of human depth.

For Baudelaire, man's poetic fate is to be the mirror of immensity; or even more exactly, immensity becomes conscious of itself, through man. Man for Baudelaire is a vast being.

Thus, I believe that I have proved in many ways that in Baudelaire's poetics, the word *vast* does not really belong to the objective world. I should like to add one more phenomenological nuance, however, which belongs to the phenomenology of the word.

In my opinion, for Baudelaire, the word *vast* is a vocal value. It is a word that is *pronounced,* never only read, never only seen in the objects to which it is attached. It is one of those words that a writer always speaks softly while he is writing it. Whether in verse or in prose, it has a poetic effect, which is also an effect of vocal poetry. This word immediately stands out from the words that surround it, from the images, and perhaps, even, from the thought. It is a "power of the word."[19] Indeed, whenever we read this word in the measure of one of Baudelaire's verses, or in the periods of his prose poems, we have the impression that he forces us to pronounce it. The word *vast,* then, is a vocable of breath. It is placed on our breathing, which must be slow and calm.[20] And the fact is that always, in Baudelaire's poetics, the word *vast* evokes calm, peace and serenity. It expresses a vital, intimate conviction. It transmits to our ears the echo of the secret recesses of our being. For this word bears the mark of gravity, it is the enemy of turmoil, opposed to the vocal exaggerations of declamation. In diction enslaved to strict measure, it would be shattered. The word *vast* must reign over the peaceful silence of being.

If I were a psychiatrist, I should advise my patients who suffer from "anguish" to read this poem of Baudelaire's whenever an attack seems imminent. Very gently, they should pronounce Baudelaire's key word, *vast*. For it is a word that brings calm and unity; it opens up unlimited space. It also teaches us to breathe with the air that rests on the horizon, far from the walls of the chimerical prisons that are the cause of our anguish. It has a vocal excellence that is effective on the very threshold of our vocal powers. The French baritone, Charles Panzera, who is sensitive to poetry, once told me that, according to certain experimental psychologists, it is impossible to think the vowel sound *ah* without a tautening of the vocal chords. In other words, we read *ah* and the voice is ready to sing. The letter *a*, which is the main body of the word *vast*, stands aloof in its delicacy, an anacoluthon of spoken sensibility.

The numerous commentaries that have been made on Baudelaire's "correspondences" seem to have forgotten this sixth sense that seeks to model and modulate the voice. This delicate little Aeolian harp that nature has set at the entrance to our breathing is really a sixth sense, which followed and surpassed the others. It quivers at the merest movement of metaphor; it permits human thought to sing. And when I let my nonconformist philosopher's daydreams go unchecked, I begin to think that the vowel *a* is the vowel of immensity. It is a sound area that starts with a sigh and extends beyond all limits.

In the word *vast*, the vowel *a* retains all the virtues of an enlarging vocal agent. Considered vocally, therefore, this word is no longer merely dimensional. Like some soft substance, it receives the balsamic powers of infinite calm. With it, we take infinity into our lungs, and through it, we breathe cosmically, far from human anguish. Some may find these minor considerations. But no factor, however slight, should be neglected in the estimation of poetic values. And indeed, everything that contributes to giving poetry its decisive psychic action should be included in a philosophy of the dynamic imagination. Sometimes, the most varied, most delicate perceptive values relay one another, in order to dynamize and expand a poem.

Long research devoted to Baudelaire's correspondences should elucidate the correspondence of each sense with the spoken word.

At times the sound of a vocable, or the force of a letter, reveals and defines the real thought attached to a word. In this connection, it is interesting to recall what Max Picard wrote on the subject, in his excellent work, *Der Mensch und das Wort:* "*Das W in Welle bewegt die Welle im Wort mit, das H in Hauch lässt den Hauch aufsteigen, das t in fest und hart, macht fest und hart.*"[21] With these remarks, the philosopher of the *Welt des Schweigens* brings us to the points of extreme sensibility at which, language having achieved complete nobility, phonetic phenomena and phenomena of the logos harmonize. But we should have to learn how to meditate very slowly, to experience the inner poetry of the word, the inner immensity of a word. All important words, all the words marked for grandeur by a poet, are keys to the universe, to the dual universe of the Cosmos and the depths of the human spirit.

V

Thus, it seems to me to have been proven that in the work of a great poet like Baudelaire an intimate call of immensity may be heard, even more than an echo from the outside world. In the language of philosophy, we could say, then, that immensity is a "category" of the poetic imagination, and not merely a generality formulated during contemplation of grandiose spectacles. By way of contrast, and in order to give an example of "empirical" immensity, I should like to consider a passage from Taine's *Voyage aux Pyrénées* (p. 96).[22] Here we shall see bad literature and not poetry in action, the kind of bad literature that aims at pictorial expression at all cost, even at the expense of the fundamental images.

"The first time I saw the sea," writes Taine, "I was most disagreeably disillusioned . . . I seemed to see one of those long stretches of beet fields that one sees in the country near Paris, intersected by patches of green cabbage, and strips of russet barley. The distant sails looked like homing pigeons and even the outlook seemed narrow to me; painters had represented the sea as being much larger. It was three days before I recaptured the feeling of immensity."

Beets, barley, cabbages and pigeons in a perfectly artificial association! To bring them together in one "image" could only be a slip in the conversation of someone who is trying to be "original." For it is hard to believe that in the presence of the sea, anyone could be so obsessed by beet fields.

A phenomenologist would be interested to know how, after three days of privation, this philosopher recaptured his "feeling of immensity," and how, on his return to the sea that had been looked at so naïvely, he finally saw its grandeur.

After this interlude, let us come back to our poets.

VI

Poets will help us to discover within ourselves such joy in looking that sometimes, in the presence of a perfectly familiar object, we experience an extension of our intimate space. Let us listen to Rilke, for instance, give its existence of immensity to a tree he is looking at.[23]

> L'espace, hors de nous, gagne et traduit les choses:
> Si tu veux réussir l'existence d'un arbre,
> Investis-le d'espace interne, cet espace
> Qui a son être en toi. Cerne-le de contraintes.
> Il est sans borne, et ne devient vraiment un arbre
> Que s'il s'ordonne au sein de ton renoncement.

> (Space, outside ourselves, invades and ravishes things:
> If you want to achieve the existence of a tree,
> Invest it with inner space, this space
> That has its being in you. Surround it with compulsions,
> It knows no bounds, and only really becomes a tree
> If it takes its place in the heart of your renunciation.)

In the two last lines, a Mallarmé-like obscurity forces the reader to stop and reflect. The poet has set him a nice problem for the imagination. The advice to "surround the tree with compulsions" would first be an obligation to draw it, to invest it with limitations in *outside* space. In this case, we should obey the simple rules of perception, we should be "objective," cease imagining. But the tree, like every genuine living thing, is taken in its being that "knows no bounds." Its limits are mere accidents. Against the accident of limits, the tree needs you to give it your superabundant images, nurtured in your intimate space, in "this space that has its being in you." Then, together, the tree and its dreamer take their places, grow tall. Never, in the dream world, does a tree appear as a completed being. According to a poem by Jules Supervielle, it seeks its soul:[24]

> *Azur vivace d'un espace*
> *Où chaque arbre se hausse au dénouement des palmes*
> *A la recherche de son âme.*

> (Vivid blue of a space
> In which each tree rises to foliation of palms
> In search of its soul.)

But when a poet knows that a living thing in the world is in search of its soul, this means that he is in search of his own. "A tall shuddering tree always moves the soul."[25]

Restored to the powers of the imagination, and invested with our inner space, trees accompany us in an emulation of grandeur. In another poem dated August 1914 (loc. cit., p. 11) Rilke wrote:

> *. . . A travers nous s'envolent*
> *Les oiseaux en silence. O, moi qui veux grandir*
> *Je regarde au dehors, et l'arbre en moi grandit.*

> (. . . Silently the birds
> Fly through us. O, I, who long to grow,
> I look outside myself, and the tree inside me grows.)

Thus a tree is always destined for grandeur, and, in fact, it propagates this destiny by magnifying everything that surrounds it. In a letter reproduced in Claire Goll's very human little book, *Rilke et les femmes* (p. 63), Rilke wrote: "These trees are magnificent, but even more magnificent is the sublime and moving space between them, as though with their growth it too increased."

The two kinds of space, intimate space and exterior space, keep encouraging each other, as it were, in their growth. To designate space that has been experienced as affective space, which psychologists do very rightly, does not, however, go to the root of space dreams. The poet goes deeper when he uncovers a poetic space that does not enclose us in affectivity. Indeed, whatever the affectivity that colors a given space, whether sad or ponderous, once it is poetically expressed, the sadness is diminished, the ponderousness lightened. Poetic space, because it is expressed, assumes values of expansion. It belongs to the phenomenology of those words that begin with "ex." At least, this is the thesis that I shall insist upon, and to which I plan to return in a future volume. Just in passing, here is a proof: When a poet tells me that he "knows a type of sadness that smells of pineapple,"[26] I myself feel less sad, I feel gently sad.

In this activity of poetic spatiality that goes from deep intimacy to infinite extent, united in an identical expansion, one feels grandeur welling up. As Rilke said: "Through every human being, unique space, intimate space, opens up to the world . . ."

Here space seems to the poet to be the subject of the verbs "to open up," or "to grow." And whenever space is a value—there is no greater value than intimacy—it has magnifying properties. Valorized space is a verb, and never, either inside or outside us, is grandeur an "object."

To give an object poetic space is to give it more space than it has objectivity; or, better still, it is following the expansion of its intimate space. For the sake of homogeneity, I shall recall how Joë Bousquet expressed the intimate space of a tree:[27] "Space is nowhere. Space is inside it like honey in a hive." In the realm of images, honey in a hive does not conform to the elementary dialectics of contained and container. Metaphorical honey will not be shut up, and here, in the intimate space of a tree, honey is anything but a form of marrow. It is the "honey of the tree" that will give perfume to the flower. It is also the inner sun of the tree. And the dreamer who dreams of honey knows that it is a force that concentrates and radiates, by turns. If the interior space of a tree is a form of honey, it gives the tree "expansion of infinite things."

Of course, we can read this line of Joë Bousquet's without tarrying over the image. But if one likes to go to the ultimate depths of an image, what dreams it can set astir! Even a philosopher of space starts to dream. And if we like words of composed metaphysics, one might say that here Joë Bousquet has shown us a space-substance, honey-space or space-honey. May all matter be given its individual place, all sub-stances their ex-stance. And may all matter achieve conquest of its space, its power of expansion over and beyond the surfaces by means of which a geometrician would like to define it.

It would seem, then, that it is through their "immensity" that these two kinds of space—the space of intimacy and world space—blend. When human solitude deepens, then the two immensities touch and become identical. In one of Rilke's letters, we see him straining toward "the unlimited solitude that makes a lifetime of each day, toward communion with the universe, in a word, space, the invisible space that man can live in nevertheless, and which surrounds him with countless presences."

This coexistence of things in a space to which we add consciousness of our own existence is a very concrete thing. Leibnitz's theme of space as a place inhabited by coexistants has found its poet in Rilke. In this coexistentialism every object invested with intimate space becomes the center of all space. For each object, distance is the present, the horizon exists as much as the center.

VII

In the realm of images, there can be no contradiction, and two spirits that are identically sensitive can sensitize the dialectics of center and horizon in different ways. In this connection a sort of *plains test* could be used that would bring out different types of reactions to infinity.

At one end of the test, we should set what Rilke said briefly and superbly: "The plain is the sentiment that exalts us." This theorem of esthetic anthropology is so clearly stated that it suggests a correlative theorem which could be expressed in the following terms: any sentiment that exalts us makes our situation in the world smoother.

Then, at the other end of the "plains" test, we could set this passage from Henri Bosco's *Hyacinthe* (p. 18). "On the plains I am always elsewhere, in an elsewhere that is floating, fluid. Being for a long time absent from myself, and nowhere present, I am too inclined to attribute the inconsistency of my daydreams to the wide open spaces that induce them."

Many a nuance could be found between these two poles of domination and dispersion if the dreamer's mood, the seasons and the wind were taken into consideration. There would always be nuances, too, between dreamers who are calmed by plain country and those who are made uneasy by it, nuances that are all the more interesting to study since the plains are often thought of as representing a simplified world. One of the charms of the phenomenology of the poetic imagination is to be able to experience a fresh nuance in the presence of a spectacle that calls for uniformity, and can be summarized in a single idea. If the nuance is sincerely experienced by the poet, the phenomenologist is sure to obtain an image at its inception.

In a more elaborate inquiry than ours, one would have to show how all these nuances are integrated in the grandeur of the plain or the plateau, and tell, for instance, why a plateau daydream is never a daydream of the plains. This analysis is difficult because sometimes, a writer wants to describe, sometimes he knows already, in square miles, the extent of his solitude. In this case, we dream over a map, like a geographer. There is the example of Loti writing in the shade of a tree in Dakar, which was his home port: "Our eyes turned toward the interior of the country, we questioned the immense horizon of sand."[28] But this immense horizon of sand is a schoolboy's desert, the Sahara to be found in every school atlas.

The images of the desert in Philippe Diolé's excellent book, *Le plus beau désert du monde!*[29] are much more valuable to a phenomenologist. For here the immensity of a desert that has been experienced is expressed through inner intensity. As Philippe Diolé says—and he is a dream-haunted traveler—the desert must be lived "the way it is reflected in the wanderer." And Diolé invites us to a type of meditation in which, through a synthesis of opposites, we can experience *concentration of wandering*. For this writer, "these mountains in shreds, these dunes and dead rivers, these stones and this merciless sun," all the universe that bears the mark of the desert is "annexed to inner space." And through this annexation, the diversity of the images is unified in the depths of "inner space."[30] This is a conclusive formula for the demonstration I want to make on the correspondence between the immensity of world space and the depth of "inner space."

In Diolé's work, however, this interiorization of the desert does not correspond to a sense of inner emptiness. On the contrary, Diolé makes us experience a drama of images, the fundamental drama of the material images of water and drought. In fact, his "inner space" is an adherence to an inner substance. As it happens, he has had long, delightful experience of deepsea diving and, for him, the ocean has become a form of "space." At a little over 125 feet under the surface of the water, he discovered "absolute depth," depth that is beyond measuring, and would give no greater powers of dream and thought if it were doubled or even tripled. By means, then, of his diving experiences Diolé *really entered into the volume of the water*. And when we have read his earlier books and shared with him this conquest of the intimacy of water, we come to a point where we recognize in this space-substance, a one-dimensional space. One substance, one dimension. And we are so remote from the earth and life on earth, that this dimension of water bears the mark of limitlessness. To try and find high, low, right or left in a world that is so well unified by its substance is thinking, not living—thinking as formerly we did in life on earth; but it is not living in the new world conquered by diving. As for myself, before I read Diolé's books, I did not imagine that limitlessness could be attained so easily. It suffices to dream of pure depth, which needs no measuring, to exist.

But then, we ask, why did Diolé, who is a psychologist as well as an ontologist of under-seas human life, go into the desert? As a result of what cruel dialectics did he decide to leave limitless water for infinite sand? Diolé answers these questions as a poet would. He knows that each new contact with the cosmos renews our inner being, and that every new cosmos is open to us when we have freed ourselves from the ties of a former sensitivity. At the beginning of his book (loc. cit., p. 12), Diolé tells us that he had wanted to "terminate in the desert the magical operation that, in deep water, allows the diver to loosen the ordinary ties of time and space and make life resemble an obscure, inner poem."

At the end of his book, Diolé concludes (p. 178) that "to go down into the water, or to wander in the desert, is to change space," and by changing space, by leaving the space of one's usual sensibilities, one enters into communication with a space that is psychically innovating. "Neither in the desert nor on the bottom of the sea does one's spirit remain sealed and indivisible." This change of *concrete* space can no longer be a mere mental operation that could be compared with consciousness of geometrical relativity. For we do not change place, we change our nature.

But since these problems of the fusion of being in highly qualitative, concrete space are interesting for a phenomenology of the imagination—for one has to imagine very actively to experience new space—let us examine the hold that fundamental images have on this author. While in the desert, Diolé does not detach himself from the ocean and, in fact, desert space, far from contradicting deep-sea space, is expressed in Diolé's dreams in terms of water. Here we have a veritable drama of the material imagination born of the conflict of two such hostile elements as arid desert sand and water assured of its mass, without any compromise with pastiness or mud.

Indeed, this passage of Diolé's shows such sincerity of imagination that I have left it uncut (loc. cit., p. 118).

"I once wrote that a man who was familiar with the deep sea could never be like other men again. Such moments as this (in the midst of the desert) prove my statement. Because I realize that, as I walked along, my mind filled the desert landscape with water! In my imagination I flooded the space around me while walking through it. I lived in a sort of invented immersion in which I moved about in the heart of fluid, luminous, beneficent, dense matter, which was sea water, or rather the memory of sea water. This artifice sufficed to humanize for me a world that was dishearteningly dry, reconciling me with its rocks, its silence, its solitude, its sheet of sun gold hanging from the sky. Even my weariness was lessened by it. I dreamed that my bodily weight reposed on this imaginary water.

"I realize that this is not the first time that unconsciously, I have had recourse to this psychological defense. The silence and the slow progress I made in the Sahara awakened my memories of diving. My inner images were bathed then in a sort of gentleness, and in the passage thus reflected by dream, water appeared quite naturally. As I walked along, I bore within me gleaming reflections, and a translucent density, which were none other than memories of the deep sea."

Here Philippe Diolé gives us a psychological technique which permits us to be elsewhere, in an absolute elsewhere that bars the way to the forces that hold us imprisoned in the "here." This is not merely an escape into a space that is open to adventure on every side. With none of the machinery of screens and mirrors installed in the box that carried Cyrano to the Sun Empires, Diolé transports us to the elsewhere of another world. He does this, one might say, merely by means of a psychological machinery that brings into play the surest, the most powerful psychological laws. In fact, his only resources are the great, lasting realities that correspond to fundamental, material images; those that are at the basis of all imagination. Nothing, in other words, that is either chimerical or illusory.

Here both time and space are under the domination of the image. Elsewhere and formerly are stronger than the *hic et nunc.* The *being-here* is maintained by a being from elsewhere. Space, vast space, is the friend of being.

How much philosophers would learn, if they would consent to read the poets!

VIII

Since I have just taken two heroic images for discussion, the diving image and the image of the desert, both of which I can only experience in imagination, without ever being able to enrich them with any concrete experience, I shall close this chapter with an image that is nearer to me, one that I shall provide with all my memories of the plain. We shall see how a very special image can command and impose its law on space.

Faced with a quiet world, on a soothing plain, mankind can enjoy peace and repose. But in an imagined world, the sights of the plain often produce only the most commonplace effects. To restore their action to these sights, it is therefore necessary to supply a new image. An unexpected literary image can so move the spirit that it will follow the induction of tranquility. In fact, the literary image can make the spirit sufficiently sensitive to receive unbelievably fine impressions. Thus, in a remarkable passage, d'Annunzio[31] makes us see the look in the eyes of a trembling hare which, in one torment-free instant, projects peace over the entire autumnal world. He writes: "Did you ever see a hare in the morning, leave the freshly ploughed furrows, run a few seconds over the silvery frost, then stop in the silence, sit down on its hind legs, prick up its ears and look at the horizon? Its gaze seems to confer peace upon the entire universe. And it would be hard to think of a surer sign of deep peace than this motionless hare which, having declared a truce with its eternal disquiet, sits observing the steaming countryside. At this moment, it is a sacred animal, one that should be worshipped." The source of the calm that is going to cover the plain is clearly indicated: "Its gaze seems to confer peace upon the entire universe." The dreamer who lets his musings follow this line of vision will experience immensity of outspread fields in a higher key.

Such a passage in itself is a good test of rhetorical sensitivity. It faces the critical slaughter of apoetic minds with lamb-like calm. It is also very typical of d'Annunzio, and can be used as an example of this writer's cumbersome metaphors. It would be so simple, positivist minds object, to describe pastoral peace *directly!* Why choose a contemplative hare as go-between? But a poet disregards this reasoning. He wants to give all the degrees of growing contemplation, all the instants of the image, and to begin with, the instant when animal peace becomes identified with world peace. Here we are made aware of the function of a seeing eye that, having nothing to do, has ceased to look at anything in particular, and is looking *at the world.* We should not have been so radically thrown back into primitiveness if the poet had told us something of his own contemplation. This, however, would be merely repetition of a philosophical theme. But d'Annunzio's animal is freed from its reflexes for an instant: its eye is no longer on the look-out, no longer a rivet of the animal machine; its eye does not command flight. Yes, this look, in an animal that is all fear, is the sacred instant of contemplation.

A few lines earlier, pursuing an inversion that expresses the dualism of observer—observed, this poet had seen in the hare's fine, large, tranquil eyes the aquatic nature of the gaze of a vegetarian animal: "These large, moist eyes ... are as beautiful as ponds on summer evenings, with their rushes bathing in water that mirrors and transfigures the entire sky." In my book entitled *L'eau et les rêves*, I collected many other literary images in which the pond is the very eye of the landscape, the reflection in water the first view that the universe has of itself, and the heightened beauty of a reflected landscape presented as the very root of cosmic narcissism. In *Walden*, Thoreau followed this enlargement of images quite naturally. "A lake is the landscape's most beautiful and expressive feature. It is earth's eye; looking into which the beholder measures the depth of his own nature."[32]

And, once more, the dialectics of immensity and depth is revived. It is hard to say where the two hyperboles begin; the one of the too sharp eye, and the other of the landscape that sees itself confusedly under the heavy lids of its stagnant water. But any doctrine of the imaginary is necessarily a philosophy of excess, and all images are destined to be enlarged.

A contemporary poet uses more restraint, but he says quite as much as in this line by Jean Lescure:

J'habite la tranquillité des feuilles, l'été grandit

(I live in the tranquility of leaves, summer is growing.)

Tranquil foliage that really is lived in, a tranquil gaze discovered in the humblest of eyes, are the artisans of immensity. These images make the world grow, and the summer too. At certain hours poetry gives out waves of calm. From being imagined, calm becomes an emergence of being. It is like a value that dominates, in spite of minor states of being, in spite of a disturbed world. Immensity has been magnified through contemplation. And the contemplative attitude is such a great human value that it confers immensity upon an impression that a psychologist would have every reason to declare ephemeral and special. But poems are human realities; it is not enough to resort to "impressions" in order to explain them. They must be lived in their poetic immensity.

9

THE DIALECTICS OF
OUTSIDE AND INSIDE

Les geographies solennelles des limites humaines . . .
PAUL ELUARD, Les yeux fertiles, p. 42

(The solemn geographies of human limits)

Car nous sommes où nous ne sommes pas.
PIERRE-JEAN JOUVE, Lyrique, p. 59

(For we are where we are not.)

Une des maximes d'éducation pratique qui ont régi mon enfance: "Ne mange pas la bouche ouverte."
COLETTE, Prisons et paradis, p. 79

(One of the maxims of practical education that governed my childhood: "Don't eat with your mouth open.")

I

Outside and inside form a dialectic of division, the obvious geometry of which blinds us as soon as we bring it into play in metaphorical domains. It has the sharpness of the dialectics of *yes* and *no*, which decides everything. Unless one is careful, it is made into a basis of images that govern all thoughts of positive and negative. Logicians draw circles that overlap or exclude each

other, and all their rules immediately become clear. Philosophers, when confronted with outside and inside, think in terms
of being and non-being. Thus profound metaphysics is rooted in
an implicit geometry which—whether we will or no—confers
spatiality upon thought; if a metaphysician could not draw, what
would he think? Open and closed, for him, are thoughts. They
are metaphors that he attaches to everything, even to his systems. In a lecture given by Jean Hyppolite on the subtle structure
of denegation (which is quite different from the simple structure
of negation) Hyppolite spoke[1] of "a first myth of outside and
inside." And he added: "You feel the full significance of this
myth of outside and inside in alienation, which is founded on
these two terms. Beyond what is expressed in their formal opposition lie alienation and hostility between the two." And so, simple geometrical opposition becomes tinged with aggressivity.
Formal opposition is incapable of remaining calm. It is obsessed
by the myth. But this action of the myth throughout the immense
domain of imagination and expression should not be studied by
attributing to it the false light of geometrical intuitions.[2]

"This side" and "beyond" are faint repetitions of the dialectics of inside and outside: everything takes form, even infinity.
We seek to determine being and, in so doing, transcend all
situations, to give a situation of all situations. Man's being is
confronted with the world's being, as though primitivity could
be easily arrived at. The dialectics of *here* and *there* has been
promoted to the rank of an absolutism according to which
these unfortunate adverbs of place are endowed with unsuper-
vised powers of ontological determination. Many metaphysical systems would need mapping. But in philosophy, all
short-cuts are costly, and philosophical knowledge cannot
advance from schematized experiments.

II

I should like to examine a little more closely this geometrical
cancerization of the linguistic tissue of contemporary philosophy.

For it does indeed seem as though an artificial syntax welded adverbs and verbs together in such a way as to form excrescences. By multiplying hyphens, this syntax obtains words that are sentences in themselves, in which the outside features blend with the inside. Philosophical language is becoming a language of agglutination.

Sometimes, on the contrary, instead of becoming welded together, words loosen their intimate ties. Prefixes and suffixes—especially prefixes—become unwelded: they want to think for themselves. Because of this, words are occasionally thrown out of balance. Where is the main stress, for instance, in *being-there* (*être-là*): on *being,* or on *there?* In *there*—which it would be better to call *here*—shall I first look for my being? Or am I going to find, in my being, above all, certainty of my fixation in a *there?* In any case, one of these terms always weakens the other. Often the *there* is spoken so forcefully that the ontological aspects of the problems under consideration are sharply summarized in a geometrical fixation. The result is dogmatization of philosophemes as soon as they are expressed. In the tonal quality of the French language, the *là* (there) is so forceful, that to designate being (*l'être*) by *être-là* is to point an energetic forefinger that might easily relegate intimate being to an exteriorized place.

But why be in such a hurry to make these first designations? One has the impression that metaphysicians have stopped taking time to think. To make a study of being, in my opinion, it is preferable to follow all the ontological deviations of the various experiences of being. For, in reality, the experiences of being that might justify "geometrical" expression are among the most indigent . . . In French, one should think twice before speaking of *l'être-là*. Entrapped in being, we shall always have to come out of it. And when we are hardly outside of being, we always have to go back into it. Thus, in being, everything is circuitous, roundabout, recurrent, so much talk; a chaplet of sojournings, a refrain with endless verses.

But what a spiral man's being represents![3] And what a number of invertible dynamisms there are in this spiral! One no longer knows *right away* whether one is running toward the center or escaping. Poets are well acquainted with the existence of this hesitation of being, as exemplified in this poem by Jean Tardieu:

> *Pour avancer je tourne sur moi-même*
> *Cyclone par l'immobile habité.*
>
> JEAN TARDIEU,
> *Les témoins invisibles*, p. 36

(In order to advance, I walk the treadmill of myself
Cyclone inhabited by immobility.)

Mais au-dedans, plus de frontières!

(But within, no more boundaries!)

Thus, the spiraled being who, from outside, appears to be a well-invested center, will never reach his center. The being of man is an unsettled being which all expression unsettles. In the reign of the imagination, an expression is hardly *proposed*, before being needs another expression, before it must be the being of another expression.

In my opinion, verbal conglomerates should be avoided. There is no advantage to metaphysics for its thinking to be cast in the molds of linguistic fossils. On the contrary, it should benefit by the extreme mobility of modern languages and, at the same time, remain in the homogeneity of a mother tongue; which is what real poets have always done.

To benefit by all the lessons of modern psychology and all that has been learned about man's being through psychoanalysis, metaphysics should therefore be resolutely discursive. It should beware of the privileges of evidence that are the property of geometrical intuition. Sight says too many things at one time. Being does not see itself. Perhaps it listens to itself. It does not stand out, it is not *bordered* by nothingness: one is never sure of finding it, or of finding it solid, when one approaches a center of being. And if we want to determine man's being, we are never sure of being closer to ourselves if we "withdraw" into ourselves, if we move toward the center of the spiral; for often it is in the

heart of being that being is errancy. Sometimes, it is in being outside itself that being tests consistencies. Sometimes, too, it is
closed in, as it were, on the outside. Later, I shall give a poetic
text in which the prison is on the outside.

If we multiplied images, taking them in the domains of
lights and sounds, of heat and cold, we should prepare a slower
ontology, but doubtless one that is more certain than the ontology that reposes upon geometrical images.

I have wanted to make these general remarks because, from
the point of view of geometrical expressions, the dialectics of
outside and inside is supported by a reinforced geometrism, in
which limits are barriers. We must be free as regards all *definitive* intuitions—and geometrism records definitive intuitions—
if we are to follow the daring of poets (as we shall do later)
who invite us to the finesses of experience of intimacy, to
"escapades" of imagination.

First of all, it must be noted that the two terms "outside"
and "inside" pose problems of metaphysical anthropology
that are not symmetrical. To make inside concrete and outside
vast is the first task, the first problem, it would seem, of an
anthropology of the imagination. But between concrete and
vast, the opposition is not a true one. At the slightest touch,
asymmetry appears. And it is always like that: inside and outside do not receive in the same way the qualifying epithets that
are the measure of our adherence. Nor can one *live* the qualifying epithets attached to inside and outside in the same way.
Everything, even size, is a human value, and we have already
shown, in a preceding chapter, that miniature can accumulate
size. It is *vast* in its way.

In any case, inside and outside, as experienced by the imagination, can no longer be taken in their simple reciprocity; consequently, by omitting geometrical references when we speak
of the first expressions of being, by choosing more concrete,
more phenomenologically exact inceptions, we shall come to
realize that the dialectics of inside and outside multiply with
countless diversified nuances.

Pursuing my usual method, I should like to discuss my thesis on the basis of an example of concrete poetics, for which I

shall ask a poet to provide an image that is sufficiently new in its *nuance of being* to furnish a lesson in ontological amplification. Through the newness of the image and through its amplification, we shall be sure to reverberate above, or on the margin of reasonable certainties.

III

In a prose poem entitled *L'espace aux ombres* Henri Michaux writes:[4]

> *L'espace, mais vous ne pouvez concevoir, cet horrible en dedans-en dehors qu'est le vrai espace.*
>
> *Certaines (ombres) surtout se bandant une dernière fois, font un effort désespéré pour "être dans leur seule unité." Mal leur en prend. J'en rencontrai une.*
>
> *Détruite par châtiment, elle n'était plus qu'un bruit, mais énorme.*
>
> *Un monde immense l'entendait encore, mais elle n'était plus, devenue seulement et uniquement un bruit, qui allait rouler encore des siècles mais destiné à s'éteindre complètement, comme si elle n'avait jamais été.*

SHADE-HAUNTED SPACE

> (Space, but you cannot even conceive the horrible inside-outside that real space is.
>
> Certain (shades) especially, girding their loins one last time, make a desperate effort to "exist as a single unity." But they rue the day. I met one of them.
>
> Destroyed by punishment, it was reduced to a noise, a thunderous noise.
>
> An immense world still heard it, but it no longer existed, having become simply and solely a noise, which was to rumble on for centuries longer, but was fated to die out *completely*, as though it had never existed.)

If we examine closely the lesson in philosophy the poet gives us, we shall find in this passage a spirit that has lost its "being-there" (*être-là*), one that has so declined as to fall from *the being of its shade* and mingle with the rumors of being, in the form of meaningless noise, of a confused hum that *cannot be located*. It once was. But wasn't it merely the noise that it has become? Isn't its punishment the fact of having become the mere echo of the meaningless, useless noise it once was? Wasn't it formerly what it is now: a sonorous echo from the vaults of hell? It is condemned to repeat the word of its evil intention, a word which, being imprinted in being, has overthrown being.[5] And we are in hell, and a part of us is always in hell, walled-up, as we are, in the world of evil intentions. Through what naïve intuition do we locate evil, which is boundless, in a hell? This spirit, this shade, this noise of a shade which, the poet tells us, desires its unity, may be heard on the outside without it being possible to be sure that it is inside. In this "horrible inside-outside" of unuttered words and unfulfilled intentions, within itself, being is slowly digesting its nothingness. The process of its reduction to nothing will last "for centuries." The hum of the being of rumors continues both in time and in space. In vain the spirit gathers its remaining strength. It has become the backwash of expiring being. Being is alternately condensation that disperses with a burst, and dispersion that flows back to a center. Outside and inside are both intimate—they are always ready to be reversed, to exchange their hostility. If there exists a border-line surface between such an inside and outside, this surface is painful on both sides. When we experience this passage by Henri Michaux, we absorb a mixture of being and nothingness. The center of "being-there" wavers and trembles. Intimate space loses its clarity, while exterior space loses its void, void being the raw material of possibility of being. We are banished from the realm of possibility.

In this drama of intimate geometry, where should one live? The philosopher's advice to withdraw into oneself in order to take one's place in existence loses its value, and even its significance, when the supplest image of "being-there" has just been experienced through the ontological nightmare of this poet. Let us observe, however, that this nightmare is not visually frightening. The fear does not come from the outside. Nor is it composed of old memories. It has no past, no physiology. Nothing in common, either, with having one's breath taken away. Here fear is being itself. Where can one flee, where find refuge? In what shelter can one take refuge? Space is nothing but a "horrible outside-inside."

And the nightmare is simple, because it is radical. It would be intellectualizing the experience if we were to say that the nightmare is the result of a sudden doubt as to the certainty of inside and the distinctness of outside. What Michaux gives us as an a priori of being is the entire space-time of ambiguous being. In this ambiguous space, the mind has lost its geometrical homeland and the spirit is drifting.

Undoubtedly, we do not have to pass through the narrow gate of such a poem. The philosophies of anguish want principles that are less simplified. They do not turn their attention to the activity of an ephemeral imagination, for the reason that they inscribed anguish in the heart of being long before images had given it reality. Philosophers treat themselves to anguish, and all they see in the images are manifestations of its causality. They are not at all concerned with living the being of the image. Phenomenology of the imagination must assume the task of seizing this ephemeral being. In fact, phenomenology can learn from the very brevity of the image. What strikes us here is that the metaphysical aspect originates on the very level of the image, on the level of an image which disturbs the notions of a spatiality commonly considered to be able to reduce these disturbances and restore the mind to a statute of indifference to space that does not have to localize dramatic events.

Personally, I welcome this poet's image as a little piece of experimental folly, like a virtual grain of hashish without which it is impossible to enter into the reign of the imagination. And how should one receive an exaggerated image, if not by exaggerating it a little more, by personalizing the exaggeration? The phenomenological gain appears right away: in prolonging *exaggeration,* we may have the good fortune to avoid the habits of *reduction*. With space images, we are in a region where reduction is easy, commonplace. There will always be someone who will do away with all complications and oblige us to leave as soon as there is mention of space—whether figurative or not—or of the opposition of outside and inside. But if reduction is easy, exaggeration is all the more interesting, from the standpoint of phenomenology. This problem is very favorable, it seems to me, for marking the opposition between reflexive reduction and pure imagination. However, the direction of psychoanalytical interpretation—which is more liberal than classical literary criticism—follows the diagram of reduction. Only phenomenology makes it a principle to examine and test the psychological being of an image, before any reduction is undertaken. The dialectics of the dynamisms of reduction and exaggeration can throw light on the dialectics of psychoanalysis and phenomenology. It is, of course, phenomenology which gives us the psychic positivity of the image. Let us therefore transform our amazement into admiration. We can even begin by admiring. Then, later, we shall see whether or not it will be necessary to organize our disappointment through criticism and reduction. To benefit from this active, immediate admiration, one has only to follow the positive impulse of exaggeration. Here I read Michaux's poem over and over, and I accept it as a phobia of inner space, as though hostile remoteness had already become oppressive in the tiny cell represented by inner space. With this poem, Henri Michaux has juxtaposed in us claustrophobia and agoraphobia; he has aggravated the line of demarcation between outside and inside. But in doing so, from the psychological standpoint, he has demolished the lazy certainties of the geometrical intuitions by means of which psychologists sought to govern the space of intimacy. Even figuratively, nothing that concerns intimacy can be shut in, nor is it possible to fit into one another, for purposes of designating depth, impressions that continue to *surge up*. A fine example of phenomenological notation may be seen in the following simple line by a symbolist poet: "The pansy took on new life when it became a corolla . . ."[6]

A philosopher of the imagination, therefore, should follow the poet to the ultimate extremity of his images, without ever reducing this extremism, which is the specific phenomenon of the poetic impulse. In a letter to Clara Rilke, Rilke wrote: "Works of art always spring from those who have faced the danger, gone to the very end of an experience, to the point beyond which no human being can go. The further one dares to go, the more decent, the more personal, the more unique a life becomes."[7] But is it necessary to go and look for "danger" other than the danger of writing, of expressing oneself? Doesn't the poet put language in danger? Doesn't he utter words that are dangerous? Hasn't the fact that, for so long, poetry has been the echo of heartache, given it a pure dramatic tonality? When we really live a poetic image, we learn to know, in one of its tiny fibers, a becoming of being that is an awareness of the *being's inner disturbance*. Here being is so sensitive that it is upset by a word. In the same letter, Rilke adds: "This sort of derangement, which is peculiar to us, must go into our work."

Exaggeration of images is in fact so *natural* that however original a poet may be, one often finds the same impulse in another poet. Certain images used by Jules Supervielle, for instance, may be compared with the Michaux image we have just been studying. Supervielle also juxtaposes claustrophobia and agoraphobia when he writes: "*Trop d'espace nous etouffe beaucoup plus que s'il n'y en avait pas assez.*"[8] (Too much space smothers us much more than if there were not enough.)

Supervielle is also familiar with "exterior dizziness" (loc. cit., p. 21). And elsewhere he speaks of "interior immensity." Thus the two spaces of inside and outside exchange their dizziness.

In another text by Supervielle, which Christian Sénéchal points out in his book on Supervielle, *the prison is outside*. After endless rides on the South American pampas, Supervielle wrote: "Precisely because of too much riding and too much freedom, and of the unchanging horizon, in spite of our desperate gallopings, the pampa assumed the aspect of a prison for me, a prison that was bigger than the others."

IV

If, through poetry, we restore to the activity of language its free field of expression, we are obliged to supervise the use of fossilized metaphors. For instance, when open and closed are to play a metaphorical rôle, shall we harden or soften the metaphor? Shall we repeat with the logicians that a door must be open or closed? And shall we find in this maxim an instrument that is really effective for analyzing human passions? In any case, such tools for analysis should be sharpened each time they are used. Each metaphor must be restored to its surface nature; it must be brought up out of habit of expression to actuality of expression. For it is dangerous, in expressing oneself, to be "all roots."

The phenomenology of the poetic imagination allows us to explore the being of man considered as the being of a *surface,* of the surface that separates the region of the same from the region of the other. It should not be forgotten that in this zone of sensitized surface, before being, one must speak, if not to others, at least to oneself. And advance always. In this orientation, the universe of speech governs all the phenomena of being, that is, the new phenomena. By means of poetic language, waves of newness flow over the surface of being. And language bears within itself the dialectics of open and closed. Through *meaning* it encloses, while through poetic expression, it opens up.

It would be contrary to the nature of my inquiries to summarize them by means of radical formulas, by defining the being of man, for instance, as the being of an ambiguity. I only know how to work with a philosophy of detail. Then, on the surface of being, in that region where being *wants* to be both visible and hidden, the movements of opening and closing are so numerous, so frequently inverted, and so charged with hesitation, that we could conclude on the following formula: man is half-open being.

V

But how many daydreams we should have to analyze under the simple heading of Doors! For the door is an entire cosmos of the Half-open. In fact, it is one of its primal images, the very origin of a daydream that accumulates desires and temptations: the temptation to open up the ultimate depths of being, and the desire to conquer all reticent beings. The door schematizes two strong possibilities, which sharply classify two types of daydream. At times, it is closed, bolted, padlocked. At others, it is open, that is to say, wide open.

But then come the hours of greater imagining sensibility. On May nights, when so many doors are closed, there is one that is just barely ajar. We have only to give it a very slight push! The hinges have been well oiled. And our fate becomes visible.

And how many doors were doors of hesitation! In *La romance du retour,* by Jean Pellerin, this tender, delicate poet wrote:[9]

> *La porte me flaire, elle hésite.*

> (The door scents me, it hesitates.)

In this verse, so much psychism is transferred to the object that a reader who attaches importance to objectivity will see in it mere brain-play. If such a document had its source in some remote mythology, we should find it more readily acceptable. But why not take the poet's verse as a small element of spontaneous mythology? Why not sense that, incarnated in the door, there is a little threshold god? And there is no need to return to a distant past, a past that is no longer our own, to find sacred properties attributed to the threshold. In the third century, Porphyrus wrote: "A threshold is a sacred thing."[10] But even if erudition did not permit us to refer to such a sacralization, why should we not react to sacralization through poetry, through a poem of our own time, tinged with fantasy, perhaps, but which is in harmony with primal values.

Another poet, with no thought of Zeus, discovered the majesty of the threshold within himself and wrote the following:

> *Je me surprends à définir le seuil*
> *Comme étant le lieu géométrique*
> *Des arrivées et des départs*
> *Dans la Maison du Père.*[11]

(I find myself defining threshold
As being the geometrical place
Of the comings and goings
In my Father's House.)

And what of all the doors of mere curiosity, that have tempted being for nothing, for emptiness, for an unknown that is not even imagined?

Is there one of us who hasn't in his memories a Bluebeard chamber that should not have been opened, even half-way? Or—which is the same thing for a philosophy that believes in the primacy of the imagination—that should not even have been imagined open, or capable of opening half-way?

How concrete everything becomes in the world of the spirit when an object, a mere door, can give images of hesitation, temptation, desire, security, welcome and respect. If one were to give an account of all the doors one has closed and opened, of all the doors one would like to re-open, one would have to tell the story of one's entire life.

But is he who opens a door and he who closes it the same being? The gestures that make us conscious of security or freedom are rooted in a profound depth of being. Indeed, it is because of this "depth" that they become so normally symbolical. Thus René Char takes as the theme of one of his poems this sentence by Albert the Great: "In Germany there once lived twins, one of whom opened doors by touching them with his right arm, and the other who closed them by touching them with his left arm." A legend like this, treated by a poet, is naturally not a mere reference. It helps the poet sensitize the world at hand, and refine the symbols of everyday life. The old legend becomes quite new when the poet makes it his own. He knows that there are two "beings" in a door, that a door awakens in us a two-way dream, that it is doubly symbolical.

And then, onto what, toward what, do doors open? Do they open for the world of men, or for the world of solitude? Ramon Gomez de la Serna wrote: "Doors that open on the countryside seem to confer freedom behind the world's back."[12]

VI

As soon as the word *in* appears in an expression, people are inclined not to take literally the *reality of the expression*, and they translate what they believe to be figurative language into reasonable language. It is not easy for me, indeed it seems futile, to follow, for instance, the poet—I shall furnish documentation on the subject—who says that the house of the past is alive in his own head. I immediately interpret: the poet simply wants to say that an old memory has been preserved *in* his mind. The exaggerated nature of the image that seeks to upset the relationship of contained to container makes us shrink in the presence of what can appear to be mental derangement of images. We should be more indulgent if we were reading a fever chart. By following the labyrinth of fever that runs through the body, by exploring the "seats of fever," or the pains that inhabit a hollow tooth, we should learn that the imagination localizes suffering and creates and recreates imaginary anatomies. But I shall not use in this work the numerous documents that psychiatry provides. I prefer to underline my break with causalism by rejecting all organic causality. For my problem is to discuss the images of a pure, free imagination, a liberating imagination that has no connection with organic incitements.

These documents of absolute poetics exist. The poet does not shrink before reversals of dovetailings. Without even thinking that he is scandalizing reasonable men, contrary to the most ordinary common sense, he actually experiences reversal of dimensions or inversion of the perspective of inside and outside.

The abnormal nature of the image does not mean that it is artificially produced, for the imagination is the most natural of faculties. No doubt the images I plan to examine could not figure in a psychology of projects, even of *imaginary projects*. For every project is a contexture of images and thoughts that supposes a grasp of reality. We need not consider it, consequently, in a doctrine of pure imagination. It is even useless to *continue* an image, or to *maintain* it. All we want is for it to exist.

Let us study then, in all phenomenological simplicity, the documents furnished by poets.

In his book: *Où boivent les loups*, Tristan Tzara writes (p. 24):

> *Une lente humilité pénètre dans la chambre*
> *Qui habite en moi dans la paume du repos*

> (A slow humility penetrates the room
> That dwells in me in the palm of repose.)

In order to derive benefit from the oneirism of such an image, one must no doubt first place oneself "in the palm of repose," that is, withdraw into oneself, and condense oneself in the being of a repose, which is the asset one has most easily "at hand." Then the great stream of simple humility that is in the silent room flows into ourselves. The intimacy of the room becomes our intimacy. And correlatively, intimate space has become so quiet, so simple, that all the quietude of the room is localized and centralized in it. The room is very deeply our room, it is in us. We no longer *see* it. It no longer *limits* us, because we are in the very ultimate depth of its repose, in the repose that it has conferred upon us. And all our former rooms come and fit into this one. How simple everything is!

In another passage, which is even more enigmatic for the reasonable mind, but quite as clear for anyone who senses the topoanalytical inversions of images, Tzara writes:

> *Le marché du soleil est entré dans la chambre*
> *Et la chambre dans la tête bourdonnante.*

> (The market of the sun has come into my room
> And the room into my buzzing head.)

In order to accept and hear this image, one must experience the strange whir of the sun as it comes into a room in which one is alone, for it is a fact that the first ray *strikes* the wall.

These sounds will be heard also—over and beyond the fact—by those who know that every one of the sun's rays carries with it bees. Then everything starts buzzing and one's head is a hive, the hive of the sounds of the sun.

To begin with, Tzara's image was overcharged with surrealism. But if we overcharge it still more, if we increase the charge of image, if we go beyond the barriers set up by criticism, then we really enter into the surrealistic action of a pure image. And the exaggerated nature of the image is thus proved to be active and communicable, this means that it started well: the sunny room is buzzing *in* the head of the dreamer.

A psychologist will say that all my analysis does is to relate daring, too daring, "associations." And a psychoanalyst will agree perhaps to "analyze" this daring; he is accustomed to doing this. Both of them, if they take the image as symptomatic, will try to find reasons and causes for it. A phenomenologist has a different approach. He takes the image just as it is, just as the poet created it, and tries to make it his own, to feed on this rare fruit. He brings the image to the very limit of what he is able to imagine. However far from being a poet he himself may be, he tries to repeat its creation for himself and, if possible, continue its exaggeration. Here association ceases to be fortuitous, but is sought after, willed. It is a poetic, specifically poetic, constitution. It is sublimation that is entirely rid of the organic or psychic weights from which one wanted to be free. In other words, it corresponds to pure sublimation.

Of course, such an image is not received in the same way every day. Psychically speaking, it is never objective. Other commentaries could renew it. Also, to receive it properly, one should be in the felicitous mood of super-imagination.

Once we have been touched by the grace of super-imagination, we feel it in the presence of the simpler images through which the exterior world deposits virtual elements of highly-colored space in the heart of our being. The image with which Pierre-Jean Jouve *constitutes* his secret being is one of these. He places it in his most intimate cell:

La cellule de moi-même emplit d'étonnement
La muraille peinte à la chaux de mon secret.

(*Les noces,* p. 50)

(The cell of myself fills with wonder
The white-washed wall of my secret.)

The room in which the poet pursues such a dream as this is
probably not "white-washed." But this room in which he is writing is so quiet, that it really deserves its name, which is, the "solitary" room! It is inhabited thanks to the image, just as one
inhabits an image which is "in the imagination." Here the poet
inhabits the cellular image. This image does not transpose a reality. It would be ridiculous, in fact, to ask the dreamer its dimensions. It does not lend itself to geometrical intuition, but is a solid
framework for secret being. And secret being feels that it is
guarded more by the whiteness of the lime-wash than by the
strong walls. The cell of the secret is white. A single value suffices
to coordinate any number of dreams. And it is always like that,
the poetic image is under the domination of a heightened quality.
The whiteness of the walls, alone, protects the dreamer's *cell*. It is
stronger than all geometry. It is a part of the cell of intimacy.

Such images lack stability. As soon as we depart from
expression as it is, as the author gives it, in all spontaneity, we
risk relapsing into literal meaning. We also risk being bored by
writing that is incapable of condensing the intimacy of the
image. And we have to withdraw deep into ourselves, for
instance, to read this fragment by Maurice Blanchot in the
tonality of being in which it was written: "About this room,
which was plunged in utter darkness, I knew everything, I had
entered into it, I bore it within me, I made it live, with a life
that is not life, but which is stronger than life, and which no
force in the world can vanquish."[13] One feels in these repetitions, or to be more exact, in this constant strengthening of an
image into which one has entered (and not of a room into
which one has entered, a room which the author bears within
himself, and which he has made live with a life that does not

exist in life), one feels, as I said, that it is not the writer's intention merely to describe his *familiar* abode. Memory would *encumber* this image by stocking it with *composite memories* from several periods of time. Here everything is simpler, more radically simple. Blanchot's room is an abode of intimate space, it is his inner room. We share the writer's image, thanks to what we are obliged to call a *general image,* that is, an image which participation keeps us from confusing with a *generality.* We individualize this general image right away. We live in it, we enter into it the way Blanchot enters into his. Neither word nor idea suffices, the writer must help us to reverse space, and shun description, in order to have a more valid experience of the hierarchy of repose.

Often it is from the very fact of concentration in the most restricted intimate space that the dialectics of inside and outside draws its strength. One feels this elasticity in the following passage by Rilke:[14] "And there is almost no space here; and you feel almost calm at the thought that it is impossible for anything very large to hold in this narrowness." There is consolation in knowing that one is in an atmosphere of calm, in a narrow space. Rilke achieved this narrowness intimately, in inner space where everything is commensurate with inner being. Then, in the next sentence, the text continues dialectically: "But outside, everything is immeasurable. And when the level rises outside, it also rises in you, not in the vessels that are partially controlled by you, or in the phlegm of your most unimpressionable organs: but it grows in the capillary veins, drawn upward into the furthermost branches of your infinitely ramified existence. This is where it rises, where it overflows from you, higher than your respiration, and, as a final resort, you take refuge, as though on the tip of your breath. Ah! where, where next? Your heart banishes you from yourself, your heart pursues you, and you are already almost beside yourself, and you can't stand it any longer. Like a beetle that has been stepped on, you flow from yourself, and your lack of hardness or elasticity means nothing any more.

"Oh night without objects. Oh window muffled on the outside, oh, doors carefully closed; customs that have come down from times long past, transmitted, verified, never entirely understood. Oh silence in the stair-well, silence in the adjoining rooms, silence up there, on the ceiling. Oh mother, oh one and only you, who faced all this silence, when I was a child."

I have given this long passage without cuts for the reason that it has dynamic continuity. Inside and outside are not abandoned to their geometrical opposition. From what overflow of a ramified interior does the substance of being run, does the outside call? Isn't the exterior an old intimacy lost in the shadow of memory? In what silence does the stair-well resound? In this silence there are soft foot-steps: the mother comes back to watch over her child, as she once did. She restores to all these confused, unreal sounds their concrete, familiar meaning. Limitless night ceases to be empty space. This passage by Rilke, which is assailed by such frights, finds its peace. But by what a long, circuitous route! In order to experience it in the reality of the images, one would have to remain the contemporary of an osmosis between intimate and undetermined space.

I have presented texts that were as varied as possible, in order to show that there exists a play of values, which makes everything in the category of simple determinations fall into second place. The opposition of outside and inside ceases to have as coefficient its geometrical evidence.

To conclude this chapter, I shall consider a fragment in which Balzac defines determined opposition in the face of affronted space. This text is all the more interesting in that Balzac felt obliged to correct it.

In an early version of *Louis Lambert*, we read: "When he used his entire strength, he grew unaware, as it were, of his physical life, and only existed through the all-powerful play of his interior organs, the range of which he constantly maintained and, according to his own admirable expression, he made *space withdraw before his advance*."[15]

In the final version, we read simply: "He left space, as he said, behind him."

What a difference between these two movements of expression! What decline of power of being faced with space, between

the first and second forms! In fact, one is puzzled that Balzac
should have made such a correction. He returned, in other
words, to "indifferent space." In a meditation on the subject of
being, one usually puts space between parentheses, in other
words, one leaves space "behind one." As a sign of the lost
"tonalization" of being, it should be noted that "admiration"
subsided. The second mode of expression is no longer, according to the author's own admission, *admirable*. Because it really
was admirable, this power to make *space withdraw*, to put
space, all space, outside, in order that meditating being might
be free to think.

10

THE PHENOMENOLOGY
OF ROUNDNESS

I

When metaphysicians speak briefly, they can reach immediate truth, a truth that, in due course, would yield to proof. Metaphysicians, then, may be compared and associated with poets who, in a single verse, can lay bare a truth concerning inner man. The following concise statement is taken from Karl Jaspers' thick volume entitled *Von der Wahrheit* (p. 50): "Jedes Dasein scheint in sich rund." (Every being seems in itself round.) In support of this unsubstantiated metaphysician's truth, I should like to present several texts formulated in schools of thought that are all oriented differently from metaphysical thought.

Thus, without commentary, Van Gogh wrote: "Life is probably *round*."

And Joë Bousquet, with no knowledge of Van Gogh's sentence, wrote: "He had been told that life was beautiful. No! Life is round."[1]

Lastly, I should like to know where La Fontaine said: "A walnut makes me quite round."

With these four texts of such different origin, it seems to me that here we have the phenomenological problem very clearly posed. It should be solved by enriching it with further examples to which we should add other data, taking care to conserve their nature of intimate data, independent of all knowledge of the outside world. Such data as these can receive nothing from the outside world but *illustrations*. We must even be careful lest the too vivid colors of the illustration make the *being of the image* lose its original light. Here the average psychologist can do nothing but abstain from action, since the perspective of psychological research must be reversed. Such images cannot be justified by perception. Nor can they be taken for metaphors as, for instance, when we say of a man who is simple and frank, that he is: "*tout rond*."[2] This roundness of a being, or of being, that Jaspers speaks of cannot appear in its direct truth otherwise than in the purest sort of phenomenological meditation.

Nor can such images as these be transported into just any consciousness. No doubt there are those who will want to "understand," whereas the image must first be taken at its inception. Others will declare ostentatiously that they do not understand, and will object that life itself is certainly not spherical. They will express surprise that this being we seek to characterize in its intimate truth should be so ingenuously handed over to geometricians, whose thinking is exterior thinking. From every side, objections accumulate to put a quick end to the discussion. And yet the expressions I have just noted are there. They are there, in relief, in everyday language, implying meanings of their own. They do not come from immoderateness of language, any more than they do from linguistic clumsiness. They are not born of a desire to astonish others. In fact, despite their extraordinary nature, they bear the mark of primitivity. They suddenly appear and, in a twinkling, they are completed. This is why, from my standpoint, these expressions are marvels of phenomenology. In order to judge them, and to like and make them our own, they oblige us to take a phenomenological attitude.

These images blot out the world, and they have no past. They do not stem from any earlier experience. We can be quite sure that they are metapsychological. They give us a lesson in solitude. For a brief instant we must take them for ourselves alone. If we take them in their suddenness, we realize that we think of nothing else, that we are entirely in the being of this expression. If we submit to the hypnotic power of such expressions, suddenly we find ourselves entirely in the roundness of this being, we live in the roundness of life, like a walnut that becomes round in its shell. A philosopher, a painter, a poet and an inventor of fables have given us documents of pure phenomenology. It is up to us now to use them in order to learn how to gather being together in its center. It is our task, too, to sensitize the document by multiplying its variations.

II

Before giving additional examples, I believe that it would be advisable to reduce Jaspers' formula by one word, in order to make it phenomenologically purer. I should say, therefore: *das Dasein ist rund*, being is round. Because to add that it *seems round* is to keep a doublet of being and appearance, when we mean the entire being in its roundness. In fact, it is not a question of observing, but of experiencing being in its immediacy. Full contemplation would divide into the observing being and being observed. In the limited domain in which we are working, phenomenology must do away with all intermediaries, all additional functions. Consequently, in order to obtain maximum phenomenological purity, we must divest Jaspers' formula of everything that could conceal its ontological value. This condition is necessary if the formula "being is round" is to become an instrument that will allow us to recognize the primitivity of certain images of being. I repeat, images of *full roundness* help us to collect ourselves, permit us to confer an initial constitution on ourselves, and to confirm our being intimately, inside. For when it is experienced from the inside, devoid of all exterior features, being cannot be otherwise than round.

Is this the moment to recall pre-Socratic philosophy, to refer to Parmenidian being and the "sphere" of Parmenides? Or, to speak more generally, can philosophical culture be the propaedeutics to phenomenology? It does not seem so. Philosophy introduces us to ideas that are too well coordinated for us to examine and re-examine them, detail after detail, as the phenomenologist must from the beginning. If a phenomenology of the logical sequence of ideas is possible, it must be acknowledged that this could not be an elementary phenomenology. In a phenomenology of the imagination, however, we receive a benefit of elementariness. An image that is worked over loses its initial virtues. Parmenides' "sphere" has played too important a rôle for his image to have retained its primitivity. Consequently, it could not be the tool required for our research on the subject of the primitivity of images of being. It would be hard to resist the temptation to enrich the image of Parmenidian being by means of the perfections of the geometrical being of the sphere.

But why speak of enriching an image, when we crystallize it in geometrical perfection? Examples could be furnished in which the value of perfection attributed to the sphere is entirely verbal. Here is one that we can use as a counter-example, in which, quite evidently, the author has failed to recognize all the values of images. One of Alfred de Vigny's characters, a young lawyer, is educating himself by reading Descartes' *Méditations*:[3] "Sometimes," writes Vigny, "he would take up a sphere set near him, and after turning it between his fingers for a long time, would sink into the most profound daydreams of science." One would love to know which ones. The author doesn't say. Does he imagine that the reading of Descartes' *Méditations* is helped if the reader begins to roll a marble between his fingers? Scientific thought develops on another horizon and Descartes' philosophy cannot be learned from an object, even a sphere. Used by Alfred de Vigny, the word *profound*, as is often the case, is a negation of profundity.

Moreover, it is evident that when a geometrician speaks of volumes, he is only dealing with the surfaces that limit them. The geometrician's sphere is an empty one, essentially empty. Therefore it cannot be a good symbol for our phenomenological study of roundness.

III

There is no doubt that these preliminary remarks are heavy with implicit philosophy. I have nevertheless felt obliged to give them brief mention because they have served me personally, and because, too, a phenomenologist must tell everything. They have helped me to "dephilosophize," to shun the allures of culture and to place myself on the margin of convictions acquired through long philosophical inquiry on the subject of scientific thinking. Philosophy makes us ripen quickly, and crystallizes us in a state of maturity. How, then, without "dephilosophizing" ourselves, may we hope to experience the shocks that being receives from new images, shocks which are always the phenomena of youthful being? When we are at an age to imagine, we cannot say how or why we imagine. Then, when we could say how we imagine, we cease to imagine. We should therefore dematurize ourselves.

But since I seem to have been seized—quite accidentally—with a neological fit, let me say again, by way of introduction to the phenomenological examination of images of solid roundness, that I have sensed the necessity here, as on many other occasions, of "de-psychoanalyzing" ourselves.

In fact, some five or ten years ago,[4] in any psychological examination of images of roundness, but especially of solid roundness, we should have laid stress on psychoanalytical explanations, for which we could have collected an enormous amount of documentation, since everything round invites a caress. Such psychoanalytical explanations are, no doubt, largely sound. But they do not tell everything, and above all, they cannot be put in the direct line of ontological determinations. When a metaphysician tells us that being is round, he displaces all psychological determinations at one time. He rids us of a past of dreams and thoughts, at the same time that he invites us to actuality of being. It is not likely that a psychoanalyst would become attached to this actuality enclosed in the very being of an expression. From his standpoint such an expression is humanly insignificant because of the very fact of its rarity. But it is this rarity that attracts the attention of the phenomenologist and encourages him to look with fresh eyes, with the perspective of being that is suggested by metaphysicians and poets.

IV

I should like to give an example of an image that is outside all realistic meaning, either psychological or psychoanalytical.

Without preparing us, precisely as regards the absolute nature of the image, Michelet says that "a bird is almost completely spherical." If we drop the "almost," which moderates the formula uselessly, and is a concession to a viewpoint that would judge from the form, we have an obvious participation in Jaspers' principle of "round being." A bird, for Michelet, is solid roundness, it is round life, and in a few lines, his commentary gives it its meaning of *model of being*.[5] "The bird, which is almost completely spherical, is certainly the sublime and divine summit of living concentration. One can neither see, nor even imagine, a higher degree of unity. Excess of concentration, which constitutes the great personal force of the bird, but which implies its extreme individuality, its isolation, its social weakness."

In the book, these lines also appear totally isolated from the rest. One feels that the author, too, followed an image of "concentration" and acceded to a plane of meditation on which he has taken cognizance of the "sources" of life. Of course, he is above being concerned with description. Once again, a geometrician may wonder, all the more so since here the bird is considered on the wing, in its out-of-doors aspect, consequently, the arrow figures could accord here with an imagined dynamics. But Michelet seized the bird's being in its cosmic situation, as a centralization of life guarded on every side, enclosed in a live ball, and consequently, at the maximum of its *unity*. All the other images, whether of form, color or movement, are stricken with relativism in the face of what we shall have to call the absolute bird, the being of round life.

The image of being—because it is an image of being—that appears in this fragment by Michelet is extraordinary for the very reason that it was considered of no significance. Literary criticism has attached no more importance to it than has psychoanalysis. And yet, it was written, and it exists in an important book. It would take on both interest and meaning if a philosophy of the cosmic imagination could be instituted, that would look for centers of cosmicity.

Seized in its center and brevity, the mere designation of this roundness is astonishingly complete. The poets who mention it, unaware that others have done the same, reply to one another. Thus Rilke, who undoubtedly did not recall what Michelet had written on the subject, wrote:[6]

> ... Ce rond cri d'oiseau
> Repose dans l'instant qui l'engendre
> Grand comme un ciel sur la forêt fanée
> Tout vient docilement se ranger dans ce cri
> Tout le paysage y semble reposer.
>
> (... This round bird-call
> Rests in the instant that engenders it
> Huge as the sky above the withered forest
> Docilely things take their place in this call
> In it the entire landscape seems to rest.)

To anyone who is receptive to the cosmicity of images, the essentially central image of the bird is the same in Rilke's poem as in the fragment by Michelet, only expressed in another register. The round cry of round being makes the sky round like a cupola. And in this rounded landscape, everything seems to be in repose. The round being propagates its roundness, together with the calm of all roundness.

And for a dreamer of words, what calm there is in the word "round." How peacefully it makes one's mouth, lips and the being of breath become round. Because this too should be spoken by a philosopher who believes in the poetic substance of speech. And for the professor who has broken with every kind of "being-there" (être-là), it is a joy to the ear to begin his course in metaphysics with the declaration: Das Dasein ist rund. Being is round. Then wait for the rumblings of this dogmatic thunder to die down, while his disciples beam with ecstasy.

But let us come back to a simpler, more tangible kind of roundness.

V

Sometimes we find ourselves in the presence of a form that guides and encloses our earliest dreams. For a painter, a tree is composed in its roundness. But a poet continues the dream from higher up. He knows that when a thing becomes isolated, it becomes round, assumes a figure of being that is concentrated upon itself. In Rilke's *Poèmes français*, this is how the walnut tree lives and commands attention. Here, again around a lone tree, which is the center of a world, the dome of the sky becomes round, in accordance with the rule of cosmic poetry. On p. 169 of this collection we read:

> *Arbre toujours au milieu*
> *De tout ce qui l'entoure*
> *Arbre qui savoure*
> *La voûte des cieux*

> (Tree always in the center
> Of all that surrounds it
> Tree feasting upon
> Heaven's great dome.)

Needless to say, all the poet really sees is a tree in a meadow; he is not thinking of a legendary Yggdrasil that would concentrate the entire cosmos, uniting heaven and earth, within itself. But the imagination of round being follows its own law: since, as the poet says, the walnut tree is "proudly rounded," it can feast upon "Heaven's great dome." The world is round around the round being.

And from verse to verse, the poem grows, increases its being. The tree is alive, reflective, straining toward God.

> *Dieu lui va apparaître*
> *Or, pour qu'il soit sûr*
> *Il développe en rond son être*
> *Et lui tend des bras mûrs.*

Arbre qui peut-être
Pense au-dedans.
Arbre qui se domine
Se donnant lentement
La forme qui élimine
Les hasards du vent!

(One day it will see God
And so, to be sure,
It develops its being in roundness
And holds out ripe arms to Him.

Tree that perhaps
Thinks innerly
Tree that dominates self
Slowly giving itself
The form that eliminates
Hazards of wind!)

I shall never find a better document for a phenomenology of a being which is at once established in its roundness and developing in it. Rilke's tree propagates in green spheres a roundness that is a victory over accidents of form and the capricious events of mobility. Here becoming has countless forms, countless leaves, but being is subject to no dispersion: if I could ever succeed in grouping together all the images of being, all the multiple, changing images that, in spite of everything, illustrate permanence of being, Rilke's tree would open an important chapter in my album of concrete metaphysics.

Notes

INTRODUCTION

1. C. f. Eugène Minkowski, *Vers une cosmologie*, ch. IX.
(*Editor's note:* Eugène Minkowski, a prominent phenomenologist whose studies extend both in the fields of psychology and philosophy, **followed Bergson in accepting the notion of "*élan vital*" as the dynamic origin of human life.** Without the vital impulse, as conceived by Bergson, the human being is static and therefore moribund. Referring to Anna Teresa Tymieniecka's book *Phenomenology and Science,* we can say that for Minkowski, the essence of life is not "a feeling of being, of existence," but a feeling of participation in a flowing onward, necessarily expressed in terms of time, and secondarily expressed in terms of space.

In view of this, Minkowski's choice of what he calls an auditive metaphor, *retentir,* is very apt, for in sound both time and space are epitomized. To understand Bachelard's reference, the following excerpt from Minkowski's *Vers une cosmologie* might be helpful:

"If, having fixed the original form in our mind's eye, we ask ourselves how that form comes alive and fills with life, we discover a new dynamic and vital category, a new property of the universe: reverberation [*retentir*]. It is as though a well-spring existed in a sealed vase and its waves, repeatedly echoing against the sides of this vase, filled it with their sonority. Or again, it is as though the sound of a hunting horn, reverberating everywhere through its echo, made the tiniest leaf, the tiniest wisp of moss shudder in a common movement and transformed the whole forest, filling it to its limits, into a vibrating, sonorous world . . . What is secondary in these images, or, in other terms, what makes these images only images for us, are the sonorous well-spring, the hunting horn, the sealed vase, the echo, the reflection of sonorous waves against the sides—in a word, all that belongs to the material and palpable world.

"Suppose these elements were missing: would really nothing living subsist? For my part, I believe that this is precisely where we should see the world come alive and, independent of any instrument, of any physical properties, fill up with penetrating deep waves which, although not sonorous in the sensory meaning of the word, are not, for this reason, less harmonious, resonant, melodic and capable of determining the whole tonality of life. And this life itself will reverberate to the most profound depths of its being, through contact with these waves, which are at once sonorous and silent ... Here to 'fill up' and 'plenitude' will have a completely different sense. It is not a material object which fills another by espousing the form that the other imposes. No, it is the dynamism of the sonorous life itself which by engulfing and appropriating everything it finds in its path, fills the slice of space, or better, the slice of the world that it assigns itself by its movement, making it reverberate, breathing into it its own life. The word 'slice' must not be taken in its geometrical sense. It is not a matter of decomposing the world virtually or actually into sonorous balls, nor of tracing the limits of the sphere determined by the waves emanating from a sonorous source. In fact, our examples, the sealed vase, the forest, because of the very fact that they fill up with sounds, form a sort of self-enclosed whole, a microcosm ...")

2. Charles Nodier, *Dictionnaire raisonné des onomatopées françaises* (Paris, 1828), p. 46. "The different names for the soul, among nearly all peoples, are just so many breath variations, and onomatopoeic expressions of breathing."

3. Pierre-Jean Jouve, *En miroir* (Mercure de France), p. 11.

4. Jean-Paul Richter, *Le Titan,* French trans. by Philarète-Chasles (1878), vol. I, p. 22.

5. Henri Bergson, *L'energie spirituelle,* p. 23.

6. J. B. Pontalis, "Michel Leiris ou la psychanalyse interminable," in *Les temps modernes,* Dec. 1955, p. 931.

7. J. H. Van den Berg, *The Phenomenological Approach in Psychology* (Springfield, Ill.: Charles C. Thomas, 1955), p. 61. An introduction to recent phenomenological psycho-pathology.

8. Pierre-Jean Jouve, loc. cit., p. 109. Andrée Chédid has also written: "A poem remains free. We shall never enclose its fate in our own." The poet knows well that "his breath will carry

him farther than his desire." (*Terre et poésie,* G.L.M. § § 14 and 25).

9. Pierre-Jean Jouve, loc. cit., p. 9: "La poésie est rare."

10. C. G. Jung, "On the Relation of Analytical Psychology to the Poetic Art," in *Contributions to Analytical Psychology,* trans. by H. G. & Cary F. Baynes (New York: Harcourt, Brace, 1928). (Bollingen Series, vol. XV.)

11. Jean Lescure, *Lapicque* (Paris: Galanis), p. 78.

12. Marcel Proust, *Remembrance of Things Past,* vol. V: *Sodom and Gomorrah.*

13. Jean-Paul Richter, *Poétique ou introduction à l'esthétique,* trans. (1862), vol. 1, p. 145.

14. C. G. Jung, loc. cit., pp. 118-19. This passage is taken from the essay entitled "Mind and the Earth."

15. Cf. *La terre et les rêveries de la volonté* (Paris: José Corti), p. 378 ff.

1: THE HOUSE. FROM CELLAR TO GARRET. THE SIGNIFICANCE OF THE HUT

1. We should grant "fixation" its virtues, independently of psycho-analytical literature, which, because of its therapeutic function, is obliged to record, principally, processes of defixation.

2. Rainer Maria Rilke, trans. into French by Claude Vigée, in *Les lettres,* 4th year, nos. 14–16, p. 11. (*Editor's note:* In this work, all of the Rilke references will be to the French translations that inspired Bachelard's comments.)

3. I plan to study these differences in a future work.

4. After giving a description of the Canaen estate (*Volupté,* p. 30), Sainte-Beuve adds: "It is not so much for you, my friend, who never saw this place, and had you visited it, could not now feel the impressions and colors I feel, that I have gone over it in such detail, for which I must excuse myself. Nor should you try to see it as a result of what I have said; let the image float inside you; pass lightly; the slightest idea of it will suffice for you."

5. *La terre et les rêveries du repos,* p. 98 (Paris: José Corti).

6. For this second part, see page 50.

7. New York: Harcourt, Brace and World.

8. Edgar Allan Poe, "The Black Cat."

9. Henri Bosco, *L'antiquaire* (1954), p. 154.

10. In my study of the material imagination, *L'eau et les rêves,* there was mention of thick, consistent water, heavy water. This was imagined by a great poet, Edgar Allan Poe; cf. ch. II.

11. *La terre et les rêveries du repos,* pp. 105–6.

12. Joë Bousquet, *La neige d'un autre âge,* p. 100.

13. Paul Claudel, *Oiseau noir dans le soleil levant,* p. 144.

14. Max Picard, *La fuite devant Dieu,* trans., p. 121.

15. I had written this page when I read in Balzac's *Petites misères de la vie conjugale* (edited by "Formes et Reflets," 1952, vol. 12, p. 1302): "When your house trembles in its beams and turns on its keel, you think you are a sailor, rocked by the breeze."

16. Francesca-Yvonne Caroutch, *Les veilleurs endormis* (Paris: Debresse), p. 30.

17. Pierre Courthion, *Courbet raconté par lui-même et par ses amis.* (Cailler, 1948), vol. I, p. 278. General Valentine did not allow Courbet to paint his city-ocean on the grounds that he "was not in prison for the purpose of amusing himself."

18. Henri Bachelin, *Le serviteur,* 6th ed. (Mercure de France), with an excellent preface by René Dumesnil, who relates the life and work of this forgotten writer.

19. Rimbaud, *Oeuvres complètes* (Lausanne: Le Grand-Chêne), p. 321.

20. Christiane Barucoa, *Antée* (Paris: Cahiers de Rochefort), p. 5.

21. Hélène Morange, *Asphodèles et Pervenches* (Paris: Séghers), p. 29.

22. G.-E. Clancier, *Une voix* (Gallimard), p. 172.

23. Erich Neumann, *Eranos-Jahrbuch,* 1955, pp. 40–41.

24. Rainer Maria Rilke, *Choix de lettres* (Stock, 1934), p. 15.

25. Richard von Schaukal, *Anthologie de la poésie allemande* (Stock), II, p. 125.

2: HOUSE AND UNIVERSE

1. Paul Eluard, *Dignes de vivre* (Paris: Julliard), p. 115.

2. Henri Bosco has given an excellent description of this type of revery in the following short phrase: "When the shelter is sure, the storm is good."

3. Henri Bachelin, *Le serviteur,* p. 102.

4. Rilke, *Lettres à une musicienne,* in French trans., p. 112.

5. Corruption of *redoute*: retreat.

6. Paris: José Corti.

7. O. V. de Milosz, 1877–1939.

8. In fact, it is interesting to note that the word *house* does not appear in the very well-compiled index to the new edition of C. G. Jung's *Metamorphosis of the Soul and Its Symbols*.

9. Jean Wahl, *Poèmes*, p. 23.

10. André Lafon, *Poésies*, "Le rêve d'un logis," p. 91.

11. Annie Duthil, *La pêcheuse d'absolu* (Paris: Séghers), p. 20.

12. Vincent Monteiro, *Vers sur verre*, p. 15.

13. Georges Spyridaki, *Mort lucide* (Paris: Séghers), p. 35.

14. René Cazelles, *De terre et d'envolée* (Paris: "G.L.M."), pp. 23, 36.

15. Erich Neumann, *Die Bedeutung des Erdarchetyps für die Neuzeit*, *Eranos* Jahrbuch, 1955, p. 12.

16. Claude Hartmann, *Nocturnes* (Paris: La Galère).

17. Jean Laroche, *Mémoires d'été* (Cahiers de Rochefort), p. 9.

18. René Char, *Fureur et mystère*, p. 41.

19. Louis Guillaume, *Noir comme la mer* (Les Lettres), p. 60.

20. Jean Bourdeillette, *Les étoiles dans la main* (Paris: Séghers), p. 48.

21. Jean Bourdeillette, op. cit., p. 28. See also (p. 64) his recollection of a house that is lost and gone.

22. Rilke, *Vergers*, XLI.

23. André de Richaud, *Le droit d'asile* (Paris: Séghers), p. 26.

24. Rilke, *Notebook of Malte Laurids Brigge* (French trans., p. 33).

25. William Goyen, *The House of Breath* (New York: Random House).

26. My imagination having been stimulated as a result of the day-dreams set in motion by reading William Goyen, I have extended the original quotation, used in 1948.

27. Théophile Briant, *Saint-Pol Roux* (Paris: Séghers), p. 42.

28. Page 361.

29. Cf. *La dialecte de la durée* (Presses Universitaire de France), p. 129.

30. André Saglio, *Maisons d'hommes célèbres* (Paris, 1893), p. 82.

31. Jules Supervielle, *Les amis inconnus*, pp. 93, 96.

32. Henri Bosco, *Le jardin d'Hyacinthe* (Paris: Gallimard, 1946), p. 192.

33. Cf. *La psychanalyse du feu*.

34. Benvenuta, *Rilke et Benvenuta* (French trans., p. 30).

35. *De Van Gogh et Seurat aux dessins d'enfants*, illustrated catalogue of an exhibition held at the Musée Pédagogique (Paris) in 1949. Dr. F. Minkowska's comments on the drawings appear on p. 137 of Mme Balif's article.

3: DRAWERS, CHESTS AND WARDROBES

1. This refers to Bergson's *Matière et mémoire,* ch. II and III.
2. Cf. loc. cit., p. 126.
3. Colette Wartz, *Paroles pour l'autre,* p. 26.
4. O. V. de Milosz, *Amoureuse initiation,* p. 217.
5. Quoted by Albert Béguin in *Eve,* p. 49.
6. Arthur Rimbaud, *Les étrennes des orphelins.*
7. Another poet, Joseph Rouffange, writes:

> *Dans le linge mort des placards*
> *Je cherche le surnaturel*
>> (In the dead linen in cupboards
>> I seek the supernatural.)
>>> *Deuil et luxe du coeur* (Rougerie).

8. Anne de Tourville, *Jabadao,* p. 51.
9. Claude Vigée, loc. cit., p. 161.
10. Denise Paulme, *Les sculptures de l'Afrique noire* (Presses Universitaires de France), 1956, p. 12.
11. Franz Hellens, *Fantômes vivants,* p. 126. Cf. the line in Baudelaire's *Les petits poèmes en prose,* p. 32, in which he speaks of "the egoist, shut up like a box."
12. Rilke, *Cahiers* (French trans.), p. 266.
13. Claire Goll, *Rilke et les femmes,* p. 70.
14. In a letter to Aubanel, Mallarmé wrote: "Every man has a secret in him, many die without finding it, and will never find it because they are dead, it no longer exists, nor do they. I am dead and risen again with the jeweled key of my last spiritual casket. It is up to me now to open it in the absence of any borrowed impression, and its mystery will emanate in a sky of great beauty." (Letter dated July 16, 1866.)
15. Jean-Pierre Richard, "Le vertige de Baudelaire," in the review *Critique,* nos. 100–1, p. 777.
16. Charles Cros, *Poèmes et prose* (Paris: Gallimard), p. 87.
17. In English in the text.
18. Jules Supervielle, *Gravitations,* p. 17.
19. Joë Bousquet, *La neige d'un autre âge,* p. 90.
20. Cf. *La terre et les rêveries du repos,* ch. I, and *La formation de l'esprit scientifique,* contribution to a psychoanalysis of objective knowledge, ch. VI.

4: NESTS

1. Victor Hugo, *Notre-Dame de Paris*, book IV, § 3.
2. Maurice de Vlaminck, *Poliment*, 1931, p. 52.
3. Ambroise Paré, *Le livre des animaux et de l'intelligence de l'homme. Oeuvres complètes*, edition J. F. Malgaigne, vol. III, p. 740.
4. Arthur Landsborough Thomson, *Birds*. Reference is to French translation (Cluny, 1934), p. 104.
5. André Theuriet, *Colette*, p. 209.
6. L. Charbonneaux-Lassay, *Le bestiaire du Christ* (Paris, 1940), p. 489.
7. A. Toussenel, *Le monde des oiseaux*, Ornithologie passionnelle (Paris, 1853), p. 32.
8. Fernand Lequenne, *Plantes sauvages*, p. 269.
9. Van Gogh, *Lettres à Théo*, p. 12 (French translation).
10. Abbé Vincelot, *Les noms des oiseaux expliqués par leurs moeurs, ou essais étymologiques sur l'ornithologie* (Angers, 1867), p. 233.
11. Jean Caubère, *Déserts* (Paris: Debresse), p. 25.
12. Jules Michelet, *L'oiseau*, 4th ed. (1858), p. 208, etc. Joseph Joubert (*Pensées*, vol. 11, p. 167) has also written: "It would be interesting to find out if the forms that birds give their nests, without ever having seen a nest, have not some analogy with their own inner constitutions."
13. Romain Rolland, *Colas Breugnon*, p. 107.
14. Loc. cit., p. 572.
15. Adolphe Shedrow, *Berceau sans promesses* (Paris: Séghers), p. 33. Shedrow also wrote: *I dreamed of a nest in which the ages no longer slept.*
16. French translation: *L'histoire de la poésie des Hébreux*, p. 269.
17. *Cahiers G.L.M.*, Autumn 1954, p. 7, translated by André du Bouchet.

5: SHELLS

1. Edouard Monod-Herzen, *Principes de morphologie générale* (Paris: Gauthier-Villars, 1927), vol. 1, p. 119. "Shells offer countless examples of spiral surfaces, on which the joining lines of the successive whorls are spiral helices." The geometry of a peacock's tail is more aerial: "The eyes in a peacock's spread tail are situated at the intersecting point of a double cluster of spirals, that are apparently Archimedean spirals" (vol. I, p. 58).

2. Paul Valéry, *Les merveilles de la mer. Les coquillages*, p. 5. Collection "Isis," Plon, Paris.

3. Jurgis Baltrusaitis, *Le moyen-âge fantastique* (Paris: Colin), p. 57.

4. Jurgis Baltrusaitis, loc. cit., p. 56. "On the coins of Hatria, a woman's head, with her hair blown by the wind, perhaps Aphrodite herself, is seen coming out of a round shell."

5. Loc. cit., p. 17.

6. Abbé de Vallemont, *Curiosités de la nature et de l'art sur la végétation ou l'agriculture et le jardinage dans leur perfection* (Paris, 1709), first part, p. 189.

7. Charbonneaux-Lassay quotes Plato and Iamblichus. He also refers the reader to *Les mystères d'Eleusis*, VI, by Victor Magnien (Payot).

8. Cf. Bachelard's *La formation de l'esprit scientifique* (Vrin), p. 206.

9. *Le spectacle de la nature*, p. 231.

10. Léon Binet, *Secrets de la vie des animaux*, Essai de physiologie animale, p. 19, Presses Universitaires de France.

11. Armand Landrin, *Les monstres marins* (Paris: Hachette), 2nd ed., p. 16.

12. Georges Duhamel, *Confession de minuit*, ch. VII.

13. Maxime Alexandre, *La peau et les os* (Paris: Gallimard, 1956), p. 18.

14. Gaston Puel, *Le chant entre deux astres*, p. 10.

15. Armand Landrin, loc. cit., p. 15. The same fable is quoted by Ambroise Paré (*Oeuvres complètes*, vol. III, p. 776). The little crab aid is "seated like a porter at the entrance of the shell." When a fish swims into the shell, the bitten shellfish shuts the shell, "then, together, they nibble and eat their prey."

16. The correct version, of course, is: *Qui vole un oeuf volera un boeuf* (He who steals an egg will steal an ox).

17. Sixteenth-century scholar, potter and enamelist. One of the creators of the ceramic arts in France.

18. Bernard Palissy, *Recepte véritable*, p. 151, published by *Bibliotheca romana*.

19. René Rouquier, *La boule de verre* (Paris: Séghers), p. 52.

20. Loc. cit., p. 78.

21. Noël Arnaud, *L'état d'ébauche* (Paris, 1950).

22. In *La revue de culture européenne*, 4th trimester (1953), p. 259.

6: CORNERS

1. *Le temps de la poésie, Cahiers G.L.M.*, July 1948, p. 32.
2. Quoted earlier, p. 127.
3. 1929.
4. Michel Leiris, *Biffures*, p. 9.
5. *Poèmes à l'autre moi*, p. 48.
6. Eighteenth-century French moralist, friend of Chateaubriand.

7: MINIATURE

1. Charles Nodier, 1780–1844. French writer of tales of fantasy.
2. Old measure, about 1/16 of a bushel.
3. *Fontaine*, French literary review published in Algiers, then in France, during the Second World War.
4. *Journal de psychologie*, April–June 1947, p. 169.
5. How many of us, once we have eaten an apple, attack the seed! In company, we restrain our innocent mania for decorticating the seeds in order to chew them. And what thoughts we have, what daydreams, when we eat the germs of plants!
6. P. de Boissy, *Main première*, p. 21.
7. Cf. Bachelard's *La formation de l'esprit scientifique*.
8. Edition *Métamorphoses* (Paris: Gallimard), p. 105.
9. *Marbre* (Paris: Laffont), p. 63.
10. Victor Hugo, *Le Rhin*, Hetzel edition, vol. III, p. 98.
11. Baron Georges Cuvier, eighteenth-century zoologist and founder of the science of paleontology.
12. *Niels Lyne* was a work that Rilke read and reread.
13. Seventeenth-century French author of many fairy tales that have become classics.
14. André Breton, *Le revolver aux cheveux blancs* (Paris: Cahiers Libres), p. 122.
15. Gaston Paris, *Le Petit Poucet et la Grande Ourse* (Paris, 1875).
16. It should be noted, however, that certain neurotics insist that they can see the microbes that are consuming their organs.
17. *"Mon père m'a donné un mari, mon Dieu, quel petit homme!"* Popular French folk song.
18. Alas, in English, the "Grand Chariot" is the "Great Bear," so this "key" will not fit the legend of our Tom Thumb. (Translator's note.)
19. Noël Bureau, *Les mains tendues*, p. 25.

20. Jules Supervielle, *Gravitations*, pp. 183–85.

21. Baudelaire, *Curiosités esthétiques*, p. 429.

22. Baudelaire, loc. cit., p. 316.

23. Joë Bousquet, *Le meneur de lune*, p. 162.

24. René-Guy Cadou, *Hélène ou le règne végétal* (Paris: Séghers), p. 13.

25. Noël Bureau, *Les mains tendues*, p. 29.

26. Claude Vigée, loc. cit., p. 68.

27. J. Moreau, "Du haschisch et de l'aliénation mentale," *Etudes Psychologiques*, 1845, p. 71.

28. In French, *mandragore*.

29. Published in *Les lettres*, no. 8, 2nd year.

30. Loys Masson, *Icare ou le voyageur* (Paris: Séghers), p. 15.

31. René Daumal, *Poésie noire, poésie blanche* (Paris: Gallimard), p. 42.

32. Max Picard, *Die Welt des Schweigens* (Rentsch Verlag, 1948, English translation, London: Harvill Press, 1952).

8: INTIMATE IMMENSITY

1. Cf. Supervielle, *L'escalier*, p. 124. "Distance bears me along in its mobile exile."

2. Pierre Albert-Bireau, *Les amusements naturels*, p. 192.

3. Marcault and Thérèse Brosse, *L'éducation de demain*, p. 255.

4. "A characteristic of forests is to be closed and, at the same time, open on every side." A. Pieyre de Mandiargues, *Le lis de mer* (1956), p. 57.

5. Pierre-Jean Jouve, *Lyrique* (Paris: Mercure de France), p. 13.

6. Pierre Guéguen, *La Bretagne*, p. 71.

7. René Ménard, *Le livre des arbres* (Paris: Arts et Métiers Graphiques, 1956), pp. 6, 7.

8. Gaston Roupnel, *La campagne française*; see the chapter entitled "*La forêt*," p. 75 ff. (Paris: Club des Libraires de France).

9. Cf. *La terre et les rêveries de la volonté*, ch. XII, § VII, "La terre immense."

10. The word *vast* is not included, however, in the excellent index to *Fusées et journaux intimes*, edited by Jacques Crépet (Paris: Mercure de France).

11. Baudelaire, *Le mangeur d'opium*, p. 181.

12. Baudelaire, *Les paradis artificiels*, p. 325.

13. Loc. cit., pp. 169, 172, 183.

14. Baudelaire, *Curiosités esthétiques*, p. 221.
15. Baudelaire, *L'art romantique*, p. 369.
16. Baudelaire, *Les paradis artificiels*, p. 169.
17. Baudelaire, *Journaux intimes*, p. 28.
18. Baudelaire, *L'art romantique*, § X.
19. Cf. Edgar Allan Poe, La puissance de la parole, *apud. Nouvelles histoires extraordinaires*, translated into French by Baudelaire, p. 238.
20. For Victor Hugo the wind is vast. The wind says: *I am the great passer-by, vast, invincible and vain* (*Dieu*, p. 5). In the three last words we hardly move our lips to pronounce the *v* sounds.
21. Max Picard, *Der Mensch und das Wort* (Eugen Rentsch Verlag, 1955), p. 15. It goes without saying that such a sentence as this should not be translated, since it obliges us to listen to the vocality of the German language. Every language has its words of great vocal value.
22. Hippolyte Taine, French philosopher, historian and critic (1828–1893).
23. "*Poème*" dated June 1924, translated into French by Claude Vigée, published in the review *Les lettres*, 4th year, nos. 14, 15, 16, p. 13.
24. Jules Supervielle, *L'escalier*, p. 106.
25. Henri Bosco, *Antonin*, p. 13.
26. Jules Supervielle, *L'escalier*, p. 123.
27. Joë Bousquet, *La neige d'un autre âge*, p. 92.
28. Pierre Loti, *Un jeune officier pauvre*, p. 85.
29. Philippe Diolé, *Le plus beau désert du monde* (Albin Michel), p. 178.
30. Henri Bosco has also written on this subject (*L'antiquaire*, p. 228): "In the hidden desert that each one of us bears within himself, and to which the desert of sand and stone has penetrated, the expanse of the spirit is lost in the infinite, uninhabited expanse that is the desolation of earth's place of solitude." See also p. 227.

    Elsewhere on a bare plateau, on the plain that touches the sky, this great dreamer gives profound expression to the analogies between the desert on earth and the desert of the spirit. "Once more emptiness stretched out inside me and I was a desert within a desert." The meditation ends on this note: "My spirit had left me" (Henri Bosco, *Hyacinthe*, pp. 33, 34).
31. Gabriele d'Annunzio, *Le feu*, French translation, p. 261.
32. Thoreau, *Walden*.

9: THE DIALECTICS OF OUTSIDE AND INSIDE

1. Jean Hyppolite, spoken commentary on the *Verneinung* (negation) of Freud. See *La psychanalyse*, no. 1 (1956), p. 35.
2. Hyppolite brings out the deep psychological inversion of negation in denegation. Later, I plan to give examples of this inversion, on the simple level of images.
3. Spiral? If we banish geometry from philosophical intuitions, it reappears almost immediately.
4. Henri Michaux, *Nouvelles de l'étranger* (Paris: Mercure de France, 1952).
5. Another poet writes: "To think that a mere word, a name, suffices to make the dividing walls of your strength come tumbling down." Pierre Reverdy, *Risques et périls*, p. 23.
6. André Fontainas, *L'ornement de la solitude* (Paris: Mercure de France, 1899), p. 22.
7. *Lettres* (Paris: Stock), p. 167.
8. Jules Supervielle, *Gravitations*, p. 19.
9. Jean Pellerin, *La romance du retour* (N.R.F., 1921), p. 18.
10. Porphyrus, *The Nymph's Cave*, § 27.
11. Michel Barrault, *Dominicale,* vol. I, p. 11.
12. Ramon Gomez de la Serna, *Echantillons* (Paris: Grasset), p. 167.
13. Maurice Blanchot, *L'arrêt de mort*, p. 124.
14. Rilke, French translation, p. 106, of *Les cahiers*.
15. Ed. Jean Pommier, *Corti*, p. 19.

10: THE PHENOMENOLOGY OF ROUNDNESS

1. Joë Bousquet, *Le meneur de lune*, p. 174.
2. Alas, in English, such a man is never "round" but "square." (Translator's note.)
3. Alfred de Vigny, *Cinq-Mars*, ch. XVI.
4. This volume first appeared in 1958. (Translator's note.)
5. Jules Michelet, *L'oiseau*, p. 291.
6. Rilke, *Poésie,* translated (into French) by Maurice Betz, under the title: *Inquiétude*, p. 95.